Advance praise for *Building Dialogue*

"Dialogue is a vital part of our existence as human beings and believers. My own experience in dialogue, over a number of years and in a number of contexts, underscores the importance of such cross-cultural work. *Building Dialogue* is an important contribution to our understanding of mutual witness and ministry."

—The Rt. Rev. Anthony Poggo, Archbishop of Canterbury's Adviser for Anglican Communion Affairs, and author of *Come Let Us Rebuild*

"If ever there was a time to reflect on peacemaking and ways to accomplish it, it is in our day of political, cultural polarization and a new threat of Empire expansion and global destruction. Richly theological and wonderfully practical, *Building Dialogue* offers the wisdom of grassroots peacebuilders who not only share their peacemaking experiences but also provide concrete models for reconciliation in other situations of conflict."

—Stephen B. Bevans, SVD, Louis J. Luzbetak, SVD Professor of Mission and Culture, Emeritus, Catholic Theological Union, Chicago

"This is a compelling read that not only provides a scriptural basis but also narrates the painful realities of the lived experience of the need for reconciliation. This collection of accessible articles from varied contexts around the Anglican Communion presents theological insights and practical suggestions to help any individual or community wanting to work towards peace and reconciliation."

—Canon Dr. Cathy Ross PhD, Pioneer Mission Training Lead, Church Mission Society, Oxford

"*Building Dialogue* provides readers with a basic course in peacebuilding, showing why doing this work in places of conflict is theologically necessary, demonstrating how it has led to change where that seemed impossible, and providing instruction for individuals and groups seeking to take up this work in their own contexts. Even more, it actually performs the kind of dialogue it advocates, being the result of years of active dialogue across difference and bringing together voices expressing numerous perspectives from regions throughout the globe. Anyone wishing to bring about a more peaceful world through dialogue will learn something helpful from this highly readable volume—and will be inspired by it, too."

—Scott MacDougall, Associate Professor of Theology, Church Divinity School of the Pacific, and author of *The Shape of Anglican Theology: Faith Seeking Wisdom*

"*Building Dialogue* is an embodied analysis and reflection on conflict and peacebuilding, with a particular emphasis on Africa and Palestine. Each of the contributors writes from within a specific context, of specific forms of conflict, and about specific processes of peacebuilding. However, their common Anglican identity, their shared embrace of scripture, and their commitment to inter-contextual, inter-cultural, and inter-textual dialogue—profoundly practiced in the book's conclusion—demonstrate that dialogue is indeed possible across particularity. The book is rich in biblical, theological, and practical resources for the many others of us who yearn to build peace through building dialogue."

—Gerald West, Professor Emeritus, University of KwaZulu-Natal, South Africa

"By thoughtfully weaving in scripture, experience, and practice in peacebuilding, *Building Dialogue* offers a fresh Christian perspective on the significance of pursuing reconciliation, restoration of trust, and healing of broken communities. Offering powerful practical insights, *Building Dialogue* not only captures the challenges and frustrations of peacebuilding in complex conflict situations but also takes us on a hope-filled pilgrimage towards Shalom."

—The Rev. Canon Dr. Anderson H. M. Jeremiah, Department of Politics, Philosophy and Religion, Lancaster University

Building Dialogue

BUILDING DIALOGUE

Stories, Scripture, and Liturgy in International Peacebuilding

Edited by
Robert S. Heaney
John Y. H. Yieh
With Jean A. Cotting

Foreword by
Archbishop Hosam Naoum,
Diocese of Jerusalem

Seabury Books
NEW YORK

Seabury Books
19 East 34th Street
New York, NY 10016

An imprint of Church Publishing Incorporated

Cover design by Jennifer Kopec, 2Pug Design
Typeset by Newgen

Library of Congress Cataloging-in-Publication Data

Names: Heaney, Robert Stewart, 1972- editor. | Yieh, John Yueh-Han, editor. | Cotting, Jean A., other.
Title: Building dialogue : stories, scripture, and liturgy in international peacebuilding / edited by Robert S. Heaney, John Y. H. Yieh, with Jean A. Cotting ; foreward by Abp. Hosam Naoum, Diocese of Jerusalem.
Description: New York, NY : Church Publishing, 2022. | Includes bibliographical references and index.
Identifiers: LCCN 2022012715 (print) | LCCN 2022012716 (ebook) | ISBN 9781640655881 (paperback) | ISBN 9781640655898 (ebook)
Subjects: LCSH: Conflict management--Religious aspects--Christianity. | Dialogue--Religious aspects--Christianity. | Peace--Religious aspects--Christianity. | Peace-building--Religious aspects--Christianity. | Anglican Communion--Doctrines.
Classification: LCC BV4597.53.C58 B85 2022 (print) | LCC BV4597.53.C58 (ebook) | DDC 204/.4--dc23/eng/20220528
LC record available at https://lccn.loc.gov/2022012715
LC ebook record available at https://lccn.loc.gov/2022012716

Contents

Foreword

Building Dialogue is a welcome and significant resource for peacebuilders and people of faith who wish to learn more about peace and reconciliation in context. Informed by Scripture and Christian liturgy, this volume's presentation of contextual peacebuilding and conflict-resolution narratives enables readers to gain a deeper understanding of different contexts within the Anglican Communion and beyond. Not only are its editors and contributors gifted theologians and lovers of peace and reconciliation, but their conceptual and practical understanding of peace in light of Christian theology reflects their genuine commitment to God's mission in and for the world.

The content of this book clearly reflects the dedication of so many Anglicans across the Communion toward peacebuilding, reconciliation, and conflict resolution. Our Anglican ethos based on Scripture, Tradition, and Reason provides both life-giving and contextual theological narratives and stories that enable peacemakers to experience the presence of the Divine within conflict, war, and alienation. In this worldview, peace is not the absence of war or conflict; it is the presence of God manifested through love, peace, and forgiveness. In other words, this book is a journey of transformation embedded in specific contexts that offer to the reader encouragement, resilience, and hopefulness.

The volume's editors and contributors remind us of both the intrinsic need for peace and the desire for reconciliation and forgiveness in our hurting world. Our local and personal stories find their way into God's story, intertwining with it in ways that shape both *who we are* and *the people we desire to become*. Peacebuilding consists of our human efforts to imagine and reimagine our place in creation, particularly by reclaiming God's image imprinted in us in creation. Indeed, peacebuilding and dialogue-building help us to become better human beings and citizens of God's Kingdom.

As Christians, we have experienced God's reconciling and redeeming love and peace in the person of Jesus Christ, who reconciled us to God and offered us the blessed ministry of reconciliation. In this, Christ has taught us that God is the God of inclusion and embrace, and not of exclusion and separation. People who live amid conflicts, divisions, and controversies diligently search for God's power to save, restore, and heal the memories, wounds, and dignity of all people.

For advancing the publication of this volume, I am personally grateful to the Virginia Theological Seminary (VTS)—an institution from which I have received three degrees—as well as for its wider commitment to Christian discipleship through theological education and training. This appreciation extends also to VTS's international partners: Saint George's College, Jerusalem; Msalato Theological College, Tanzania; and Cuttington University, Liberia.

Let me conclude with a word of thanks to all the ambassadors of peace who have contributed to this work. For as Jesus himself said: "Blessed are the peacemakers, for they shall be called the children of God" (Matt. 5:9).

Hosam Naoum
The Anglican Archbishop in Jerusalem
Lent 2022

Contributors

Kofi Ankrah, President, Trinity Cathedral Youth Fellowship, Episcopal Church of Liberia.

The Rev. Herman B. Browne has served as the President of Cuttington University in Liberia. Earning his PhD in systematic theology at the University of London in 1994, he became the first clergyman from the Episcopal Church of Liberia to earn a terminal degree in Theology. His published works include *Theological Anthropology: A Dialectic Study of the Africa and Liberation Traditions*; *50 Things Your Pastor Forgot to Tell You About God, You and the Bible*; *Grasshoppers No Longer: Critical Essays in Western Cultural History, Theology and Philosophy*; and *A Theologian's Advice: How to Avoid Sincere, but Misguided Talk about God.*

C. Patrick Burrowes, PhD is Vice President for Academic Affairs, Cuttington University and Liberian Historian.

Julia Duncan Cassell is Former Minister of Gender and Women's Advocate. She is a member of the Board of Trustees, Episcopal Church of Liberia.

The Rt. Rev. Dickson Chilongani, PhD, has been Bishop of Central Tanganyika since his consecration at the Cathedral of the Holy Spirit, Dodoma, on November 23, 2014. He was educated at St. Philips Theological College, Kongwa; Durham University and the University of Bristol.

Chris Cole is a Seminarian at Virginia Theological Seminary.

The Rev. Canon Anne Fredericks Cooper DMin is a Priest at Trinity Cathedral, Monrovia and Member of the Board of Trustees, Cuttington University.

Jean Cotting is Research Assistant, Center for Anglican Communion Studies, Virginia Theological Seminary.

The Rev. Stephen Crippen is a Seminarian at Virginia Theological Seminary.

The Rev. Canon Fuad S. Dagher currently serves as the Canon for Reconciliation in the Diocese of Jerusalem, seeking to bring together Christians, Jews, and Muslims in dialogue throughout the Galilee region. He also serves as the Rector of St. Paul's Church in Shafaram in the Palestinian territory.

Ebonee Davis is Associate for Multicultural Ministries Programming and Historical Research for Reparations, Virginia Theological Seminary.

The Rev. Wadie N. Far is Vicar of the Arabic Speaking Congregation at St. George's Anglican Cathedral, Jerusalem.

The Rev. Allen V. Gaye is a Priest at Trinity Cathedral, Monrovia.

The Rev. Robert S. Heaney, PhD, DPhil, is Professor of Theology and Mission, Virginia Theological Seminary, USA. He has experience in research, teaching, ministry, and consultation on three continents. Widely published, his most recent works include *Post-Colonial Theology: Finding God and Each Other Amidst the Hate*; *The Promise of Anglicanism* with William L. Sachs; and *God's Church for God's World* (Senior Editor).

The Rev. Hilda Kedmond Kabia is Principal, Msalato Theological College, Dodoma.

The Rev. Jamil Khadir is Vicar of St. Philip and The Good Shepherd Episcopal Church in Nablus and Rafedia and Director of the Christian National Kindergarten, Nablus.

The Rev. Susan Ackley Lukens is Associate Dean Emerita, St. George's College, Jerusalem.

The Rev. Pendo Gilberth Magayo is Parish Priest, Mata Parish, Dodoma, Diocese of Central Tanganyika.

Vannessa McCormick is Administrative Coordinator, Office of the Dean and President, Virginia Theological Seminary.

The Rev. David Wilson Mdabuko is Assistant Lecturer and Assistant to the Head of Department of Theology and Religious Studies, Faculty of Humanities and Education, St. John's University of Tanzania.

The Rev. Jonathan Musser is Administrative Assistant to the Associate Dean of Chapel and the Office of Church and Community Engagement, Virginia Theological Seminary.

The Rev. Canon Charles Azariah Mwihambi is Principal, Diocese of Central Tanganyika, Ibihwa Christian Education and Vocational Training Center (retired).

The Rev. Fares Naoum is Vicar of Emmanuel Episcopal Church, Ramla.

The Rev. Canon Ernest Godwin Ndahani is Administrator, Msalato Theological College, Dodoma.

Shadia Qubti is an experienced practitioner and researcher in peacemaking and reconciliation education within the context of Israel and Palestine. She has served as a manager for *World Vision* Jerusalem, West Bank, Gaza, designing and implementing numerous peace promoting projects. She is the creator of the podcast *Women Behind the Wall*, an endeavor to give voice to the unique perspective of Palestinian and Israeli women.

The Rev. Nael Abu Rahmoun is Vicar of Christ Church, Nazareth.

Canon Sarah Snyder is the Archbishop of Canterbury's Advisor for Reconciliation. This role has a particular emphasis on supporting the Anglican Church in contexts of violent conflict or post-conflict and helping the Church to be an agent of reconciliation and conflict-transformation. Sarah is the Founding Director of the Rose Castle Foundation, an international centre of reconciliation, based in the north of England, offering safe space in which to address misunderstanding of the "other," particularly those of different religious traditions.

Hartley Wensing is Associate Director, Center for Anglican Communion Studies, Virginia Theological Seminary.

The Rev. A. Siede Williams is Archdeacon, Southeastern Region, Episcopal Church of Liberia.

The Rev. John Yueh Han Yieh, PhD, is the Molly Laird Downs Professor in New Testament at the Virginia Theological Seminary (VTS) in Alexandria, Virginia. He joined the faculty at VTS in 1995. His research focuses on the Gospel of Matthew and the Johannine Literature from the vantage of sociological and history-of-effects approaches. His published works include *Conversations with Scripture: The Gospel of Matthew*; *A History of Biblical Interpretation in China*; *One Teacher: Jesus' Teaching Role in Matthew's Gospel Report*; and numerous journal publications.

The Rev. Anna Samweli Yohana is Parish Priest, Ntyuka Parish, Dodoma, Diocese of Central Tanganyika.

Acknowledgments

The journey of this book was only possible with the support and contributions of several individuals and institutions. The editors wish to express their gratitude to the leaders of the institutions that fostered the work of this project. These include the Rt. Rev. Dickson Chilongani, PhD, Diocese of Central Tanganyika, The Anglican Church of Tanzania and the Rev. Canon Hilda Kabia, Principal, Msalato Theological College; The Most Rev. Jonathan Hart, Primate of the Church of the Province of West Africa and Bishop of Liberia and the Rev. Herman B. Browne, PhD, President, Cuttington University; The Most Rev. Suheil Dawani, former Anglican Archbishop in Jerusalem; and the Very Rev. Ian S. Markham, PhD, Dean and President, Virginia Theological Seminary (VTS); Dr. Mitzi J. Budde, Professor and Head Librarian, VTS and Mr. Vincent Williams, User Services Manager, Bishop Payne Library, VTS.

The Most Rev. Hosam Naoum, Anglican Archbishop in Jerusalem; the Very Rev. Richard Sewell, Dean of St. George's College, Jerusalem, and the Rev. Susan Ackley Lukens, D. Min., Associate Dean Emerita, St. George's College, extended hospitality to all the authors in Jerusalem fostering life-giving community and connection to the local context. We are delighted that Archbishop Naoum was willing to write the foreword. Appreciation goes to the authors of individual chapters in the book whose presentations at the writing workshop in Jerusalem resourced and provoked much conversation and insight. We acknowledge with gratitude all the authors of chapters for their dedication and commitment to the vision of the book over two years of work on the project.

There are several individuals at VTS whose dedication made the project possible: Linda Dienno, Vice President for Institutional Advancement; Hartley Wensing, Associate Director of Center for Anglican Communion Studies; Molly O'Brien, Administrative Coordinator of the Center for Anglican Communion Studies; Curtis Prather, Director of Communications; and Valerie Mayo, Garrett Ayers, and Jean Cotting, Center for Anglican Communion Studies Research

Assistants. The help, advice, and support of Nancy Bryan and Airié Stuart made it a joy to work with Church Publishing. Finally, the project would not have been possible without the generous financial support of Trinity Church Wall Street, New York.

Method and Themes in *Building Dialogue*

Robert S. Heaney and John Y. H. Yieh

Building Dialogue is intended to help the Church think about intercontextual analysis of conflict and practices of peace. This resource emerges from intercultural relationships and discernment. Thus, *Building Dialogue* is more than a text. It is also a community of scholars and practitioners from across the Anglican Communion who for two years reflected on the nature of conflict in relation to Christian visions of peace. By way of introduction, we set before the reader the methodology at work in *Building Dialogue* and the major themes that leaders from East Africa, West Africa, the Middle East, and North America thought of as particularly important in faithful witness to the Gospel of Jesus Christ.

Method

The method at work in this study is characterized by three priorities and principles. The first methodological characteristic at work in this study is contextualization. While the practice and theology of contextualization is complex and, at times, controversial, it also provides a point of departure that acknowledges all theology is located and all theology is only ever a partial view of the issues.[1] This book does not claim to present universal or exhaustive insight into the nature of conflict and peacebuilding. Further, we do not presume to present an even-handed or objective reading of contextual conflicts or visions of peace. Rather, the contextualizations at work in these chapters arise from preexisting institutional relationships or partnerships between Virginia Theological Seminary (VTS), Alexandria; Msalato Theological College, Dodoma;

1. See Stephen B. Bevans, *Models of Contextual Theology*, rev. ed. (Maryknoll: Orbis Books, 2004); William L. Sachs and Robert S. Heaney, *The Promise of Anglicanism* (London: SCM, 2019), 57–83; Victor I. Ezigbo, *The Art of Contextual Theology: Doing Theology in the Era of World Christianity* (Eugene: Cascade, 2021).

Cuttington University, Suacoco, and the Episcopal Church of Liberia; and St. George's College, Jerusalem. These are institutions that share a history of relationship and partnership. Each of these institutions has historic links and contemporary commitments one to another. Each context is also marked and shaped by historical conflict. In the runup to the fifteenth Lambeth Conference, a group of scholars and practitioners, with links to each of these institutions, determined to provide a contextual and inter-contextual resource on the Church's call to witness peace amidst conflict.

Second, the qualitative method at work in this study belongs broadly to approaches often associated with narrative enquiry or narrative analysis.[2] That is to say, while we do not eschew scripture and theology as indispensable resources (see section A) we take it that a contextual theology also relies on testimony or story arising from experience. Such textualized experience or reflection is limited and only ever partial. The majority of the provinces of the Anglican Communion are not represented in this study. We do not claim that any reading of contextual conflict is "objective" or "neutral."[3] Leaving aside to what extent objectivity or neutrality is attainable in contexts of conflict, a narrative-based analysis is concerned with the particularity of experience and not with a presentation of a "balanced" view (readers should consult the footnotes for broader studies). The experience of conflict and the vision and frustrations of peacebuilding of particular actors in particular African, North America, and Middle Eastern contexts is our concern here. This we take to be a strength of the study but not a final word on any of the issues under consideration. This book is an invitation to listen and pray with siblings from around the Communion. In more formal terms, the method admits and encourages a reflexivity or co-construction at a number of levels.[4] This book is an invitation for authors to read, and

2. See Jerome Bruner, *Acts of Meaning* (Cambridge: Harvard University Press, 1990); David Polkinghorne, *Narrative Knowing and the Human Sciences* (Albany: SUNY Press, 1988); Anna De Fina and Alexandra Georgakopoulou eds., *The Handbook of Narrative Analysis* (Chichester: Wiley-Blackwell, 2015); Catherine Kohler Riessman, *Narrative Analysis* (Newbury Park: Sage, 1993); Jerome Bruner, "The Narrative Construction of Reality" *Critical Inquiry* 18, no. 1 (1991): 1–21.

3. Bruner, *Acts*, 85.

4. See Gary Barkhuizen, "Narrative Knowledge in Second Language Teaching and Learning Contexts" in De Fina and Georgakopoulou eds., 98–115. Barkhuizen proposes the importance of "narrative knowledging" in narrative analysis that identifies a certain instability of

write, their contexts alongside scripture and published theology. It is also an invitation for readers to resource readings of their own. As will be seen, the authors center this desire by inviting readers into biblical reflection and into prayer. Here, methodologically, is a move away from formational outcomes predicated on content-focused products to the work of formation in the Church as process and testimony locally across a myriad of contexts. In other words, not only is this study contextual and, therefore, partial—its partiality is itself an invitation to further creative work in congregations and study groups. Here is an invitation, in light of particular conflicts and particular readings of conflict and peacebuilding, to reflect on how that experience and vision relate to contexts of conflict readers may find themselves in.

Third, while the method at work emerges from a commitment to narrative analysis, because of a prior (theological) commitment to the necessity and inevitability of contextualization, the project design did not insist on particular philosophical (or cultural) commitments to that method.[5] Instead, taking the object of analysis to be external to the text in social phenomena (conflict events), we grounded a narrative-based approach in research questions to invite narrations of conflict, peace, and practice from a variety of leaders in East Africa, West Africa, the Middle East, and North America.[6] Each author and each group from each context were invited to center their analysis and vision on three research or reflective questions. What is the primary conflict in my context? What is the Christian vision for peacebuilding? Given answers to the first two questions, what are the practices or priorities the Church should pursue as witnesses to peace amidst conflict? In defining these questions, we

---

narratives in their construction and various readings. This study does not seek to undertake the formalized research that Barkhuizen assumes but, nonetheless, the potential for such "narrative knowledging" in the production of this book over two years and its reception by readers has to be acknowledged.

5. It should also be noted that the very definition of "narrative" is contested in the theoretical and methodological literature. See Anna De Fina and Alexandra Georgakopoulou, *Analyzing Narratives: Discourse and Sociolinguistic Perspectives* (Cambridge: Cambridge University Press, 2012), 1–25 for typologies of narrative analyses. While we are aware of this, we have prized the freedom that authors have taken to narrate conflict, peace, and priorities in Christian peacebuilding. This is a book arising from the local church in dialogue with the academy. While informed and resourced by narrative analysis we have avoided being bound to narrowly defined theory or method.

6. De Finna and Georgakopoulou, *Analyzing*, 24.

sought both to deepen a type of narrative analysis (that often focuses on local-level interaction, the contextualizing potency of narrative, and commitments to better understandings and practice in response to societal needs)[7] while providing authors with space to foreground their own approaches to conflict and peacebuilding. The research questions uncovered a range of contextual narrations that included engagement with scripture and theology. How Christian communities experience and analyze conflict and peace is shaped by readings of scripture, theology, and liturgy. Therefore, the chapters belonging to the first section of the book sought to anticipate some of the biblical, theological, and liturgical resources that would be at work in contextual peacebuilding (see chapters 1–5). These chapters, it should be noted, are not written by scholars independent of the *Building Dialogue* process. Each of these scholars and practitioners was involved in some or all of the stages of the process. In the final chapter of this study, we will return to how major themes in individual chapters relate to each other (see also chapter 8). At this juncture, and by way of introduction, we simply identify major and related themes at work in each of the chapters.

Themes

To facilitate a deep reflection on the process and purposes of building dialogue for peace, five essays in the first section of the book address the central theme of "conflict vs. peace" from five distinctive yet interrelated perspectives—Old Testament, New Testament, systematic theology, history of Anglicanism, and practical theology—in the Christian tradition. They provide a broad horizon for a Christian view of peace and several valuable resources for the tasks of conflict-resolution and peace-making intended to inspire and assist the churches to tackle clashes and violence in social, political, economic, and religious settings and to organize and strategize conciliatory efforts to promote justice and concord.

Dickson Chilongani (chapter 1) opens this section with a careful survey of the various meanings and practices of peace (*šālôm*) in the narratives of the Hebrew Bible. He shows that, amidst the events of

7. Anna De Fina and Alexandra Georgakopoulou, Introduction, *The Handbook of Narrative Analysis*, 3.

covenant, conflict, and compromise it is always Yahweh who gives peace, which means well-being, proper relation, and restitution or recompense. He also discusses the controversial narratives of the Exodus and the Conquest and the prophecies of the Exile and the Return to show that peace means more than the absence of war. Because peace is a gift from God, God-fearers are obliged to be agents of peace.

John Y. H. Yieh (chapter 2) explains that peace (*eirēnē*) in Greek culture denotes the "tranquility of order" in harmonious relationship with self, others, and enemies. He then examines three narrative contexts in the New Testament in which peace appears: invocation, kerygma, and paraenesis. An exegetical and inter-textual analysis of the various uses of "peace" across main traditions in the New Testament results in a multifaceted vision of peace as the tranquility of order from God, with God, and with each other. The peace that surpasses human understanding contains abundant blessings from God, gracious reconciliation with God, and genuine concord with others, all of which are made available through the Son by the Holy Spirit. Peace is the heart of the gospel, the character of Jesus' disciples, and the mission of the Church. It is both a gift and a mandate.

Herman Browne (chapter 3) offers a theological analysis of the peacebuilders' task. He reflects on the project, product, and price of peacebuilding in the light of the doctrine of salvation, the worshipping community, and the eschatological hope. To build peace is to redeem the time, reconcile the space, and restore relationship, that is, to manifest God's saving work in Christ. Eucharist not only consolidates our identity as a redeemed people but also commissions us to serve the broken world in need of peace. Insofar as peacebuilding is God's restorative and sacramental work, its final goal is eschatological. Insofar as it involves human finitude and fallibility, its current result will be partial and incomplete. The imperfect peace is but the foreshadow of heaven's perfect peace. The Church should carry on the task, cost what it may.

Robert S. Heaney (chapter 4) examines the Church of England and Anglicanism from a historical–theological perspective and reminds us that the call of the Church is to reconciliation. Just as the Church of England was conceived in contestation between the British crown and the Pope, Anglicanism proper begins in intercultural dialogue, contextualization, and controversy. Samuel Ajayi Crowther respected traditional African religions and was accused of syncretism by the

Church Missionary Society (CMS) Commission of Inquiry. John William Colenso believed African people had already heard God's voice before the arrival of missionaries and was tried for heresy and condemned by the first Lambeth Conference in 1867. In the postcolonial era, theologians such as John S. Mbiti and J. N. K. Mugambi, began to write back on the issues of overlapping interests between colonialist and missionary, justification of imperialism, imposed theologies, racism, and sectarianism. By 2014, Archbishop Justin Welby was making a public statement on the need of the Church of England to say sorry for her betrayal of Bishop Crowther. Such corporate repentance models contrition, confession, penance, and absolution for the ministry of reconciliation. It also leads to a new understanding of holiness. The Church is holy because of God's presence, and it is becoming holy because of her mission of reconciliation.

Sarah Snyder (chapter 5) defines reconciliation (*katallage*) as healing what is broken between God and creation and among people. From a practical point of view, the call to reconciliation is a call to deep listening. We understand the past through story by creating meaningful narratives of life. Reconciliation involves re-membering our own stories, re-humanizing the stories of others, and re-imagining shared elements between all our stories for a new future. Snyder also recommends twelve habits that a "reconciled reconciler" needs to develop: hospitality, curiosity, generosity, empathy, vulnerability, humility, lament, forgiveness, gratitude, hope, stewardship, and creativity. There is an Anglican instinct for holding opposites in creative tension to channel conflict constructively, and there are useful tools (common worship, Eucharist, and sacred scripture) to facilitate reconciliation. Reconciliation is a challenge, but it is a journey every Christian is called to embark on.

To listen deeply to the voice of those who actively engage in daily struggles to build dialogue and make peace and begin to relate that witness to the readers' context is the task of the second section of this book. Two peace activists in Israel–Palestine offer biographical accounts of their experience and struggle as agents for social change and share personal reflections on their despair and hope as Christian peacemakers among warring peoples and religions in a land of discrimination, oppression, conflict, hatred, and violence. The organizations and projects they are leading on the ground obviously do not represent all the peacemaking efforts in the Holy Land, but the honest and thoughtful reflections on social-political contexts and their programs to promote justice and peace give us two good samples of peace activism that may shed some light on the challenges and potentials of a contextualized and participatory approach to peacemaking amidst conflict.

Fuad S. Dagher (chapter 6) considers the calling of the Church in the Middle East to be an instrument of peace and love in a world of violence and hatred. The Church strives to build bridges to reach the other and refuses to build ghettos or walls. He cites Archbishop Elias Chacour's appeal to turn the Palestinians' story of land loss into a story of reconciliation by organizing multiethnic and multireligious youth camps and schools. To build peace, Palestinians and Jews need to regard each other as neighbors and recognize each other as children of God. He comments on the impact of the organization, *Parent Circle*, started by a Jewish father and a Muslim father whose children were killed in the Israeli–Palestinian conflict. The shared grief unites parents of diverse ethnic groups, and the work of that organization shows four steps toward peacebuilding in community: discover and assess, focus and commit, build and launch, and evaluate and maintain. Dagher sees local peace groups that organize activities for children and discussions over local issues and opportunities as increasing mutual understanding and trust among Jewish, Druze, Christian, and Muslim neighbors. He then identifies some benchmarks to assess the progress of peacebuilding, warning peace activities to avoid fear, intolerance, and hatred and raising planning questions concerning representation, leader, process, outcomes, impact, and connection.

Shadia Qubti (chapter 7) tells her story of changing views on peacebuilding as a Palestinian Christian woman. Her unique identity and experiences reveal the complexity of her life context through which, however, a new way of engagement for peace is found. Growing up, her first church taught her to focus on individual salvation and to stay neutral on social and political issues. Indigenous theologies, however, help her to reclaim her Palestinian identity, and contextual Bible reading leads her to foreground the suffering of her people. After years of community work for peacemaking, she discovers that women who bear the brunt of suffering and frustration have important perspectives and voices and deserve to take leadership roles in the communal efforts to survive and thrive. Disappointed by Palestinian theology and Messianic theology, both of which fail to recognize gender injustice, she started a podcast, "Women Behind the Wall," to feature the stories of Palestinian Christian women. These women's life testimonies need to be heard if true peace is to be built.

Jean Cotting (chapter 8) provides for readers an initial means to engage the theological and existential issues raised in sections A and B. She also provides a bridge to the contextual team chapters in section C of this study. Cotting suggests three practices for approaching this material especially in the context of small group study. First, effective study begins in hospitality. This hospitality is framed by prayer, prizes informal conversation, takes account of personality types, and nurtures a culture where sharing distinct perspectives is encouraged. Second, intentional reflection is marked by a willingness to be open to new ideas, patience in struggling with concepts, and attention to one's own social location. Third, identifying major themes is an important exercise in orientating readers as they approach material written from a variety of contexts and cultures. Cotting names three major themes that readers might hold onto as they reflect on *Building Dialogue*: the ongoing presence and impact of history, the importance of recognizing trauma, and the vital voice of the Church in contexts of conflict.

The final section of this study comprises four chapters written by each of the teams involved in the *Building Dialogue* project. In each chapter authors define a particular contextual conflict, narrate how their community relates this conflict to Christian tradition (particularly scripture), and provide resources for addressing peacebuilding.

In chapter 9, the Palestine team highlight the 2017 Israeli Identity Law as deepening conflict in their context. This law threatens the multifaceted identity of Christians living in the Holy Land. Ethnicity, religion, nationality, citizenship, and denomination intersect and resource Christian identity. However, the richness and complexity of such identity is now under threat due to the recent legislation that defines Israel as "the national state of the Jewish people." It seems Christians—along with Samaritans, Druze, Muslims, and Bahá'í—are to be regarded now as outsiders. In understanding this threat to identity, the team turn to the book of Ruth and the Gospel of Mark. In the story of Ruth, issues of identity and dignity are central. Amidst displacement and loss, hope remains because God moves people to compassion and honors the relationship between land and identity. God, in Christ, remains close to his followers through all kinds of storms (Mark 4). Christians continue to hold onto this image of Jesus calming the storm in the Holy Land. Peace comes first, then, in lives centered on Christ. The call of the Church in the "storm" created by this legislation remains to model peace and service that prioritizes and celebrates diversity. In the diocese of Jerusalem, such witness is grounded particularly in institutions of education and art open to all, worship and worship space for all, celebrations of the diversity of faiths in the land, centering the importance of water and land rights for peaceful coexistence, and providing means for dialogue across difference.

Civil unrest dating back to 1979 and two civil wars define conflict for the Liberia team in chapter 10. Between 150,000 and 300,000 people were killed, over 1 million people displaced, and over 200,000 people fled into exile. The trauma of violence continues to impact daily life. In this chapter, the roots and ongoing impact of the conflict related to colonial history, international migration, ethnic identities, economic challenges, military coups, and religious animosities are outlined. The chapter particularly focuses on the impact such trauma has had on young people. In turning to scripture and Christian tradition, the team recognize that conflict is part and parcel of holy writ. Isaac, Jacob, and Esau were in constant conflict (Gen. 32). Yet, facing fear, Jacob embraced and was embraced by his brother. Community has been undermined by conflict in Liberia, and the Church's witness continues to be an example of community building that will embrace all. From the example of a fifth-century saint, Moses the Black, this chapter calls the Church to repentance and reconciliation. In ecumenical and interreligious endeavor (often led by women) practices of dialogue, human rights advocacy, conflict prevention, collective religious action, and processes of mediation are prioritized.

The Tanzania team (chapter 11) identify land disputes as a particularly pressing problem in the context of Dodoma city. In defining this conflict, they narrate how it impacts family relationships, relationships between individuals and the Church, and relationships between the Church and the government. Each case involves the displacement of people, threats to family homes, controversy over places of worship, and disruption of traditional custom. All of these factors are exacerbated by tribal identities. Such conflicts over land, rights, and identity are not foreign to scripture. Turning to both the New Testament (Eph. 2) and the Old Testament (Gen. 26; 1 Kings 21), this chapter raises the question of how the witness of scripture impacts understandings and practices of reconciliation. It is in the work of Christ that enemies find common ground and a renewed community. At the same time, scripture recognizes that disputes may continue, that uneasy coexistence is an interim solution, and that justice delayed need not be justice denied. The reality is, then, that the Church is called to witness amidst conflict that is unresolved or partially resolved. For the Tanzania team, this means that the Church's fundamental witness amidst land disputes is evangelistic. For it is only in God's work to change lives that deeper forms of resolution and justice can be realized.

In chapter 12, the U.S. team define conflict as polarization. Communities in the United States of America have become more divided in recent years over a number of issues that include race relations, human sexuality, increasing homogeneity in local communities, and a lack of social cohesion. The Anglican tradition in the United States of America has often been an exemplar of such polarization and not a prophetic voice for reconciliation and justice. As the team is made up of members of VTS, it was to this institution that the team turned in reflection. Polarization is at work in the United States of America, in the Episcopal Church, and in theological education. VTS in many respects can be treated as a microcosm of the broader U.S. context especially in its relationship to the history of slavery (slave labor was used to build some of the structures at VTS and some members of the VTS faculty were slave owners) and racism (members of the VTS community have experienced racism). Turning to scripture, this chapter reflects on Cain and Abel (Gen. 4), as well as the story of Joseph (Gen. 37–50). These narratives are identified as biblical examples of polarization that led to breakdown, violence, and sometimes reconciliation. It is in this context of the Cain and Abel story that the first mention of sin emerges in the Bible. In the context of the Joseph story, the depths of psychological struggle that conflict creates are identified and a process of reconciliation emerges. As the Church seeks to witness to God's peace amidst polarization, certain priorities are identified. These include a Christian witness to "common kinship," an ongoing commitment to ministries of reflection, and practices of repentance and reparation.

We are delighted that Archbishop Hosam Naoum agreed to write the foreword to this study. Not only did he welcome all the teams to Jerusalem in the summer of 2019, he himself is part of an international network of Virginia Seminary graduates that reaches across the Anglican Communion. The gospel of peace rises from the city of Jerusalem; it was deeply moving that the international and intercultural authors of this study could walk together, listen together, and witness together in the context of pilgrimage in the Holy Land. It is a kind of pilgrimage that we invite readers to as they pick up this book. We invite you to listen and reflect with siblings in Christ from diverse and wounded contexts. It is our prayer that you may know more of the risen Christ and the peace of God in your own context as you reflect on the struggles and hopes of others from throughout the Communion.

SECTION A

Peacebuilding as Christian Vision

CHAPTER 1

What Does the Old Testament Say About Peace?

Dickson Chilongani

Introduction

In the view of many Christians, it is almost impossible to turn to the Old Testament as the basis for peace and peacemaking. In fact, "the Old Testament and its God have been caricatured as violent, exclusivist and lacking in the love and grace we associate with peacemaking."[1]

In this chapter, we overview the rich meaning of peace (*šālôm*) in the Old Testament. As will be seen, *šālôm* is more than the absence of war, it is well-being, it is relational, it is restitution or recompense, and it is a gift from God. However, the history of Israel also includes the failure of diplomacy and the waging of war. This too must be faced in a consideration of *šālôm*. For the people were tempted to trust in their own power more than the sovereign power of Yahweh. Eventually, their lack of trust led to exile. The true prophets constantly and consistently called the people back to trust in Yahweh and his true gift of *šālôm*.

It is true that Old Testament concepts of peace are rather complex and somehow different from our modern understanding of peace. Nonetheless, as will be seen, the Old Testament is a significant theological witness for peace and peacemaking.

---

1. Bruce C. Birch, "Old Testament Foundations for Peacemaking in the Nuclear Era," *The Christian Century* 102: 38 (December 2004): 1115.

Peace in the Old Testament

The Hebrew word *šālôm* is the basis for expressing notions of peace. Old Testament lexicons generally agree that *šālôm* entails wholeness or completeness, welfare, prosperity, good health, tranquility, friendship, and harmony.[2] Gerhard von Rad points out that the word's root means "well-being" with a strong emphasis on the material side.[3] This well-being is frequently wished to others in meetings, letters, and conversations. It is also wished through prayers in which it signifies bodily health, or well-being with the related satisfaction.[4]

In the Old Testament, *šālôm* commonly, though not exclusively, refers to a group such as a city or a nation enjoying harmony or prosperity.[5] Whenever it occurs, the emphasis is not on an inward spiritual peace, or peace of the soul. Rather, it is on something that manifests itself in the form of external well-being; something that is visible for others to see.[6] If a person claims to possess inner peace but has an outer struggle, then that is not *šālôm*. *Šalôm* can only be present when the totality of existence, both inner and outer, is whole or complete.[7] There are passages such as Lamentations 3:17, where *šālôm* seems to refer to an individual rather than a group. Even here, *šālôm* is not something that is hidden or inward (see also Judg. 6:23).

It is important to grasp this definition of *šālôm* for it shows from the outset how the Hebrew concept of *šālôm* is much richer than the English translation "peace." It covers more than the English *peace* and embraces health, wholeness, and alignment with God's structures of creation and existence. It also keeps the spiritual and the material, the

---

2. See, for instance, Francis Brown, Samuel R. Driver and Charles A. Briggs eds., *A Hebrew and English Lexicon of the Old Testament* (Oxford: Clarendon Press, 1952), 1022f.

3. Gerhard von Rad, "מולש in the OT," in *The Theological Dictionary of the New Testament,* vol. 2, eds. Gerhard Kittel and Gerhard Friedrich (Grand Rapids: William Eerdmans, 1964), 402. He cites, for instance, Judges 19:20; 1 Samuel 16:5; 2 Samuel 18:28. The idea here is not any sort of materialism as in Karl Marx and Marxism, but simply the lack of dualism. In the Hebrew Bible there is no separation between the "material" and the "spiritual."

4. von Rad, "מולש," 402.

5. von Rad, "מולש," 402.

6. von Rad, "מולש," 406.

7. Claus Westermann, "Peace (Shalom) in the Old Testament," in *The Meaning of Peace: Biblical Studies*, ed. Perry B. Yoder and Willard M. Swartley, trans. Walter Sawatsky (Louisville: John Knox, 1992), 20.

inner and the outer, closely interconnected. John I. Durham has correctly pointed out how the English version of the Hebrew *šālôm* is inadequate and misleading.[8]

Šalôm is More Than the Absence of War

In our modern understanding, peace is often described as the absence of war. To a certain extent, this is also true in the Old Testament. As Qoheleth says: there is "a time for war and a time for peace" (Eccl. 3:8). However, the concept of *šālôm* goes beyond this. When David wants to know about the welfare of Joab, his soldiers, and of the war, he asks Uriah about the *šālôm* of Joab, of the soldiers, and of the war (2 Sam. 11:7). Obviously in this context *šālôm* does not imply peace in the sense of the absence of war. Rather, it implies the welfare of those involved in the war and its progression. It is not an exaggeration to say that in this context *šālôm* comes close to indicating the success of Joab and the soldiers in the field.[9]

Bruce C. Birch is even more direct in pointing out that *šālôm* should be understood as the opposite or the absence of chaos.[10] From the creation stories, we understand that Yahweh created *ex nihilo.*[11] Birch argues that this should rather be said that he created out of chaos. Through his act of creating, Yahweh brought order (*šālôm*) out of chaos. The character of that order, according to Birch, was harmony and wholeness of *šālôm*. God brought chaos under control, and in so doing he gave us the gift of whole life.[12] Birch then goes on to describe war as one form of chaos: "within this broad concern for the things that bring chaos and destroy peace, war certainly has a special place. War is that form of chaos which results from the violent attack of one group of people on another."[13] Since war brings chaos to *šālôm*, this means that "any concern for peace must place our

---

8. John I. Durham, "םוֹלָשׁ and the Presence of God," in *Proclamation and Presence: Old Testament Essays in Honour of Gwynne Henton*, eds. John I. Durham and Joshua R. Porter (London: SCM Press, 1970), 272.

9. Ulrich Mauser, *The Gospel of Peace: A Scriptural Message for Today's World* (Louisville: John Knox Press, 1992), 15.

10. Bruce C. Birch, "Old Testament Foundations for Peacemaking in the Nuclear Era," *The Christian Century* 102, no. 38 (December 4, 1985): 1115–1116.

11. Out of nothing, as in Genesis 1:1.

12. Birch, "Old Testament Foundations," 1115.

13. Birch, "Old Testament Foundations," 1116.

opposition to war alongside an equal concern for every enemy of well-being and wholeness: Injustice, oppression, exploitation, disease, famine, etc."[14]

This understanding of *šālôm* as the absence of chaos, and of war as a form of chaos, does justice to the wider definition of *šālôm*. It helps us understand why war is an enemy of *šālôm*. Just imagine another world war broke out today, with all the nuclear weapons that the nations have accumulated. What would be the resulting chaos to the human world, animal kingdom, and the environment? Yes, the absence of war is necessary for *šālôm*. As we shall see, presently, further analysis of the Old Testament's *šālôm* provides an even greater vision of peace.

Šalôm as Well-Being

In the Old Testament, the term *šālôm* appears more than 250 times in over 200 separate verses. About 10 percent of its usage is in the context of greetings and farewells.[15] When two people meet, they ask each other "is it peace?" When Naaman sees Gehazi, Elisha's servant, running after him he asks him "is it peace?" (2 Kings 5:21).[16] Upon meeting his brothers, Joseph greets them by inquiring about their *šālôm* and the *šālôm* of their father (Gen. 43:27). In response, the brothers assure him that their father is *šālôm* and still alive (Gen. 43:28). When Joseph says farewell to them, he tells them to "Go in *šālôm*" (Gen. 44:17). When Jacob wants to know about the well-being of his uncle Laban, he asks about his *šālôm* (Gen. 29:6).

Although Durham perceives *šālôm* in the context of greetings as merely a formal term with no special content, he admits that its usage in the various Old Testament contexts suggests that much more is involved.[17] Gillis Gerleman is more to the point in arguing that, although the questions are weakened to a formula of greetings, they are meant to inquire about someone's external and internal state of satisfaction.[18]

14. Birch, "Old Testament Foundations," 1116.

15. Durham, "שָׁלוֹם and the Presence of God," 275–276.

16. See the use of this term in the context of Diplomacy below.

17. Durham, "שָׁלוֹם and the Presence of God," 275–276.

18. Gillis Gerleman, "שׁלם šlm to have enough," in *Theological Lexicon of the Old Testament*, vol. 3, ed. Ernst Jenni with Claus Westermann, trans. Mark E. Biddle (Peabody, MA: Hendrickson, 1997), 1344.

Put differently, they express a genuine concern for someone else's well-being, health, wealth, and general standard of life.[19]

The Relational Dimension of *Šalôm*

Von Rad has examined the use of *šālôm* in other contexts where the term emphasizes a relational aspect. In some contexts, *šālôm* is linked with *emet* (truth, stability, firmness, security), whereby the conjunction shows that in such a context peace implies stability of relationship. In 2 Kings 20:19, for instance, Hezekiah takes Isaiah's prophecy for granted since he expects stability of relationships (*shälôm weémet*) among his people to last for his entire generation. In other settings, *šālôm* is connected with *darash* (to seek or to be concerned for) to imply the well-being of a people. Thus, the prophet Jeremiah tells those in exile to seek (*darash*) the well-being (*šālôm*) of the city (Jer. 29:7).

This relationship can be between people such as in Deuteronomy 20:10 where Israel is instructed to offer *šālôm* before attacking a city. It could also be between individuals such as a friendly alliance between Solomon and Hiram (1 Kings 5:12). Very frequently, these friendly alliances are accompanied by a covenant (*berith*) either to inaugurate or seal a relationship of *šālôm*.[20] Whenever this occurs, it is described as a covenant of peace (*berit šālôm*). Very frequently, *šālôm* occurs when there is a reference to a covenant. The prophet Ezekiel points out repeatedly that Yahweh makes a covenant of peace with his people, where the relationship of *šālôm* is the result (Ezek. 34:25; 36:22–32; 37:26–28; see also Isa. 54:10).

Šalôm as Restitution or Recompense

Gerleman explains how the *piel* verb of the root *šlm* means "pay or repay" and that the concept of requital underlies all forms of the root. He further points out that the covenant code attests *šlm* (*piel*) as a significant legal term. It involves legislation concerning property law devoted to the performance of restitution for damages and reparation.[21] In Exodus 21:33–34a, for instance, we read:

---

19. Paul A. Barker, "Rest, Peace," in *Dictionary of the Old Testament Pentateuch*, ed. T. Desmond Alexander and David W. Baker (Downers Grove: IVP, 2003), 687–691.

20. von Rad, "םוֹלָשׁ," 403.

21. Gerlemann, "םלשׁ šlm to have enough," 1340.

If someone leaves a pit open
Or digs a pit and does not cover it
And an ox or a donkey falls into it
The owner of the pit shall make restitution (*šlm*).

Gerleman further notes in all fourteen laws in Exodus 21–22 with a similar context, *šlm* (*piel*) is used. He admits that it is questionable whether the legal usage reflects the original and proper basic meaning of *šlm* (*piel*) or should be evaluated as a secondary specialized usage of a more comprehensive concept. In either case, Gerleman insists that the use of the *piel* is in no way restricted to legal affairs but refers to a much broader semantic sphere. Essentially "to pay" means to satisfy obligations, claims, and every kind of promise. It means that *šlm* as in English, "to repay" can have the twofold senses of a positive "to satisfy" and a negative "to requite."[22] This positive sense is used in 1 Samuel 24:20 when after David spares Saul's life, Saul says to him "May the Lord repay you with good." By contrast, in Deuteronomy 32:41, God says to Israel: "I shall requite those who hate me."[23]

Šalôm as a Gift from Yahweh

Edwin M. Good in his discussion of *šālôm* and its cognates speaks of secular and religious peace.[24] In the modern world, it is easier to distinguish between the religious and the secular; the Hebrew worldview does not allow such a distinction. In the Hebrew worldview, life was experienced religiously. There was no separate domain of secular, inner, or private life. Durham thus dismisses out of hand the arbitrary division of *šālôm* into "secular" and "religious," describing it as misleading. He correctly points out that *šālôm* is entirely a religious and theological term.[25] Ulrich Mauser shares a similar view in his argument that the separation of secular peace from the sacred domain is a modern construct, something that ancient Israelites would not have comprehended.[26] Von Rad sums this up rather persuasively when he says:

---

22. Gerlemann, "שׁלם šlm to have enough," 1340–1341.

23. John Wycliffe's version, for instance, renders such translation.

24. Edwin M. Good, "Peace in the OT," in *Interpreter's Dictionary of the Bible*, vol. K-Q, ed. Keith Crim (New York: Abingdon Press, 1962), 704–706.

25. Durham, "שָׁלוֹם and the Presence of God," 272.

26. Mauser, *The Gospel of Peace*, 17.

> Naturally the goods and values associated with [*šālôm*] were always referred in Israel to Yahweh, whether in prayers for them, or in recognition that they are His gift when present. This religious use must not be regarded as a deduction or a later development. On the contrary, if we said above that there is a basic material element in [*šālôm*] we must acknowledge that when it is used in its full compass [*šālôm*] is a religious term. In this respect it is more likely that an original religious significance was to some extent lost in the course of time than the reverse.[27]

In the Old Testament, Yahweh is considered the giver of *šālôm*. Several instances of God's manifestations are connected with the giving of *šālôm*. Following his dream-theophany at Bethel where he felt the presence of Yahweh, Jacob makes a promise that if God watches over him and God returns him safely (*šālôm*) then God will be his God (Gen. 28:21). In this sense, Jacob portrays Yahweh as the giver of *šālôm*.

Following the theophany that confirms his call to generalship, Gideon declares with terror, "Help me, Lord God, for I have seen the angel of the Lord face to face" (Judg. 6:22). In response to Gideon's request for help, the Lord gives him peace saying, "Peace (*šālôm*) be with you; do not fear, you shall not die" (Judg. 6:23).

Known as a theophany psalm, Psalm 29 provides theophanic language that Artur Weiser describes as "the hymnic response to the appearance and revelation of God at the climax of the festival cult."[28] Psalm 29:11 concludes the hymn by asking God's blessing upon God's people, "The LORD gives strength to his people. The Lord blesses his people with *šālôm*" (Ps. 29:11). In Psalm 85, we also get a similar concept of God promising peace upon his people:

> I will listen to what God the LORD says
> He promises *šālôm* to his people, his faithful servants
> But let them not turn to folly.
>
> (Ps. 85:8)

27. von Rad, "םוֹלָשׁ," 403.

28. Artur Weiser, *The Psalms: A Commentary* (Philadelphia, PA: The Westminster Press, 1962), 261. Weiser is of the view that the psalm was sung on the last day of the Feast of Tabernacles.

Based on verse 1b, some scholars consider this Psalm to be postexilic, written to reflect the great change in the fortunes of Israel as prophesied by Deutero-Isaiah. Since we are not certain that verse 1b refers to deliverance from exile, it makes sense to assume that it is preexilic. Based on verse 12, it is very convincing to argue that the Psalm was written in the tradition of the festival cult celebrated at the autumn feast when the cult community remembered the Exodus.[29] The Exodus story reminded them of God's gracious deliverance from slavery and guidance to the Promised Land. It is important to note how the Lord's promises for peace relate to the faithfulness of his people. The Lord requires the people to be faithful before the Lord grants them *šālôm.*

Two of the psalms of pilgrimage, Psalms 125 and 128, portray God as the giver of *šālôm*. Both psalms begin by commending those who trust in Yahweh, who are righteous and upright. While God's protection is promised upon them, the wicked are warned of God's judgment. At the end of each of these psalms, a blessing is invoked on the Israelite covenant community as a whole, "Peace (*šālôm*) be upon Israel" (Pss. 125:5; 128:6). Weiser insists that this must not be considered as later interpolation. Rather, it should be taken as part of the current contexts as it fits well both with the cultic tradition and the thought-sequence of the two psalms.[30]

The view that Yahweh is the giver of *šālôm* is also expounded by the prophets including Isaiah of Jerusalem (26:12), Deutero-Isaiah (45:7), and Jeremiah (33:6; 33:9). It is especially portrayed in the Aaronic blessing in Numbers 6:24–26 which reads:

> The Lord bless you and keep you
> The Lord make his face to shine upon you
> The Lord Lift up his countenance upon you
> And give you peace (*šālôm*).

With regard to its present context, George Buchanan Gray has argued persuasively for an early origin of the blessing.[31] He believes it was preexilic and it was probably a blessing used in the temple in Jerusalem

29. Weiser, *Psalms*, 571–572.

30. Weiser, *Psalms*, 759.

31. George Buchanan Gray, *Critical and Exegetical Commentary on Numbers* (Edinburgh: T&T Clark, 1903), 71.

for daily sacrifices.[32] Stephen Cook shares a similar view and locates its original setting within the context of the ordination of priests (Lev. 8) and the inauguration of the daily sacrifices (Lev. 9).[33] This view is further strengthened by ancient Israelite amulets, which show that the priestly blessing was in use already in the sixth century BC.[34]

Gray argues that when the Aaronic blessing was used, the sacred name was pronounced and not replaced by Adonai.[35] This is significant with regard to *šālôm* because as Gray points out, when Yahweh's face was hidden all creatures were troubled (Pss. 30:7; 44:24; 104:29). When God's countenance turned toward them, their welfare was secure. Gray interprets *šālôm* in this context to mean welfare in the sense of freedom from all disasters.[36]

The Place of War in the Old Testament

As has already been seen, *šālôm* means much more than the absence of war. The opposite of *šālôm* is not war but chaos. How, then, is war to be accounted for in the Old Testament? Some of the most important questions that must be addressed here include: How is *šālôm* understood in the context of diplomacy? What do we say about all the battles that Israel fought in Yahweh's name? How can a good God who desires *šālôm* authorize Israel to kill other people? And what implication does this have in peacemaking?

Šalôm and Diplomacy

D. J. Wiseman has explored the use of *šālôm* and especially the term "is it peace?" in the context of diplomacy.[37] He builds on the work of Durham

---

32. Gray, *Critical*, 72.

33. Stephen L. Cook, "Priestly Blessing and Its Setting in Life," August 27, 2019, accessed September 30, 2019, https://youtu.be/F1n8d-oqOJ8.

34. "Priestly Benediction on Amulets," at the Israel Museum in Jerusalem, accessed September 30, 2019, https://artsandculture.google.com/asset/priestly-benediction-on-amulets/WgGs7fls-QiYdw. These amulets are from burials and they show that the blessing of shalom was appropriated by the dying so that God's light and peace should accompany them after their deaths.

35. Gray, *Critical*, 72.

36. Gray, *Critical*, 73 as in Job 21:9 and Leviticus 26:6.

37. Donald J. Wiseman, "'Is It Peace?': Covenant and Diplomacy," *Vetus Testamentum* 32, no. 3 (July 1982): 311–326.

who contends that the word *šālôm* is used in a "state of non-hostility," as opposed to a state of war (Eccles. 3:8) involving calamity (Isa. 47:7; Jer. 29.1). Durham further notes, in addition to its association with law and order, peace was something that had to be sought (Ps. 34:14; see also Deut. 23:6). Wiseman explores the way diplomacy leading to the making of peace and a full covenant relationship was conducted in the ancient Near East. He then discusses how this sheds light on peace and diplomacy in the Old Testament. He points out that in the Old Testament asking for peace, especially, using the phrase "is it peace?" which was often accompanied by a gift, marked the beginning of diplomatic negotiations. Likewise, the dismissal "go in peace" marked the conclusion of successful negotiations between officials of high rank.[38] Wiseman cites several biblical examples to support his argument. Five are particularly significant.

First, Wiseman considers that this diplomatic procedure of asking for peace is part and parcel of 2 Kings 9. Jehu had been anointed king and intends to kill the rival king, Joram. When Jehu arrives in Jezreel to confront Joram, he is met by a horseman who asks, "is it peace?" Jehu's answer is "what do you have to do with peace?" A second horseman receives the same response. Fearing the worst, Joram and Ahaziah (king of Judah) get in their chariots to meet Jehu. Joram asks, "is it peace, Jehu?" This is not a greeting nor an acknowledgment of Jehu's superior position. It indicates a genuine desire for negotiation.[39] Jehu responds, "how can there be peace, as long as all the idolatry and witchcraft of your mother Jezebel abound?" Alarmed by Jehu's rejection of negotiations, Joram tries unsuccessfully to escape while crying out to Ahaziah: "Treachery!"

Second, Wiseman considers that in some instances the war regulations outlined in Deuteronomy 20:10–14 reflect a similar diplomatic procedure. The law requires that when Israel besieges a town, they must proclaim peace. If the answer is peace, the people must submit to Israel and work for them under vassal obligations. If the people refuse to declare peace and decide to engage in battle, then the Israelites may attack it.[40]

38. Wiseman, "Is It Peace?" 314–317.

39. Wiseman, "Is It Peace?" 317–325.

40. Of course, the Lord does command some exceptions to seeking terms of peace. In Deuteronomy 20:16–17, God tells the Israelites that they are to annihilate certain groups in the Promised Land. This, however, needs to be understood within its cultural context. The destruction of all inhabitants of a conquered land was the cultural norm and this Hebrew concept of *herem* did in fact remove the incentive to conquer and destroy based on a desire

Third, Wiseman sees that this diplomatic use of the phrase "to ask for peace" may also apply to the Joseph narratives. In Genesis 43:27, Joseph privately asks about the health and well-being of his brothers and father. Prior to this, he had received the gifts brought by his brothers, including Benjamin, and asked them of their *šālôm* and the *šālôm* of Jacob. For Wiseman, this was an indication to them of his willingness to enter negotiations that would lead to *šālôm*.

Fourth, the story of Moses and Jethro is important to a diplomatic understanding of *šālôm*. Following Moses' success with Pharaoh, Jethro, his father-in-law and chief priest of Midian, pays him a visit in Sinai with Moses' wife and her two sons. When Moses goes out of the tent to meet Jethro, he bows down and kisses him. Then they ask each other for peace. While this can be a normal greeting after a long separation, it can also be part of a diplomatic procedure between persons of high rank. This is borne out by their entry into the tent (indicating a more intimate meeting), and the discussion that follows (Exod. 18:7).

Fifth, Wiseman also documents several examples that demonstrate how the term "go in peace" is widely used in the Old Testament to conclude successful diplomatic negotiations. Abimelek seeks reconciliation with Isaac in Genesis 26. Isaac raises the question of why he had mistreated him. In response, Abimelek reminds Isaac that while they told him to leave their land—they did not do him any harm but told him "to go in peace." As a result of this diplomatic negotiation, Isaac makes a feast for them; they eat and drink. They then make a peaceful agreement between them (Gen. 26:16; see also 26–31). When Moses asks permission from Jethro to leave his wife and family for a period of unknown duration, he is told to "go in peace" (Exod. 4:18). When the praying Hannah responds to the ill-founded rebuke of Eli, the high priest, she is told to "go in peace" as an assurance that her prayer for a child would be granted (1 Sam. 1:17). When Absalom requests permission from David to let

for personal gains. It designated that all "booty" from conquered lands belonged to God and so the conquered people could not be kept or sold as slaves, nor could the Israelites retain any material wealth from their conquests. Those who violated this mandate, such as Achan (Josh. 7:1), brought disaster upon themselves and the people as a whole. For a more comprehensive discussion, see for example Daniel G. Reid and Tremper Longman III, "When God Declares War: The Violence of God Can Only Be Understood in the Shadow of the Cross," *Christianity Today* 40, no. 12 (October 28, 1996): 14–21.

him go to Hebron to fulfill his vow to Yahweh, David agrees saying, "Go in peace" (2 Sam. 15:9).

Wiseman's explanations are very important in this context for they show not only that diplomatic conversations happened in the Old Testament, but also that *šālôm* was the basis and the goal of those negotiations. Sometimes, however, war and not diplomacy prevailed.

Šalôm and War

According to Millard C. Lind, most scholars agree that one similarity between Israel and their neighbors was that all ancient people claimed the gods' participation in battles. Outside Israel this meant that while the gods fought, the warriors were expected to fight even harder. In Israel, however, divine involvement made it unnecessary for the warriors to fight.[41] Lind notes that the disagreements among scholars have to do with whether this interpretation was late or early and how it relates to historical events.[42]

Even though Lind does not directly address these questions, the first question can be addressed based on Brevard Child's prominent work on canonical shaping.[43] The Old Testament texts on warfare were shaped theologically to reenvision the meaning of violence in a clear direction away from mere bloodshed. On the second question of authenticity, it is canonically held that these texts related to actual events that unfolded in the history of Israel. Through oral circulation, they slowly formed portions of Israel's highly valued traditions. They were eventually edited in accordance with the Mosaic tradition and became part of Deuteronomy.[44]

Beginning with the narratives of the patriarchs, Lind sees that in most cases these are peaceful narratives with very minor cases of violence. He wonders why very few traditions of patriarchal violence were handed to us. We do not know whether there were no more traditions or this

41. Stephen L. Cook, "Prof. Cook Interacts with the Ark of the Covenant," August 21, 2019, accessed September 30, 2019, https://youtu.be/Vvq7luJ9IKk.

42. Millard C. Lind, *Yahweh Is a Warrior: The Theology of Warfare in Ancient Israel* (Pennsylvania: Herald Press, 1980), 24.

43. See, for instance, Brevard Childs, *Biblical Theology in Crisis* (Philadelphia: Westminster Press, 1970).

44. Stephen L. Cook, *Reading Deuteronomy: A Literary and Theological Commentary* (Macon, GA: Smyth & Helwys Publishing, 2015), 6–9.

was due to the selectivity of the redactor. In contrast, the story of Exodus (especially chapters 1–15) is a story of conflict, the conflict of an enslaved people with the most powerful empire of its time. Despite the scholarly debate on how to read this section, Lind suggests that it should be read as a unified entity. He perceives the Exodus and wilderness period as more significant for assessing Yahweh's involvement in Israel's war than either the period of the Judges or the conquest.

In the Exodus narratives, Yahweh is portrayed as a warrior, but not in the sense of deploying human fighters in the ancient Near East. In contrast, Yahweh delivers his people from Egypt by a prophetic leader, and the nature of this deliverance takes the form of miracles. The Red Sea experience as accounted in the Song of the Sea (Exod. 15:1–21; 15:1–20 is sometimes called the Song of Moses, and 15:21 the Song of Miriam) is particularly significant for understanding Yahweh's involvement in this deliverance. Three verses provide the message of the song: Verse 1 gives the context of the song, which is a celebration of Yahweh's victory over Pharaoh and his chariots at the sea.

Verse 3 provides the theme of Yahweh as a warrior. Verse 4 explains what Yahweh has done: Pharaoh's chariots and his army are cast into the sea; his best officers are sunk in the Red Sea. Explaining the nature of Yahweh's victory, Lind points out that Yahweh's victory, though described as a battle, is not a battle in the conventional sense. For God's military power is exercised neither by Israel nor through Israel. Yahweh defeats Pharaoh and redeems his people by performing miracles rather than through military weapons.

The conquest narratives differ from those of Exodus in that they feature human participation in the battle, although victory is ascribed to Yahweh. The story of the conquest involves aggressive warfare in which Israel fights under the leadership of Joshua who is seen as the warrior. Just as the Exodus story is followed by the Song of the Sea, the defeat of the Canaanite cities by Barack is followed by the Song of Deborah (Judg. 5). By comparing these two songs, one can begin to see a shift from an emphasis on Yahweh alone fighting the battle to human participation. Verse 2 gives the theme of the song, which is a celebration of the fact that people and commanders "offered themselves willingly." Verse 7 praises Deborah as the hero—nobody else could fight and win a battle until she arose. This celebration of human participation in war has led Charles L. Echols to classify the Song of Deborah as a "heroic victory song," the purpose of which is to praise human characters for their actions. For him, this generic classification explains why Yahweh plays such a small role.[45]

Prior to the time of the kings, Israel did not have a professional army; it was the militia that participated in battle.[46] Israel did not rely on sophisticated weapons to defeat her enemies. For instance, David's rise to his kingship began with his battle with Goliath, and he did not rely upon instruments of warfare. During the first part of his reign, however, we begin to see the battle being fought by his personal troops, but even so, he went to battle only in response to Yahweh's oracle based on Israel's tradition of the Exodus and Sinai. During the monarchal period, and especially the later period of King David's reign, we begin to see a professional army fighting alongside the militia. In 2 Samuel 11:1, David sends Joab out with "his men/officers/servants," that is, David's personal (professional) army and the militia ("all Israel"), to fight against the Ammonites while he remained in Jerusalem.

The dialogue between David and Uriah, the husband of Bathsheba, sheds further light on Old Testament understandings of war. When David tells him to go and spend the night at his house, Uriah does not go but spends the night at the entrance of the king's house. When David interrogates him, Uriah's response is:

> The ark and Israel and Judah remain in booths; and my lord Joab and the servants of my lord are camping in the open field; shall I then go to my house, to eat and to drink, and to lie with my wife? As you live, and as your soul lives, I will not do such a thing.
>
> (2 Sam. 11:11)

It is significant to note the dualism that exists here: the ark and Israel (the militia) are in the tents while Joab and David's servants (his professional army) are camping in the fields. This dualism is given theological significance in 2 Samuel 12:26–31 by the way in which Rabbah, the Ammonite city, is taken. While Joab and his professional army fight the decisive battle (2 Sam. 12:26), they deliberately avoid capturing the

---

45. Charles L. Echols, *Tell Me O Muse: The Story of Deborah (Judges 5) in the Light of Heroic Poetry* (New York: Continuum Press, 2008), 162.

46. A group of civilian rather than professional forces.

city. Instead, it is David and the militia who eventually take the city (2 Sam. 12:29):

> This contrived "division of labor" was no doubt an attempt to tie the new age to the old. In the old tradition a military crisis was responded to by a voluntary militia which depended for victory upon the intervention of the divine. Miracle was now replaced by professional army.[47]

Birch argues persuasively that the ominous turning point in the story of Israel's experience with war came when its elders asked the prophet Samuel to provide a king like other nations. The elders said: "Give us a king to govern us . . . so that we also may be like other nations, and that our king may govern us and go out before us and fight our battles" (1 Sam. 8:6, 20). The result of this was what might be termed the "secularization of war."[48] Many prophets did not support this secularization of war. They opposed some of the policies of these kings and were against the false prophets who prophesied peace to entertain evil kings. As von Rad has pointed out, "From Micaiah to Ezekiel there is a minority of prophets of doom who passionately resist the message of salvation [*šālôm*] proclaimed by false prophets."[49] For von Rad, the problem of the false prophets was not that they prophesied peace but that they ignored the people's sin and failed to see the judgment that was soon to fall.[50]

One of the most interesting encounters is that of the prophet Micaiah with the 2 kings and the 400 prophets (1 Kings 22). In this story, Jehoshaphat, the king of Judah, and Ahab, the king of Israel, conspire to fight against Ramoth Gilead. Jehoshaphat requests Ahab to summon the prophets to ascertain if it is God's will to go to war. Ahab summons 400 false prophets who prophesy the same message that it is God's will to go and fight against Ramoth Gilead. At Jehoshaphat's request, Ahab sends a messenger to summon Micaiah, the son of Imlah. Along the way, the messenger tries to convince Micaiah to prophesy a message of peace like that of the false prophets. Micaiah refuses to listen and underlines that he

---

47. Lind, *Yahweh Is a Warrior*, 118.

48. Birch, "Old Testament Foundations," 1118.

49. von Rad, "שָׁלוֹם," 404.

50. von Rad, "שָׁלוֹם," 404.

will only deliver a message that comes from the Lord. When he delivers a message of doom rather than of peace as the false prophets, Ahab orders that Micaiah should be put in prison and given nothing to eat except bread and water. The two kings eventually go to battle and Ahab is killed as Micaiah had prophesied.

In their condemnation of war, the prophets declared that Israel had abandoned trust in Yahweh and trusted their own powers. They had abandoned Yahweh's goal of *šālôm* in favor of the pursuit of prosperity and power. The prophet Hosea declared that because trust was placed in "the multitude of . . . warriors" then injustice had been reaped (Hosea 10:13) and war and destruction would be inevitable (Hosea 10:14; see also Isa. 31:1). While these prophets confronted kings on the issue of war policy, other prophets, such as Jeremiah and Ezekiel, continued to battle with false prophets and challenged their prophecy. This confrontation focused on what was *šālôm* and what was "not *šālôm* (*ayin šālôm*)." Jeremiah prophesied, "*šālôm*, *šālôm*, they say when there is no peace (*ayin šālôm*)" (Jer. 6:14; 8:11; see also Ezek. 13:10, 16). Failure to pay heed to the message of the prophets in maintaining *šālôm* through greed and lack of internal social justice eventually led to the calamity of 587 BC. Jerusalem was destroyed and its ruling class was taken into exile. This came as Yahweh's judgment on nationalistic pride and trust in human power and wealth. This destruction was also a defeat of false prophets:

> If Jeremiah and Ezekiel brought the battle between *šālôm* and *ayin šālôm* to its supreme climax, the defeats of 597 and 586 led to a certain relaxation of tension in this respect, and the promise of *šālôm* in a new and larger sense became one of the most important elements in their prophecy.[51]

In his message to the exiles, Jeremiah gives them hope by assuring them that Yahweh still has thoughts of *šālôm* for them and not of evil (Jer. 29:11). Other nations will tremble at the *šālôm* that Yahweh will bring upon his people (Jer. 33:9). Building on this theme, Ezekiel announces that God will make a covenant of *šālôm* with the people (Ezek. 34:25) and this covenant will be everlasting (37:26). Deutero-Isaiah also reminds

51. von Rad, "שָׁלוֹם," 404–405.

his people that if they had listened to Yahweh, its *šālôm* would have rolled down like a river and its righteousness like waves of the sea (Isa. 48:18).

Conclusion

What does the Old Testament say about peace? The answer is that the Old Testament says *šālôm*. This *šālôm* is much richer than simply the absence of war. It means well-being expressed especially in terms of material possession, good health, and strong relationships. The concept of *šālôm* involves recompense or restitution in both the positive and negative sense. Good deeds are repaid; deeds that threaten peace can be requited. Because God is the giver of *šālôm*, God-fearers have a role to play as agents of *šālôm*.

A variety of texts foreground the diplomatic nature of *šālôm* and the negotiations toward peace. Despite this, war was also waged in the Old Testament. The Exodus narratives show violence particularly in relation to Israel's redemption from slavery in Egypt. Yahweh himself fights miraculously through Moses as his prophet to bring redemption. This concept of Yahweh fighting miraculously for his people begins to erode at the time of the judges where we see human participation in the battles of Israel. With the rise of the monarchy, a professional army emerges and false *šālôm* is pursued. Exile becomes a confirmation that the *šālôm* of the false prophets was empty and meaningless, and the true prophets warning of judgment were speaking on behalf of God.

Israel's loss of *šālôm* was a result of its failure to trust and adhere to the early tradition of Yahweh as sovereign. The consequence of this failure was the devastation of war and exile. It meant that Israel had lost its credibility as the vehicle of bringing Yahweh's gift of *šālôm* to God's people. A return to Yahweh through the messages of the prophets was necessary to regain credibility.

CHAPTER 2

"Peace That Surpasses All Understanding"

A New Testament Perspective

John Y. H. Yieh

Introduction

The world has witnessed many conflicts and experienced too much suffering. We know that we are in desperate need of God's peace that may dispel violence, reduce rivalry, and restore relationship. What precisely does God's peace have to offer to our broken world? This chapter will examine the life-giving message of God's peace in Christ as conveyed in the concepts, narratives, and contexts of New Testament (NT) traditions. It will also reflect on why God's peace can bring comfort to people in distress, and how it may guide the Church's mission to reconcile all humanity with God and with itself to enjoy enduring peace.

The Greek word for peace in the NT is *eirēnē* (εἰρήνη), which is an antonym to *polemos* (πόλεμος), meaning war which connotes the destruction of life. Peace is not simply the absence of conflict or stress. In Stoic moral philosophy, it is identified with *homonoia* (ὁμονοία meaning, "of the same kind, concord or harmony") referring to good personal relationship and *galēnē* (γαλήνη meaning, "calm or tranquility") describing a person's inner state as undisturbed and under self-control. The word *eirēnē* thus describes a contented and orderly state of what St. Augustine calls "tranquility of order" (*tranquillitas ordinis*), referring to the harmonious relationship with oneself, others, and even enemies.[1]

We need to remember that a major theological concept in the scripture is often expressed not simply by a single word with one straight definition, but by the various ways in which that word is used literally or metaphorically in various biblical accounts. The connotations and nuances of its meaning are usually made explicit in discourses, narratives, or arguments to address specific social contexts or rhetorical situations. As a result, a cluster of definitions, connotations, and nuances are interconnected to form the full range of the meaning of the concept. To understand the NT concept of peace, therefore, three social-rhetorical contexts in which peace is evoked must be considered—invocation (salutation and benediction), *kerygma* (gospel proclamation), and *paraenesis* (moral exhortation).

Invocation (Salutation and Benediction): Peace from God and Jesus Christ

Peace as *eirēnē* appears 91 times in the NT and as *shalom* more than 250 times in the Old Testament. Like many other NT concepts, the meaning of *eirēnē* is grounded in and enriched by its corresponding Hebrew word in the OT, *šālōm* (שלם), which is translated as *eirēnē* in the Septuagint (LXX). Peace as *shalom* denotes the state of well-being in every realm of human life, granted by the merciful God to the community of God's people. Its rich meaning is most clearly illustrated in the priestly benediction of Numbers 6, a traditional ritual prayer to invoke the almighty God's goodwill to bestow abundant blessings on people:

> [May] The Lord bless you and keep you. The Lord make his face to shine upon you and be gracious to you. The Lord lift up his countenance upon you and give you peace.
>
> (Num. 6:24–26)

Here we see *shalom* is the climax of six benefits conferred by God to people. A person receiving peace (*shalom*) is one who is blessed (*bārak*)

1. Augustine of Hippo, *The City of God*, Book XIX, Chap. 13, in *St. Augustine's City of God and Christian Doctrine*, Nicene and Post-Nicene Father, Series 1, Vol. 2 (Grand Rapids: Eerdmans, 1983), 409–410.

with good things, kept/guarded (*šāmar*) from all evil, favored (*yā'ēr*) by the Lord God, treated with divine grace (*ḥānan*), and stands under God's watchful care (*yisā'*). A person receiving *shalom* from God is therefore one who is safe, feels joyful, lives under God's care, and feels fulfilled and complete. This traditional priestly benediction shows us how loaded the meaning of *shalom/eirēnē* in the Old Testament is, and yet more can be found on its uses in several narratives and contexts in the NT.

Peace is frequently found in the stylized salutations and benedictions in Paul's letters to his churches. Paul prays for peace to be conferred upon his recipients and emphasizes its divine source. In his salutation to the Church in Rome and in Corinth, for instance, Paul writes: "To all God's beloved in Rome, who are called to be saints: Grace to you and peace from God our Father *and* [emphasis added] the Lord Jesus Christ" (Rom. 1:7) and "Grace to you and peace from God our Father *and* [emphasis added] the Lord Jesus Christ" (1 Cor. 1:2–3). Notice how Paul pairs "grace" (χάρις), which reads and sounds like the customary Greek salutation of health (χάρειν), with "peace" (εἰρήνη), a translation of the Jewish greeting *shalom*. Instead of the usual Greek idea of health, Paul now wishes for his Christian readers to receive God's grace of salvation made available through Jesus Christ. To the churches that include Jews and Gentiles, it is also appropriate to include both Greek and Jewish salutations, and it is theologically significant to combine the grace of salvation with the gift of peace. Also notice that Paul believes both grace and peace come not only from "God our Father" but also from "the Lord Jesus Christ." Jesus Christ is honored as the source of grace and peace, just as God is the giver of grace and *shalom*. In his letter to the Romans, Paul's benediction invokes God's goodwill on both Jews and Gentiles that they might live in harmony with one another and welcome one another as Christ has welcomed them (Rom. 14:5, 7). Paul prays, "May the God of hope fill you with all joy and peace in believing, so that you may abound in hope by the power of the Holy Spirit" (Rom. 15:13). God will give joy and peace to those who believe in Jesus Christ so that they, with the help of the Holy Spirit, may have abundant hope in seeking reconciliation and unity in the Church.

The conviction that Jesus Christ is God's co-granter of grace and peace indicates a high Christology in Paul's mind. It may evince the early

Christian devotion to Jesus Christ as divine.[2] It may also reflect an early Church memory of Jesus' greetings to the disciples in his post-Easter appearance, "Peace be with you!" (Luke 24:36; John 20:19, 21, 26). In the Johannine tradition, Jesus then breathed the Holy Spirit into them (John 21:22). Jesus' greeting of peace after resurrection dramatically fulfills the promise he made to the disheartened disciples in the "Farewell Speech":

> [Peace] I leave with you. My peace I give to you. I do not give to you as the world gives. Do not let your hearts be troubled, and do not let them be afraid.
>
> (Jn. 14:27)

For the small band of disciples trying to escape Roman arrest, the gift of peace given by the risen Lord Jesus Christ, who had conquered death, is precisely what they needed to sustain faith and hope amidst a hostile and violent world.

Kerygma (Gospel Proclamation): Peace with God as the Gospel of Christ

The most noteworthy element of peace in the NT is that it defines the gospel of Christ in the major texts authored by Paul, Peter, Luke, and John. Peace is often found in the phrase "peace with God" to indicate that the purpose of peace is to restore right relationship between sinful humanity and a holy God, which is the central message of the gospel.

For Paul, God will reveal God's righteousness in dealing with humanity and grant the status of righteousness to all people who accept Christ's redemption, because Christ has died on the cross for our sake in faithful obedience to God's salvation plan (Rom. 3:21).[3] If God and Christ have done their parts, what should humans do? Paul argues, just as Abraham, the Patriarch of the people of Israel was reckoned righteous for his faith in God's promise not by his works of the law (Rom. 4:23), so will all humans be justified by their faith in Jesus Christ. Thus, believers will receive "peace with God" (Rom. 5:1).

---

2. See Larry Hurtado, "Binitarian Worship," in *Lord Jesus Christ: Devotion to Jesus in Earliest Christianity* (Grand Rapids: Eerdmans, 2003), 134–154.

3. Ernest Käsemann, *Commentary on Romans* (Grand Rapids: Eerdmans, 1980), 21–32. Joseph Fitzmyer, *Romans* (New York: Doubleday, 1993), 253–268.

This peace with God (reconciliation) is the direct outcome of being justified and is the first gift of new life in a series of many—access to grace, hope of glory, victory over sin, perseverance in suffering, life in the Spirit, and love of God (Rom. 5–8). Reconciliation with God takes a pivotal position in the theological argument of Romans. It connects the story of God's power to save all people through Jesus Christ (Rom. 1–4) and the story of God's power to sustain all the saved to live a new life (Rom. 5–8). Ralph Martin has argued that reconciliation, broadly conceived, represents "the *centrum Paulinum*," that is to say, "the overarching core" of Paul's teaching on salvation (soteriology).[4] This language of reconciliation, as a key gospel category, may well have been adopted by Paul to help explain God's work in Christ to an audience unfamiliar with Israel's covenant relationship with God.[5]

When Peter visited Cornelius, the Roman centurion in Caesarea, he began the earliest *kerygma* (proclamation of the gospel of Jesus) by saying that God's message of peace to Israel has come in Jesus who is "Lord of all" (Acts 10:35–36). Peter told the truth-seeking Cornelius what Jesus did in his ministry in Galilee, why he died in Jerusalem, and how the disciples became witnesses to his resurrection. In Peter's view, Jesus was sent by God to preach the gospel of peace to the people of Israel and to all nations. Jesus' ministry, death, and resurrection gave the world the much-needed gift of reconciliation with God, so that all people may be forgiven of their sins and enjoy the all-encompassing well-being from the almighty and merciful God.

For Luke, who investigated and collected traditions from Paul and Peter, it was right and appropriate for the angels and heavenly hosts to sing "peace" to the shepherds on the night of Jesus' birth (Luke 2:14). Jesus' birth was "good news of great joy for all the people" (Luke 2:10) because hope for peace with God was ready to be realized. All people can receive God's favor like the prodigal son returning to his father. Jesus was anointed by the Holy Spirit "to proclaim the year of the Lord's favor" (Luke 4:19). While Paul used peace to describe the effect of Jesus' redemptive death, Peter used peace to summarize the message

4. Ralph Martin, "New Testament Theology: A Proposal. The Theme of Reconciliation," *Expository Times* 91 (1980), 364–368.

5. Ralph Martin, *Reconciliation: A Study of Paul's Theology*, rev. ed. (Grand Rapids: Zondervan, 1989), 151–153.

of Jesus' ministry for all, and Luke used peace to explain the purpose of Jesus' birth. In these three NT traditions, peace is used as a catchword to summarize the main contents of the gospel of Jesus.

If peace is so quintessential for the gospel of Jesus, one may ask, why did Jesus himself say that he had *not* come to make peace but to bring a sword (Matt. 10:34)? Jesus was clearly using hyperbole. He contrasted peace with the sword to provoke his audience, especially his opponents, to think seriously about the impact of his ministry. They believed that Jesus was a social reformer who called for nonviolent resistance to Rome and just distribution of land and food.[6] Jesus' contemporaries might wish that he had preached comforting messages of peace as they desired to hear, such as freedom, happiness, and prosperity. However, Jesus preached an upsetting call for repentance (Gk: *metanoia*) that demanded a change of mind to live a life according to the Holy Spirit and against human impulses. Such a changed mind would lead to a changed conduct, a return (Heb: *shūb*) to the way of the Law as exhorted by the prophets. Jesus refuses to be a false prophet who preaches fake peace. Only a transformed life can enjoy true peace.

For John, Jesus' death on the cross—not the resurrection or ascension—was the symbolic and thematic climax of the gospel story. On the cross, Jesus was lifted up as the Savior of the world and at that very hour both the Father and the Son were glorified (John 12:32–33; 17:1). It is a great irony that the holy and almighty God should choose the sign of humiliation and suffering to reveal God's love and glory to the world. The moment when Jesus was sacrificed on the cross, he became the Paschal Lamb to take away the sins of the world and the peace between God and humanity was made and became available. By believing in Jesus' name, all can receive eternal life (John 20:30).

In John's passion narrative, right before giving up his last breath Jesus said: "*Tetélestai*" (Τετέλεσται, perfect tense passive voice of τελέω), often translated as "It is finished" (John 19:30). The Greek word *teleō* (τελέω) means "to finish," "to complete," or "to be perfect," so commentators often interpret John 19:30 as Jesus' final declaration that his mission on earth has been accomplished. Since Jesus also cried out in Aramaic: "*Eloi, Eloi, lema sabachthani*" ("My God, my God, why have you forsaken me?"

6. John Crossan, *Jesus: A Revolutionary Biography* (San Francisco: HaperOne, 2009), 61–84.

Mark 15:34)—a lamentation of the suffering righteous (Ps. 22:1) familiar to pious Jews—it is highly probable that Jesus also said his last word in his mother tongue. What might the Aramaic word behind the Greek *teleō* be? Allow me to share three brief linguistic notes that will shed important light on the meaning of Jesus' last word that has implications for the concept of peace.

1. The ancient Syriac translation (a cousin language of Aramaic) of *tetélestai* (John 19:30) in the *Peshitta* (an Ancient Syriac version of the Bible) is *mshalam* (ܡܫܠܡ, משלם), the passive participle of the *pael* form of the verb *shalem* (ܫܠܡ, שלם) that means "to end," "to complete," or "to fulfill."[7] In his English translation of the *Peshitta*, George Lamsa takes the third meaning of *shalem* and renders John 19:30 as "It is fulfilled,"[8] suggesting that Jesus has not only "accomplished" his earthly mission but has "fulfilled" God's foreordained plan to redeem the world.
2. It is to be noted that the root of *shalem* in Syriac and Aramaic (Š-L-M) is the same as the root of *shalom* in Hebrew (Š-L-M), which means "peace." This suggests that the two words are semantically connected.
3. Recent lexicographers[9] have found new examples in Targumic and Rabbinic literature that indicate *shalem* in Syriac and Aramaic signifies not only "to complete or to end," but also "to restore or to give peace" (in *pael*), "to make friends or to surrender" (in *hiphil*), and "to make peace" (in *af'el*).[10]

---

7. J. Payne Smith ed. *A Compendious Syriac Dictionary Founded upon the Thesaurus Syriacus of R. Payne Smith* (Oxford: Clarendon, 1903, 1985), 581. Cf. Marcus Jastrow, *Dictionary of the Targumim, Talmud Babli, Yerushalmi and Midrashic Literature* (New York: Judaica Press, 1985), 1585–1586; Michael Sokoloff, *A Dictionary of Jewish Palestinian Aramaic of the Byzantine Period* (Rmat-Gan, Israel: Bar Ilan University, 1990), 554–555.

8. George Lamsa tr. *Holy Bible from the Ancient Eastern Text* (San Francisco: HarperOne, 2014).

9. See Smith, *A Compendious Syriac Dictionary* and Jastrow, *Dictionary of the Targumim*, 581. Sokoloff, *A Dictionary of Jewish Palestinian Aramaic*, 555.

10. In one instance cited by Marcus Jastrow in his *Dictionary of the Targumim*, the *hiphil* passive participle form of *shalem* is used in *Numeri Rabbah* (Midrash to Numbers Rabbah) 7:4 to mean that the Israelites are "at peace with" God (adhered to him sincerely). Michael Sokoloff cites another example in Deuteronomy 20:12 in Targum Neofiti (*The Neophyti Targum of the Pentateuch*, ed. A Diéz-Macho, Madrid-Barcelona: Consejo Superior de Investigaciones Científicas, 1968–78), which reads: "[When you draw near to a city to fight it, offer it terms of peace.] . . . If it (the city) does not make peace with you [cf. Masoretic Text as translated in NRSV: 'submit to you peacefully'] . . . then you shall besiege it."

If the Aramaic *mshalam* is behind the Greek *tetélestai*, what Jesus said at the end of his life carried a very significant nuance indeed. He was saying that his mission on earth to reveal God's love and redeem the world had been "accomplished," and his death as the Paschal Lamb on the cross connoted that "peace with God" had now been restored and given. In other words, Jesus' last word was not a self-pitiful exclamation ("My life is finished") as if he was lamenting over his untimely death, nor was it a triumphant cry ("My mission is accomplished") as if he was shouting to the devil with a shrug of pride. Rather, Jesus was humbly reporting to God: "The work you sent me to do, Father, has been completed"; at the same time, he solemnly declared to the world: "Peace (with God) has now been restored and given."

With the connotation of peace-restoration and peace-giving in the Aramaic *mshalam*, a trajectory of peace dramatically emerges in John's passion narrative. In the last supper, Jesus promises to give his disciples his own peace unlike that of the world ("Peace I leave with you, my peace I give to you" 14:27; 16:33). While dying on the cross, he declares to the world that the peace with God has now been restored and given to them through his death ("It is accomplished/The peace is restored" 19:30). After the resurrection, he greets his disciples with the peace from God ("Peace be with you" 20:19, 21, 26) and breathes in them the Holy Spirit.

If peace with God is restored and given at Jesus' death on the cross, it is easy to understand why an early Church's "Christ Hymn" confesses that God reconciles all things to Godself "by making peace through the blood of his cross" (Col. 1:20). Having been reconciled with God, all Christians are called to proclaim the same "gospel of peace" with the divine armor of truth and righteousness (Eph. 6:13–15).

Paraenesis (Moral Exhortation): Peace with Others as Character and Mission

Peace is highlighted often in the *paraenesis* (a popular form of moral exhortation used by Greco-Roman philosophers to give general instruction, counsel, and encouragement) in the NT as a virtue of personal character that Christians should cultivate and as a task of social mission that they should engage in. It is peace in terms of keeping good relationship with others and building a harmonious community. For

Jesus, peace-loving is a divine characteristic. Like their heavenly father, Jesus' disciples should love peace and be "at peace with one another" (Matt. 9:50). They are called to serve as peacemaking agents between rivals (Matt. 5:9) and to transform the norm of the world by radical actions of loving one's enemies and praying for them (Matt. 5:48).

Jesus practiced what he preached. He brought peace by standing firm against evildoers and unjust authorities. He showed compassion for the poor and defended the dignity of the downtrodden. He used divine power to heal the sick and cast out demons. He befriended the untouchables who were despised and shunned. Moreover, he humbled himself to die a painful death on the cross to redeem sinners and reconcile all to God. In his life and death, Jesus tore down the high wall that separated God from humanity and built strong bridges to reconcile friends and foes. To be his disciples is to imitate God the Father and learn from him to make peace where conflict and violence are found. For Stanley Hauerwas, this means that the task of Christian social ethics is to create a peaceable kingdom on earth. The way to do this, Hauerwas proposes, is for Christians to take responsibility for their personal character and for the Church to become a critical community of virtues.[11]

Paul considered peace an important character of Christian virtue, so he listed it as a fruit of the Holy Spirit with other virtues such as love, joy, patience, and kindness (Gal. 5:22). New life in Christ should exhibit the character of peace, that is to say, the temperament to remain calm under pressure and the ability to relate to others in harmony. Such inner peace cannot be attained by one's own effort, so believers should follow the ways of the Holy Spirit to overcome negative fleshly inclinations and mature into a person of peace. In his ministry, Paul faced many conflicts and struggles in his churches over issues of doctrine, membership, leadership, and lifestyle. In Antioch, for instance, he saw racial discrimination and insisted that Peter treat Gentile believers as equals to Jewish believers at the table for the sake of the gospel (Gal. 2:11–21). To the Galatians, he debunked Jewish privilege of religious heritage and defended new Gentile members as legitimate offspring of Abraham by faith. He declared a vision of unity that breaks through ethnic, social, and gender boundaries

---

11. Stanley Hauerwas, *The Peaceable Kingdom* (Notre Dame: The University of Notre Dame Press, 1983), 35–49, 72–95, 96–115. See Richard Burridge, *Imitating Jesus: An Inclusive Approach to New Testament Ethics* (Grand Rapids: Eerdmans, 2007), 31–32.

(Gal. 3:27–29). With this vision, Paul was not simply advocating social equality but constructing a new social identity.[12]

To the Church in Corinth, fraught with factional tensions, power struggles, shocking chaos in worship, and audacious claims for spiritual gifts, Paul provided the powerful image of the Church as "Body of Christ" to urge them to seek reconciliation (1 Cor. 12:12).[13] To keep peace in the Church is to remember we are the one Body of Christ, serving one God, one Lord, and one Spirit. As the way to keep peace is to love one another, Paul composed the inspirational "Love Hymn" (1 Cor. 13). It is important to keep the Church in concord and harmony because "God is not a God of disorder, but of peace" (1 Cor. 14:33). For the same reason, he pled with them to "live in peace" (2 Cor. 13:11). Peace with one another is so important for the Church's identity and unity that Paul encouraged the Church in Colossae to "let the peace of Christ rule in your hearts" (Col. 3:15).

The Church in Rome was an ethnically mixed Church with Jewish and Gentile Christians living in tension. James Dunn has reviewed recent critical scholarship and summarized Paul's three purposes in writing his letter to the Romans as missionary (Rom. 15:18–24, 28), apologetic (1:16–17), and pastoral (11:17–25; 12:3, 16; 14:3).[14] In order to address the increasing rift between Jewish believers and Gentile converts, Paul used a parable of olive trees (Rom. 11:17–36) to remind Gentile leaders that they are wild olive shoots grafted into the original olive tree to share the rich root because some natural branches (that is to say, unbelieving Jews) were broken off. If they were boastful over the branches, Paul warned, they could also be cut off from the olive tree. So, he implored the Romans: "Let us then pursue what makes for peace and for mutual upbuilding" (Rom. 14:19). Many interpreters have thought Paul's main concern in Romans was to explain the purpose and means of reconciliation between God and humanity (i.e., justification by grace through faith), but Corneliu Constantineanu makes a convincing case to

---

12. Bruce Hansen, *All of You Are One: The Social Vision of Galatians 3.28; 1 Corinthians 12.13 and Colossians 3.11* (London: T&T Clark, 2010), Ch. 3, 67–106.

13. Margaret Mitchell, *Paul and the Rhetoric of Reconciliation: An Exegetical Investigation of the Language and Composition of 1 Corinthians* (Tübingen: Mohr, 1991), 267–269.

14. James Dunn, *Romans 1–8* (Word Biblical Commentary, Vol. 38A; Thomas Nelson, 1988), liv–lviii.

argue that Paul also intended to encourage reconciliation among different peoples. Constantineanu calls attention to the fact that, while presenting the story of Jesus and reconciliation with God, Paul's final purpose was "to bring about the obedience of faith among all the Gentiles" (Rom. 1:5). The argument of Romans is to be understood, on the one hand, as an exposition of the inner logic of the gospel in terms of divine intervention to redeem the world and a new way of life for those who are in Christ and, on the other hand, as a response to a historical situation in which the Church was divided by differences and dissensions over issues of ethnicity, religious practices, and relationship with outsiders.[15] Constantineanu further argues that Paul's exhortation in Romans 12–15 is an ethical imperative that shows the Christian practice of reconciliation has social significance. Romans 12–13 provide concrete advice on how to welcome fellow believers into the community and how to relate to outsiders, and Romans 14–15 address the clash between "the weak" and "the strong" in the Church. Most important of all, the story of Christ in Romans 5–8 illustrates that God's reconciliation with humanity in Christ became the basis and model for the believers' welcoming and reconciling life toward "the other."[16]

For John, peace with others is also a vital sign for the community of faith. If Jesus' disciples fight for primacy with one another, they would not be able to survive the attacks of a hostile world. The only way to keep a community in peace and unity is for all members to practice mutual love, self-sacrificial love modeled on their Teacher and Lord who washed the disciples' feet and died on the cross. Thus, at the last supper, Jesus gave them a "new commandment" to love one another (John. 13:34; 15:12). Jesus also prayed that "they may all be one" as God the Father and Jesus the Son are one (John. 17:21). Peace with one another will enable the disciples to join the oneness that exists between God and Jesus.[17] For John, therefore, peace in community means more than harmony and coherence among members. It is unity, modeled on the perfect union

---

15. Corneliu Constantineanu, *The Social Significance of Reconciliation in Paul's Theology: Narrative Readings in Romans* (London: T&T Clark, 2010), 141.

16. Constantineanu, *Social Significance*, 183.

17. Richard Bauckham, "Divine and Human Community," *Gospel of Glory: Major Themes in Johannine Theology* (Grand Rapids: Baker, 2015), 21–42.

and mutual love between the Father and the Son and refers to a mutual in-dwelling in total integration.[18]

In summary, as we look at the diverse ways in which the concept of peace is expressed in the contexts of invocation, *kerygma*, and *paraenesis*, it becomes clear that it is indeed a major theological theme in the NT. The rich meanings of peace from various NT traditions are intersected to form a coherent theme with enormous significance. Peace is qualified in three phrasings—peace from God, peace with God, and peace with others—to indicate the origin, the goal, and the scope of peace. Peace serves as a catchword to describe the abundant blessings of God for humanity, the reconciling gospel of Jesus Christ, and the new life in the Holy Spirit. Peace brings forth reconciliation with God and reconciliation among people. It also demands those who have received God's peace by grace to preach the gospel of Christ's peace to all people and to make peace in the world with the power of the Holy Spirit. Peace-loving is a Christ-like characteristic, and peacebuilding is the unequivocal task of the Church in its role as a critical community of virtue in society.

Conclusion

On November 5–6, 1998, nine Nobel Peace Laureates gathered in the University of Virginia at Charlottesville to convene a meeting on "human rights, conflict, and reconciliation." They signed a joint declaration urging the international community to support their initiatives to "bring about a more peaceful world." What are their initiatives? Betty Williams (Laureate 1976), for instance, tried to build a safe haven for the children of war in Northern Ireland. Archbishop Desmond Tutu (1984) tried to reconcile Black and white South Africans after Apartheid with restorative justice and genuine forgiveness. Aung San Suu Kyi (1991) pled for the human rights of ethnic groups in Burma. Bishop Carlos Belo and José Ramos-Harta (1996) sought independence for the oppressed people in East Timor. Seeing what they each have tried to do, we realize that to make peace is not only to stop wars and violence, but also to

18. This is often referenced in terms of the so-called *perichoresis*. See Jürgen Moltmann, "God in the World—the World in God: Perichoresis in Trinity and Eschatology," in *The Gospel of John and Christian Theology*, eds. Richard Bauckham and Carl Mosser (Grand Rapids: Eerdmans, 2008), 369–381, esp. 372.

reconcile the victims with their violators and to lift up the marginalized and the downtrodden. Peace here, as in Christian theology, is not only the absence of conflict but a transforming movement toward a different reality.

Christians are blessed, because we have experienced the peace of God in Christ that may transform individual lives and make bridges in our polarized world. As God's children, we learn to love peace and are duly charged to preach peace and make peace, a costly and dangerous mission. But that peace is precisely what the world needs! As we strive to resolve conflict and resist violence, let us remember Reinhold Niebuhr's famous prayer for serenity:

> Lord,
> give us the courage to change that which should be changed,
> the tranquility to accept that which cannot be changed,
> and the wisdom to know the difference.

Christians believe that we can find peace in God even when our efforts to make peace seem wrecked, because ultimately the peace of God is eschatological; and what the Lord wants from us is faithfulness. May we be persistent in loving peace and making peace. As we strive to build dialogues for peace, let us remember one final piece of advice from Paul which he gave to the Church in Philippi:

> Do not worry about anything, but in everything by prayer and supplication with thanksgiving let your requests be known to God. And the peace of God which surpasses all understanding will guard your hearts and your minds in Christ Jesus.
>
> (Phil. 4:6–7)

CHAPTER 3

The Peacebuilder

A Theological Commentary

Herman B. Browne

Introduction

This reflection, from the perspective of conflict, is an attempt to interpret from a theological perspective what I see going on in the project of peacebuilding, peacemaking, and peacekeeping. This exercise consumes much of our energy, time, and passion. How does it fit within God's will (as far as we can tell from the Christian revelation) for the world? Is this project fit for his purpose? Is "making peace" and "waging reconciliation" conformable to God's glory? How does peacebuilding feature in God's purpose for his world? How seriously does he take it? Why are we so convinced that this exercise is valued by God and central to his concern for us? In this chapter, the enterprise of peacebuilding will be clarified, the cost inherent to the enterprise of achieving peace will be considered, and the goal of peace itself will be explored.

We hope to demonstrate and highlight the core place peace enjoys in the providence of God for his world, and by extension show how attentive he is to our pursuit of peacebuilding.[1] He is as much delighted at our attempts at peacebuilding, as he is at our successes at it. We will

1. The first point made to his disciples after Jesus resurrects is his desire that they might have peace, and that it might endure, remain with them in ways they had not experienced before (John 14:27; 16:33). God desires not only that we live in peace (1 Sam. 25:6; Rom. 2:18; 2 Cor. 13:1), but that we also pursue it (Ps. 34:14; Rom. 14:19; 1 Pet. 3:11).

consider the role of the Church and how it is that God brings about "peace and goodwill towards all" through its ministry.[2]

The first field or object of interest is a task, an initiative, an enterprise, the journeying together, the putting together of elements that make peaceable living possible. This is the *project*.[3] This project is a time-consuming process that produces a product that comes at a price. The second field of interest is a focus on the result, what emerges, the relationships we cherish and describe as fruitful and constructive, the desired state of affairs that give meaning to the exercise of reconciliation, this is the *product*. The third field of interest is exploring the costs to achieve this, what must we endure or sacrifice to enjoy this peace. What kind of peace is possible under these circumstances? We look here at the *price* we pay for the product we seek. We will explore these basic elements (of project, product, and price) from the logic gleaned by the language used in the Christian revelation about our salvation, sanctification, and ultimate purpose.

Peace as Theology

Theologically, there are at least three standpoints from which to consider how crucially valuable the project, product, and price are to God. I believe there are dimensions of this remedial enterprise that are profoundly soteriological, ecclesiological, and inescapably eschatological. From these three standpoints or dimensions, we will get a sense of just how important peacebuilding must be to God's purpose for humankind. What are the elements in this project that are identical to what we, through revelation, have come to know that God did for us in Christ Jesus? When we reflect on peacebuilding, what thoughts and practices around us approximate to how we have traditionally described God's redeeming work in the world? In what ways does this project conform to what God wishes us to do

2. 2 Corinthians 5:18 sees reconciliation as the Church's task. Peace and goodwill occasion the birth of a Son of David in Bethlehem (Luke 2:14) tied to the presence of God among humankind. Therefore, a gift of the incarnation.

3. In some sense, because peacebuilding is generally undertaken in contexts of conflict, the enterprise is a remedial, not an ideal one. One's involvement comes as a result on "the hardness of our heart." It is not an effort originally within the pristine will of God. Much in the same line of Jesus in relation to divorce (Mark 10:5–6); and Samuel in relation to the monarchy in Israel (1 Sam. 8:22), this remedial enterprise can well be a redemptive feature of God's world. The worthwhileness of what we do does not lie in the relentless pursuit of charity, nor the delicate complexity of what we do; it rests in the delight it brings to the Father who, by it, is sufficiently moved to call us "children of God."

(ethics), and in what other sense is it an extension and reflection of God's own workings (divine agency)? I hope to bring us closer to understanding more theologically the project on which we embark, the product we seek, and the price we pay to attain it.

When we build peace, we are essentially resetting ourselves to try the same things, but this time in a new way with new attitude and expectation. We are given a real chance to make it work this time. We are entrusted with more political, moral, cultural, and self-estimable awareness this time round. We are given another chance to do better, always at a time when we have seen a glimpse of the alternative course of actions and attitudes, the results of not choosing to do things differently this time around.[4] This enlightens the situation and raises the stakes. We live our lives in old relationships, but with new opportunities to take those relationships to new heights and into more fruitful ways of living.

This is what we mean by "redeeming the time."[5] Whereas, for whatever reason, one was conflicted with the other, new opportunities for better relationships have now arisen to be lived and cherished. This turnaround of situations that provide a second chance is the essence of redemption. It is not a change of situation that gives redemption its true import, but the emergence of opportunities surrounding the situation. Suddenly, one's actions have the real and unfettered potential to display, manifest, and demonstrate one's true character and soul in a different way, providing an opportunity to express better one's truest ambition for the other. This "altered" opportunity gives the participant a fighting chance to undo somewhat the effect of his prior inactions or actions.

In doing so, the peacebuilder's time is redeemed, as well as the time spent in conflict. In a football analogy, a slow-scoring team can be every bit as successful as a fast-scoring team. They may not be as riveting to watch but can certainly be a winning team. For the race is not given to the swift but the enduring. The more the peace is sustained, the more possible it becomes to redeem the time that has been lost to conflict.[6]

---

4. See Isaiah 9:6, Matthew 5:9 alerts us to the virtue inherent in peacemaking.

5. See Ephesians 5:16; Colossians 4:5.

6. The redemption of the Lord is often described in terms of making up for lost "time," to be and do what one could not in time past. "I will free you from the burdens of the Egyptians and deliver you from slavery to them. I will redeem you with an outstretched arm" (Exod. 6:6); "I will repay you for the years that the swarming locust has eaten" (Joel 2:25); "I am appealing to you for my child, Onesimus ... he was separated from you for a while, so that you might have him back for ever...no longer as a slave but as more than a slave, a beloved brother" (Philem. 10–16)

Beginning with the Old Testament, the scriptures highlight a distinction between the former time from the latter time, the former years from the latter years in order to draw attention to new opportunities.[7] The scriptures describe a new dispensation of the strange and unlikely: the Spirit on all flesh, the young dreaming dreams, and the elderly having visions; a time in which we will know more clearly and directly for ourselves what the will of God is for us.[8] The emphasis here is not on the novelty of the changed circumstances, but possibilities inherent in the dawn of a new moment.

When relationships are reconfigured and people are reconciled with each other, their communities are safer and the common spaces and institutions they share are experienced as fairer and more equitable.[9] Reconciliation is nothing if it does not mean reconciled relationships, and the feeling that one belongs in spaces in which they were previously unwelcome. Shared spaces create mutual respect and trust. We render the mutual ownership or belongingness to each other's space a reconciliation of *space*; where it is not your space or my space, nor neutral space, but our space, shared space.

It is in this *reconciliation* of space (spaces of conflict) and the *redemption* of time (spent in conflict), that the concept of restoration has its fullest import. In so far as the redemption of time and reconciliation of space are quintessential to peacebuilding, then the peacebuilding project is a manifestation of God's saving work in Christ. It is not enough simply to say that it is soteriological in nature nor even Christological in character. One must admit it is salvific, in so far as the peacebuilding endeavor, spurred on by God's holy and unpredictable Spirit, continues the saving, reconciling, and redeeming work of Christ. It has a saving and restorative value. The vocation (enterprise, project, task, exercise) is a deliberate step in *redemption* (time) and *reconciliation* (space). In our talk of redemption and reconciliation, time and space are cleansed and set anew, thereby effecting the salvation of history itself, by renewing and transforming God's world painstakingly before our very eyes.

---

7. Jeremiah 23:20; Ezekiel 38:8; Daniel 10:14; Haggai 2:9; Zechariah 8:11, 10:1; Malachi 3:4.

8. Joel 2:28; Isaiah 11:6; Acts 2:5–11; 2 Corinthians 5:17; Revelation 21:4.

9. God who has reconciled us gives us a ministry of reconciliation (2 Cor. 5:18, 20), that the world may be reconciled (Col. 1:20, 21).

The Liturgical Nature of Peace

The Church is classically considered to be a group of people called out of the world to transform it by the Lord and Giver of Life.[10] It is a gathered people called to testify to his love and manifest the glory of God in the world. Just as in the very calling of what became the *ekklesia*, a *new* people emerged, in the calling of people for peacemaking, a new people will emerge from a tired people for whom peace is a desired end. God is not a God of "Christian" peace, but of all peace. The people who embrace peace become the new people among whom the spirit dwells.

The Church in teaching us how to be fully alive to the world and true to our calling sets before us a pattern, an ordering of our public worship. Public worship in the Anglican tradition is guided by what we call liturgy. This involves a preferred sequencing of essential components of worship.

The Sequence of the Eucharistic Liturgy

How does the liturgy call us to peace? The liturgical tradition of Anglicanism centralizes and places a high premium on "the product" of peace. It is an end-value, a desired state of affairs to which the Church testifies, for which she works, and of which she believes is possible, desirable, and achievable on earth.[11] The practice of "sharing" the peace is to publicly and collectively begin to demonstrate what we should eventually become: peacebuilders. In that moment, we become a foreshadowing of our future selves.[12] In a real sense, the movement of the liturgy leads us from hearing the revealed word to confessing a common

---

10. Exodus 3:16, 35:1; Leviticus 8:3; Numbers 1:16. The gathering or calling together of the Hebrews has been an essential feature of Israel's life. As a hen would her chicks, so the people are gathered together. It was upon the assembled in Jerusalem that the Holy Spirit descended (Acts 4:31).

11. Peace as a product should be an "end" value. It is not something to be desired for some other purpose other than peace itself. This should be an end in itself. It is not desired as an instrument in the service of something else. There should be no strategic purpose for peacebuilding beyond the desire for conditions that make for human flourishing. I owe this distinction between use-value (hypothetical) and end-value (absolute) to Juan Luis Segundo in his *Faith and Ideologies*, vol. 1 (New York: Orbis Books, 1982).

12. This moment in the liturgy is meant to bring security, especially to the newly baptized. They are now part of a family and can rely on their welcome. It recognizes a common, shared space with the stranger where our interests are mutually bound up together, both lost and found. Stuart Hall, *Doctrine and Practice in the Early Church* (London: SPCK, 1994), 22.

faith (in the creed). With this faith, we are moved to peacebuilding action and prayer, dramatizing our unity of purpose and at-one-ness with the suffering of Christ in the Eucharist.[13]

At the close of the eucharistic liturgy, inner peace with ourselves and outer peace with our neighbor become the refrain of the liturgy pronounced upon worshippers in sending them out into the world to love and serve the Lord. "The peace of God which passes all understanding, keep your hearts and minds in the knowledge and love of God, and of his son Jesus Christ."[14]

The highlight for Anglicans at the Eucharist is not in the consecration of the elements of bread and wine, nor in their distribution, but in the fellowship that ensues as the result. It is a moment where barriers of all sorts are ignored, and the equal valuing of everyone by God is demonstrated. Our fellowship with God and one another at the shared meal *via* "one bread, one cup" at that moment signals the kind of peace we seek. We seek the joy of his heavenly banquet and demonstrate there at that moment what we will be, or how we should be on earth. The Eucharist simultaneously announces who and whose we are (we are one and we are God's). At the same time, importantly, it reminds us of the possible, but not yet realized. It dramatizes what the *world* should be like, were it not for its unredeemed time and unreconciled relationships. The Eucharist therefore is not just about consolidating and recommitting to the identity of a redeemed people, but is also for the benefit of a broken world itself in need of peace. So, the valued place of peacebuilding is at the heart of the Eucharist. Peacebuilding can also be discerned in the language used to describe how we understand the sacraments more generally.

Sacraments

The life of the Church testifies to the empowering work of the Holy Spirit. God continues to embolden and empower God's people, being actively present when we gather. It is the symbolic reference of God's interface with the world that we call sacraments. They generally are moments in the life of the Church that reveal or demonstrate the work of the Holy Spirit in the life of God's people. These moments occur on

13. Romans 14:17, 15:35.

14. Philippians 4:7; Colossians 3:5.

occasions when the Church of God gathers and ritualizes with specific symbolic elements, such as water, oil, bread, and wine.

Importantly in the Anglican tradition, the outward signs of these moments are both symbolic and effectual. They are more than symbols. They generate and are part of bringing about what it is they symbolize.[15] It is at these moments that the people of God should recognize the realness of God's presence and the awesome difference God's love makes to this broken world. What God does is literally a precursor, a sample or prototype of what is to come.

When the people of God gather to seek each other's good, but are prevented by conflict, we can glimpse through our peace efforts the difference ritual actions make to our broken world. When we glimpse a handshake, an embrace, an overture of neighborliness, a pact or covenant, anything that gets us a little closer to our prize of peace, we should celebrate. We should celebrate, not because there is no more work ahead, nor because it is a perfect document, nor because it is the best that can be done. We celebrate not because the effort is complete or perfect. We celebrate because in these rare and unexpected moments, we are glimpsing what perhaps would not have been possible at this exact time without *our* efforts, prompted as they were by the Spirit of God working in us, doing more than we had thought possible.[16] Therefore, every consultation and sign of mutual respect or consideration by people in conflict becomes a sign of God's full presence, a symbol of his redeeming work and evidence of his fidelity to us.

It is in these moments that the new people of God should rightly see the hand of God at work in our conflicts, our histories, our lives, our futures. These transforming moments may be signs that restoration is taking place, and these overtures and instances of grace may well themselves be catalysts to the peaceable future they seek. In so far as these moments are signs of the better future we seek, they play a role that is both symbolic and effectual in bringing about this future in a real

---

15. I owe the importance of symbols in my own thinking to Frederick W. Dillistone's work on how "symbols connect" in his classic work, *The Power of Symbols* (London: SCM, 1986), 226–236.

16. He who is the Prince of Peace presides over the peace we enjoy; it is to him we ultimately look to for the peace that abides: "flesh and blood has not revealed this to you" (Matt. 16:17); "Unless the Lord guards the city, the guard keeps watch in vain" (Ps. 127:1); "Those of steadfast mind you keep in peace—in peace because they trust in you" (Isa. 26:3).

way. In celebrating these moments, we are announcing their sacramental character and drawing attention to moments when God interfaces with God's world, literally in plain sight. The peacebuilder is analogous to a gatherer, an assembler of the people of God, who calls them together in the name of peace to find and live in peace. She or he mediates, negotiates, and creates the neutral or common spaces that make meaningful conversation and dialogue possible. It is the peacebuilder as gatherer, who takes the lead in celebrating these sacramental acts of peace. Just as priests celebrate the holy sacraments of the Church, peacebuilders may rightly celebrate the sacraments of the enterprise, always, as do priests, in the context of thanksgiving to God.

How enduring are these "sacramental" moments? What is their status in the scheme of things, and why do they count? What is certain is that their value does not rest in their permanence, their scale, or impact. It rests in the initiative, the sacrifice it took, and the result achieved. When Jesus said, "Blessed are the peacemakers" he did not add "but only the successful ones." The value is in making the effort and taking the project sufficiently seriously to make that effort count. You will be called "children of God" because in you (and this effort) not only is God pleased, but he sees his work in Christ unfold "to the glory of the Father."[17] And the sacrifices made in pursuit of this effort will not go without reward by a God who, having seen what is done in secret, rewards one openly. This brings us to why we believe that there is a dimension to this project that accords well with the goal of God's world.

The Eschatology of Peace

Eschatology is the study of all things, in so far as all things have endings. Things eschatological refer to ultimate ends in terms of destination, completion, termination, or purpose, which are inexorably in the future. Classically, it includes matters to do with heaven, hell, judgment, purgatory, the Parousia (the return of Christ), and the consummation of all things. The project as we know it is an earthly endeavor and nowhere in the Christian revelation are we given to understand or believe that there is room for peacemaking in the afterlife, or heaven, more specifically.

---

17. Matthew 5:9.

What then is specifically *eschatological* about our product? And why do we consider it inescapably so?

We have spoken of peacebuilding as a project, and the goal as a product. It is the product that now concerns us. It is fundamentally strange, I think, that even as we work so hard and often thanklessly for peace, we must additionally pray for it. But why should we pray for it if peace is a guaranteed result of all our efforts? Should peace not follow automatically from our efforts? True peace is sustained by the attitude and acts of the heart. Our efforts set the stage for it and bring it to life, displaying peace's full productive potential, but we must want and truly desire it to "enjoy the fruits of the land."[18] It is not something that the force of words can produce, political accommodation can generate, nor our best efforts at resolving conflicts possibly guarantee. Yet we work as though it does. Why? Because we know that our best efforts create the best chance of making peace possible. Peace, though often facilitated by outsiders, is sustained by the heart-driven commitment of insiders.[19]

When asked how we should pray to the Father, our Lord Jesus instructed his disciples that in their approach to him they should request, "May your will be done on earth as it is in heaven."[20] He wished peace upon us. He did not think it was enough only in heaven to experience peace. It was not enough for him that all was well in heaven. It was not good for him that what he met on earth should not be transformed into the home he left in heaven. He knew that his disciples deserved better, and he knew the source of that "better." In heaven, there is perfect peace. When we attempt the task of peacebuilding, and especially when we begin to see signs of hope, we bring into the present what we clearly know and believe characterizes the eschatological future. We make a conscious move to "May your will be done on earth as it is in heaven."

---

18. The place of a deep-seated desire for peace cannot be underestimated. It fuels an imagination of a world without conflict, without destructive attitudes of mind and will. It is the necessity of this kind of imagining that makes peace more likely and sustainable, and for which John Paul Lederach argues well in his book, *The Moral Imagination: The Art and Soul of Building Peace* (Oxford: Oxford University Press, 2005).

19. We believe all things ultimately end up reconciled under Christ. 1 Corinthians 15:28; Colossians 3:11; Hebrews 2:8; 1 Corinthians 15:52.

20. In this sense Jesus articulates a genuine "realized eschatology" which brought the future of what we will become into the present, enabling us to experience our future selves "living in peace" even *now*, before we get to heaven.

More graphically, we open up heaven and pull down here what we believe should be here.[21] In other words, the Lord's prayer has the effect of reaching up and opening the clouds of heaven and pulling down onto the earth what the Father willed for heaven. When we experience a semblance of peace, we experience something celestial. We experience only pangs of peace now, but we wait, travailing until the full season when "peace and justice" will flow like streams of living water. For as much as this careful, delicate, and time-consuming project is part of God's restorative and sacramental work among his people, its goal and product is an eschatological gift, "one which passes all understanding" and for which we are called to pray daily (Phil. 4:7).

What is the price we pay for praying upon ourselves the peace we seek? For who "builds a house without first counting the cost" (Luke 14:28)? The price we pay for having the project undertaken by human peacebuilders is that the resultant product will inevitably take on the traits of the human. The gift of peace will reflect the limitations that restrict and constrain all human's activity and agency. This perhaps is the real irony, as celestial as the gift might be, being molded by human hands means a peace that shares in all the dimensions of our finitude, inexactitude, and fallibility. It will be partial and incomplete; temporary and not everlasting; situated and located in a specific geographical space; centered primarily on the interests of the competing parties; dependent on significant actors to make it work; and subject to misrepresentations in both the letter and the spirit of the agreement. This imperfect peace is but a foreshadow of heaven's perfect peace. We cherish it as a gift to be fully lived, until God brings it to perfection by his gift of infinity. With this gift of infinity, finitude is perfected by infinitude, and our finite efforts are validated; since infinity admits of no change or improvement.[22] The limited efforts we apply to redeeming our time and reconciling our relationships result in a limited restoration of our world, in a way that is then taken to a new level of infinitude where full restoration occurs in a world "without end."

---

21. "Those of steadfast mind you keep in peace—in peace because they trust in you." (Isa. 26:3). The peace that comes from God rules "in your hearts" (Col. 3:15).

22. 1 Peter 1:4; 1 Corinthians 15:53–54.

The scriptural language of eternity helps us to see clearly the ultimate prize God reserves for earthly peace and by extension our efforts in building it. Eternity is a gift that God grants to our "life (and work)" in him and our "fellowship" with him. This gift enables us to work as Christ did selflessly for the kingdom's values of peace and goodwill. It alters our life in his service, strengthened by our fellowship with him. However, eternity is not a part of the stuff that makes up the created order. It is extraneous to it.[23] "Eternal" refers to that which has neither beginning nor end. Or, its beginning has no starting point, and its ending has no end. As creatures, we have beginnings. There was a time when we were not. We are therefore not and can never be eternal. When we say that we "share in" eternal life, we share something of eternity that is peculiar to it and it alone. We also share in its unending nature. We are granted "everlastingness," "forever and everness."[24] So, distinct from the fullness of life we share in Christ, it is also the unending, perpetual nature of it that is equally granted.

We make this point to say that the promise then of "eternal life" (salvation) and "eternal fellowship" (heaven) with God validates and perfects both life and fellowship, as we know them, and raises both to a new and unalterable dimension. This gift of eternity allows us Christians to refer both to our life in Christ and our fellowship with God, in the end, as "eternal rest," "everlasting life," and "perfect peace." What, therefore, God calls us to desire for ourselves, he promises the world, imperfect as it is.

Conclusion

The foregoing reflection was intended to bring to clearer focus how the project of peacebuilding is by no means peripheral to God's concerns for his world. We showed how the project is *patterned after Christ* himself *in* his reconciling and redeeming work in our earthly continuum of time

23. The created order, however, was created with the potential for rising beyond its limits. In creaturehood, natural and native to it is the potential to negotiate its relationship with the uncreated. So, we get a glimpse of St. Paul's view that at some point our mortality will be transformed into immortality, thereby granting infinitude to not just life and fellowship with God, but our mortal bodies as well (1 Thess. 4:17). The point I make is that while the gift of everlasting life is our end, it is not native or intrinsic to what it means to be created.

24. 1 Thessalonians 4:17; James 3:18.

and space, restoring both opportunities and relationships. We attempted to show also how the Anglican worshipping community reaffirms and dramatizes, in liturgy, the Church's *promotion of peace* among the faithful and in the world and identifies with the price (Christ's broken body at the Eucharist) it must bear to attain it. Peacebuilding, being at the heart of the Church's service to Christ, we employed sacerdotal language, analogously, in order to highlight for us the *sacred value* of what is taking place in this undertaking as we seek peace. Lastly, we drew attention to the logic intrinsic to the language used in the scriptures to describe the ultimate end of the created order. The purpose of this was to get a sense of the enduring *significance* lent (or better still, granted) to the product. After all, our human transient and corruptible efforts are "caught up in incorruptibility." The project, price, and product we speak of are all based on this promise.

We hope these reflections give us a sense of how well suited we are to embark upon this enterprise with all the resources of our Christian heritage. We do so with confidence in knowing how conformable it is to the mind of Christ, to the will of God for our world, and to the glory of the Father.[25]

25. We are brought constantly in the scriptures to see that peace is not just part of the nature of God, but that it is his passion. He desires it for his children, his family, his church, his creatures, his universe. When, in the NT epistles the Father of our Lord Jesus Christ is announced, peace is announced as part of his identity. He is described at once both "Father" and the "God of peace." See Hebrews 13:20; 2 John 1:3; 2 Peter 1:2; 1 Thessalonians 5:23; Colossians 3:15; Romans 1:7; 2 Corinthians 13:11; Romans 15:33; Philippians 4:9.

CHAPTER 4

The Call of the Church

A Historical and Theological Perspective

Robert S. Heaney

According to Paul, the person and work of Christ decisively changes the Christian's view of history and humanity (2 Cor. 5:11–17). For it is through Christ that God reconciles the world to God's self. Nothing less than a renewed Israel and a renewed humanity is being created in God's reconciliatory mission. The call of the Church is to reconciliation. The Church is to be a community of reconciliation and Christians are to be ambassadors of reconciliation (2 Cor. 5:17–21). The Church as holy is to be a community of peace, love, unity, acceptance, welcome, and friendship. The work of God in Christ, in other words, has implications not only at the personal level but also at the social and political level.[1] This theological and ethical vision has not always been borne out historically. The Church is as much known for conflict as it is for reconciliation. Given this historical reality, and the ongoing consequences of conflict, a practical approach to reconciliation that has implications for an understanding of holiness will be submitted in this chapter.

The Church in Conflict

The Church of England and Anglicanism proper were conceived in contestation. Famously, the Church of England emerged out of disputes between the British crown and the Pope. Acts of Supremacy in 1534 and

1. See Corneliu Constantineanu, *The Social Significance of Reconciliation in Paul's Theology* (London: T&T Clark, 2010), 99–183.

1559 made the monarch head of the Church on earth. Since that time, various movements for reform and renewal have claimed continuity, and discontinuity, with the reforming Catholicism of Henry VIII and Elizabeth I. Arguably, it was not until the nineteenth century that an Anglicanism distinct from the Church of England, or an expansionist Church of England in colonial outreach, emerged. Elsewhere I have argued that Anglicanism proper begins in intercultural dialogue, contextualization, and controversy in this period.[2] For example, the ministries of Bishop Samuel Ajayi Crowther (1809–1891) and John William Colenso (1814–1883) illustrate an emerging intercultural Anglicanism. This movement was characterized by translation, dialogue with traditions and philosophies beyond the West, and local leadership. It was opposed by a dominant Anglicanism that we might call imperialist. In Rowan Strong's work, imperial Anglicanism was characterized by a belief that England was gifted overseas territories by divine providence, that the salvation she brought was compensation enough for any material loss the colonized would suffer, and that Britain was called to establish a just empire in competition with Catholic nations.[3]

Samuel Ajayi Crowther was a crucial advocate of the Church Missionary Society (CMS) antislavery work in West Africa. He himself had been rescued from slavery in 1822 and by 1825 had been baptized. He was priested in 1843 and consecrated as a missionary bishop in 1864. His ministry was marked by an intercultural sensitivity that emphasized respect for traditional African religions, a cautious approach to ending polygamy, and a commitment to biblical translation. It was this ministry that would begin to establish the Africanness of the Church. This same ministry would also come under suspicion by white missionaries who worried that his approach fell into a syncretism that quashed the distinctiveness of the gospel. Between 1871 and 1874, controversy erupted over Crowther's mission. This led to the setting up of a CMS Commission of Inquiry in 1880. By 1890, the commission had dismissed twelve out of the fifteen African missionaries working under Crowther. Bishop Crowther died in 1891. In this chapter of an emerging

---

2. For a more detailed study of the witness of Crowther and Colenso see William L. Sachs and Robert S. Heaney, *The Promise of Anglicanism* (London: SCM, 2019), 57–83.

3. See Rowan Strong, *Anglicanism and the British Empire* (Oxford: Oxford University Press, 2007), 111–117.

Anglicanism, imperialism won out. Tragically, in a series of contexts, imperial Anglicanism would continue to belittle contextualizations, indigenous wisdom, and local leadership. Sixty years would pass before an African was appointed as diocesan bishop.

As Crowther's evangelicalism prioritized adaptation and contextualization for the sake of Christ's gospel so too John William Colenso's liberalism would attempt a similar intercultural witness. Like Crowther, Colenso was a scholar interested in translation and the wisdom of indigenous cultures. For Colenso, his theological opinions emerged from exchange and dialogue with Zulu thinkers. Colenso was no anti-colonialist. He had hopes that British imperialism would be used, by God, for good. His writing employed language that did not rise above common colonialist tropes and his theological views today may not seem shocking. However, at that time, his published theology and his practiced interculturality were considered controversial. Here, we get but a glimpse of an intercultural Anglicanism beyond the crown and beyond the Church of England. But it is, nonetheless, a glimpse of a different kind of Church and future.

The controversy surrounding Colenso would loom large at the first gathering of the Lambeth Conference in 1867. Six years prior to the first Lambeth Conference, Colenso published a commentary on the epistle to the Romans from a "missionary point of view."[4] To study scripture from this missional perspective meant, for Colenso, serious study of language and culture that would lead toward entering the "secret chambers of light, which may be written by God's own finger there."[5] The role of a missionary was not to instill fear but to go as a "voice of comfort and love . . . to whisper of Him, Who has been with them all along—Who has *not* left them alone . . . Whose Voice they have heard already, though they knew it not . . . ."[6] In his Romans commentary, he praised Zulu thought and questioned established theological orthodoxy. It was in dialogue with Zulu thinkers, especially William Ngidi, that drew Colenso to question and reject a series of doctrines. He would come to reject both

4. John William Colenso, *St. Paul's Epistle to the Romans: New Translated, and Explained from a Missionary Point of View* (Cambridge: Macmillan and Co., 1861), 122.

5. Jeff Guy, *The Heretic: A Study of the Life of John Willian Colenso, 1814–1883* (Pietermaritzburg: Natal University Press, 1984), 77.

6. John William Colenso, *Village Sermons* (Cambridge: Macmillan and Co., 1853), 139–140.

the doctrine of eternal punishment and substitutionary atonement. He apparently taught a form of universalism emphasizing that the love of God was available to all people everywhere. Thus, the sacraments were in no way peculiar vehicles of grace. For Christians, reasoned Colenso, baptism cannot be some sort of "charm upon our breasts, as if *that* would save us from His judgement."[7] Amidst a variety of overlapping and intersecting attitudes toward race, revelation, empire, and polity, Colenso was tried and found guilty of heresy and condemned by the first Lambeth Conference.

Amidst these controversies and contestations, in the context of colonial expansion and a planting of an English Church overseas, we see something different in the thought and witness of Crowther and Colenso. We do not have to pass judgment on the theological content of their work to see a distinct approach to Christian witness that begins in presence and listening. Here is an intercultural discernment and theology that possesses a confidence in an already present Holy Spirit speaking to and not just through foreign missionaries. Many church leaders of their time were suspicious precisely of this approach to the gospel and culture. Unfortunately, the judgment passed on Crowther and Colenso would be passed on others in a variety of contexts in the nineteenth and twentieth centuries. Those who often suffered most at the hands of an imperialist Anglicanism were indigenous peoples. But the emerging communion would suffer too as a whole range of contextual Anglican theologians were inevitably forestalled because of attitudes similar to those faced by Crowther and Colenso.

In the postcolonial era, as nations were gaining flag independence from former colonies, published theologies from beyond the so-called West began to "write back." This postcolonial theology included criticism of imperial Anglicanism as it especially related to the so-called modern missionary movement. Several criticisms were identified that might be summed up as *overlapping* colonialist and missionary interests, *justification* of imperialism, *imposed* theologies, *racism*, and *sectarianism*.

Colenso hoped that the mission of the Church and empire would overlap. He had faith in a British empire that would help "civilize" the world. This, despite his adjudged heterodoxy, was a commonly held belief

7. Colenso, *Village*, 145.

among British missionaries. Bishop Charles James Blomfield (1786–1857) in an 1827 sermon could ponder:

> An empire so vast, so interspersed amidst the different nations of the world, so unaccountable in its growth, so singular in its structure, as fully to justify a belief that Providence has ordained it for some purpose of vast importance to mankind; and . . . a commerce so wonderfully extended and extending that we may seem to discern the finger of the Most High.[8]

For R. S. Sugiratharajah, it was the broadened horizons brought by empire that led to the rediscovery of the "unfashionable" text of Matthew 28:19.[9] For CMS missionary Johannes Rebmann, writing in 1856, ". . . 'where the power of a Christian nation ceased to be felt, there is also the boundary, set by Providence, to missionary labour.'"[10] For postcolonial theologians, this kind of thinking, and the practice that followed in its wake, compromised Anglican theology. Overlapping colonialist and missionary interests are adjudged to have forestalled contextual theology, local leadership, and worked against movements for self-determination.

Not only was empire seen as providential but some leaders in the Church of England explicitly justified imperialism and its myriad colonizing projects. A clear, and late, example of such justification is Max Warren's *Caesar The Beloved Enemy*.[11] Warren was secretary of the CMS from 1942 to 1963. Making "every necessary qualification as to the sinfulness of those who exercise power," Warren submitted that it is possible to theologically (and biblically) justify the subordination of one group of people by another. It is possible to ". . . envisage circumstances in which imperialism has a place in the purpose and providence of God." As with Warren's imperialist Anglican forebears' imperialism must be justified according to its missional efficacy. Colonization is legitimate if

8. Daniel O'Connor, *Three Centuries of Mission: The United Society for the Propagation of the Gospel 1701–2000* (London: Continuum, 2000), 52–53.

9. Robert S. Heaney, *From Historical to Critical Post-Colonial Theology: The Contribution of John S. Mbiti and Jesse N.K. Mugambi* (Eugene: Pickwick, 2015), 214.

10. Cited by Robert W. Strayer, *The Making of Missionary Communities in East Africa: Anglicans and Africans in Colonial Kenya, 1875–1935* (London: Heinemann, 1978), 33.

11. Max Alexander Cunningham Warren, *Caesar The Beloved Enemy: Three Studies in the Relation of Church and State* (London: SCM Press, 1955).

it serves "... the purpose of God in history ... to bring mankind to a true knowledge of Himself who is Love, Power and Justice."[12] In reference to providence, Christian vocation, social order, and the greater good, Warren justified imperialism. Empire, he argued, functions as a preparation for the reception of the Christian Gospel. A universal vision of empire is superior to the "localism" of traditional religions. It inspires vocation and it brings order through political legislation. Empire provides its subjects with a greater view and thus a grander sense of the common good. Those "writing back" would protest such thoughts. For example, J. N. K. Mugambi considered the association of Christian mission with colonialism a "scandal." He asked, "How can a liberating God condone oppression?"[13]

Crowther and Colenso sought a dialogic method toward a theology that connected with and spoke to the people they ministered among. In translation and reception, doctrine inevitably shifts, adapts, and changes. However, this cannot veil the fact that for some missionaries their intent was to impose their version of the faith on peoples they considered less enlightened or enthralled by Satan. John S. Mbiti witnessed a "bulldozer mentality" among missionaries assuming that indigenous traditions were demonic and, thus, needed to be "swept aside."[14] In not a few contexts, the Church sought to suppress traditional rituals in regard to birth, adulthood, marriage, elderhood, and death. This was done, argued Mbiti, "without . . . clear theological justification."[15] For some critics, evangelization worked with or amounted to Europeanization.[16] For Mbiti, such attempts at "cultural conditioning" resulted in a "rebellion" by African Christians.[17] Such resistance was seen especially in the rise of African Initiated Churches that grew particularly rapidly in countries like South Africa, Zimbabwe, and Kenya, where a small

---

12. Warren, *Caesar*, 24.

13. Jesse N.K. Mugambi, *Christian Theology and Social Reconstruction* (Nairobi: Acton, 2003), 70.

14. John S. Mbiti, "Confessing Christ in a Multifaith Context with Two Examples from Africa," *Metanoia* 4, nos. 3–4 (1994): 138–145.

15. Cited in Heaney, *Historical*, 43.

16. Jesse N.K. Mugambi, "A Fresh Look at Evangelism in Africa," *International Review of Mission* 87 (1998): 343.

17. Cited in Heaney, *Historical*, 41.

conservative community of white settlers sought to rule along racialist and racist lines.[18]

Racism was at work in settler societies and was not absent, as we have already seen, in missionary attitudes and practices. During the nineteenth century, the notion of the superiority of white people was a trope employed to justify colonialism. So-called social evolutionism depicted a hierarchy of peoples with Europe at the top and Africa at the bottom.[19] Such pseudoscience did not emerge in a vacuum. Anti-Semitism and racialized hierarchies were at the heart of what would be vaunted as European enlightenment and modernity. No less a figure than Immanuel Kant (1724–1804), considered foundational for modern Western philosophy and theology, would imagine hierarchies of race. On the basis of skin color (phenotype), Kant constructed four "racial distinctions"—white, Black, Mongul, and Hindustani.[20] These races existed along a continuum between the two poles of Black and white. The white pole was considered superior. Those races furthest from whiteness were furthest from the human ideal. For Kant it was the white race, living in a near perfect climate, that was closest to Adam and Eve.[21] On the way to perfection, the white race was spreading its ideals and its peoples throughout the world. In contrast, "Black flesh" lacked "universal gravitas. It was trapped in its particularity . . . ."[22] Against this backdrop, it is of some significance that, in 1908, the Dean of Westminster, Armitage Robinson, depicted an international family of Anglican churches bound together by a belief in the "providential mission" of the Anglo-Saxon race.[23] A Christian intercultural theology will stand against the racism of white supremacy and the concomitant sin that elevates as supreme so-called Western thought.

---

18. Jesse N.K. Mugambi, *The Biblical Basis of Evangelization: Theological Reflections Based on an African Experience* (Nairobi: Oxford University Press, 1989), 56–62. See Norman Etherington, Introduction in Norman Etherington ed., *Missions and Empire* (Oxford: Oxford University Press, 2005), 4.

19. See Herbert Spencer, *The Principles of Sociology Volume 1* (New York: D. Appleton and Company, 1895), 537–563.

20. See J. Kameron Carter, *Race: A Theological Account* (Oxford: Oxford University Press, 2008), 84.

21. Carter, *Race*, 88.

22. Carter, *Race*, 90.

23. See Alan M. G. Stephenson, *Anglicanism and the Lambeth Conferences* (London: SPCK, 1978), 8; Sachs and Heaney, *Promise*, 59.

Anglican missionaries have been accused of creating, solidifying, or exacerbating sectarianism. The criticism has some justification as the message that missionaries communicated, and more often the means of its communication, divided communities into those who had accepted the gospel and those who had not. Colonialists themselves objected to such apparent divisiveness. They feared it would create instability in society that would challenge their power and the supply chain for goods they sought to develop and protect. The company directors of the British East India Company, for example, forbade its chaplains from evangelizing indigenous peoples. By 1813, under the influence of evangelical leaders and in light of the loss of thirteen colonies in North America, the charter of the East India Company allowed for missionary activity. As was feared, social instability ensued as Christians, Hindus, and Muslims contended for power and voice. Particularly controversial was the missionary opposition to widow burning (*sati*). Along with Indian reformers, missionaries campaigned for the banning of *sati*. It was abolished in 1829. This along with Christian opposition to the caste system, and the competing demands of Muslims and Hindus, eventually led to the downfall of the Company's power with the Great Rebellion of 1857–1858.[24] Such histories speak to the complexities of pluralism, politics, and faithful Christian witness. In the wake of rebellion and the fall of the Company's power, Anglican mission leadership sought to develop a more cautious or careful approach to Christian witness. George Edward Lynch Cotton (Bishop of Calcutta, 1858–1866) discerned two goals for the Church: enter into deeper understanding of India's religions and deal fairly with non-Anglican Christians.

Given that Church history, and Anglican history, is as much marked by conflict as reconciliation—how might reconciliation be understood and, more importantly, how might it be practiced? This will be the focus of the next section.

The Church in Practical Reconciliation[25]

In 2002, the Church of the Province of Southern Africa revisited the case of Colenso. The Diocesan council of Durban submitted a resolution

24. See Sachs and Heaney, *Promise*, 158–162.

25. For a fuller treatment of this issue see Robert S. Heaney, *Post-Colonial Theology: Finding God and Each Other Amidst the Hate* (Eugene: Cascade, 2019), 143–159.

stating that Colenso had "sought to rethink Christian theology and the interpretation of Scripture in the light of his understanding of the Zulu people in their culture." The council also recognized that the Colenso family had fought for "the preservation of Zulu culture and autonomy, and for justice for the Zulu people." In 2014, the Rev. Canon Philip Mountstephen, executive leader of CMS, publicly repented the sin against God and Crowther. Young English missionaries had "effectively tried to place the shackles back" on Bishop Crowther. At the same service of "thanksgiving and repentance," the Most Rev. and Rt. Hon. Justin Welby, Archbishop of Canterbury, said: "We in the Church of England need to say sorry that someone was properly and rightly consecrated Bishop and then betrayed and let down and undermined. It was wrong."[26] How are these practices to be understood? In this section, it will be argued that such practices only have theological and ethical significance when placed within a broader understanding of how reconciliation relates to the holiness of the Church of Christ.

For Jeremy Bergen, corporate repentance as a practice of reconciliation is a distinct witness that emerges in the twentieth century.[27] Ecclesial repentance means a church and/or denominational body making a public and official statement or confession that requests forgiveness for what once was official practice or policy.[28] Such confession and repentance does not, in itself, define reconciliation but it can be a practice that arises from a commitment to the reconciling mission of God in Christ. That is to say, the practice of corporate repentance might be understood as the Church's ongoing response and reception of the gospel of Jesus Christ. Such reception is made particularly plain in the Church's own liturgy and ministry of reconciliation in contrition, confession, penance, and absolution.[29] That liturgical pattern might suggest or frame broader practices of reconciliation beyond the liturgy.

Contrition is a heartfelt sorrow for a particular sin and a heartful commitment to not sin in such a manner again. It is evidence of the work of the Holy Spirit. For the Spirit witnesses to the truth (John 14:6). It

---

26. Sachs and Heaney, *Promise*, 78.

27. Jeremy M. Bergen, *Ecclesial Repentance: The Churches Confront Their Sinful Pasts* (London: T&T Clark, 2011).

28. Bergen, *Ecclesial*, 3, 70–71.

29. Bergen, *Ecclesial*, 243–283.

is only in the power of the Spirit that those benefitting from imperialist Anglicanism will practice a contrite witness. It is only in the power of the Spirit that those suffering under the consequences of imperialism will weigh that contrition and practice a "forgiving witness."[30] As an example of contrition, Bergen cites the work of the 1993 National Native Convocation of the Anglican Church of Canada. During the Convocation, First Nations peoples testified to mistreatment in Church-governed residential schools. After a weeklong gathering and after numerous testimonies of abuse, the Primate of the Church, Michael Peers, offered an apology. In listening to the suffering of indigenous people in residential schools, he confessed to feeling "shame and humiliation." The Church, he confessed, failed indigenous young people and failed God. "I am sorry, more than I can say" continued Peers, "that we were part of a system which took you and your children from home and family" in a mission to "remake" indigenous people in the image of white people.[31]

Contrition should lead to a particular and specific *confession*. As has been seen, in both the cases of Crowther and Colenso, the Church gathered and leaders confessed their sin. Particular sins were committed and particular sins were confessed. While such confession might be ritualized, in gathering and in specific liturgy, there is also danger in such ritual. Such ritual can be designed in a way, intentionally or unintentionally, that sets up an expectation (or power dynamic) that public confession be met with immediate acceptance or even absolution. Given the depths of sin and the repercussions of sin associated with imperial Christianities, it is not the case that confession be lightly, quickly, or automatically received by those wronged or those suffering from historical wrong. In 1986, the United Church of Canada (UCC) issued an "Apology to First Nations" for the sin committed against indigenous peoples by white Christians. In responding to the apology, two years later, Native leaders received it but did not accept it. In their response, they explained that in Native American cultures apologies are lived out. Instead of a simple acceptance, what was proposed was that a stone cairn be erected on the site of the apology. Further stones would

30. Amos Yong, *Mission After Pentecost: The Witness of the Spirit from Genesis to Revelation* (Grand Rapids: Baker Academic, 2019), 282–283.

31. Heaney, *Post-Colonial*, 145.

be placed at the site as reparative or penitential progress was made and specific movements of healing entered into.[32]

Penance and absolution can be ordered in distinct ways depending on the theology of reconciliation at work in any given context. For example, absolution might come first and penance be seen not as preparation for absolution but as a reparative witness in the light of absolution. For the purposes of this chapter, I will follow the order as outlined by Berger. Penance is a witness that the Church has heard from those who have been sinned against and has entered into the witness of reparative action. On the twentieth anniversary of the UCC apology, more stones were added to the cairn in recognition of a specific reparative witness. This included new contextual education programs and a Healing Fund for survivors of Indian residential schools.[33] In more broader terms, those associated with imperialist Christianities might begin to think of theology in penitential mode. That is to say, white theologians might do the deep work associated with a critical awareness of the particularity of their historical, cultural, theological, and spiritual locatedness.[34] This will include an openness to theology formed in cultures beyond dominant cultures and theologies that critique imperialist Christianities.

Absolution comes from God (1 John 1:9) and is embodied in pastoral and sacramental action. Yet, it seems counterintuitive to take from these two realities that those who sin, or their descendants, are the ones to declare absolution on themselves. How might such tension be resolved in reconciliatory practice? Again, an emphasis on the work of the Spirit in the mission of God must be kept in view. In God's mission in creation and to creation, it is the Spirit that comes first. The Spirit of God hovers over the waters (Gen. 1:2); the Spirit gives life (Gen. 2:7); the Spirit empowers prophetic speech (Ezek. 2:2); the Spirit renews and restores life (Ezek. 36:25–28; 37:1–14); the Spirit births the mission of Christ (Luke 1:35, 4:18–19; Matt. 3:16); the Spirit births, teaches, and leads the Church as a fellowship or communion (John 14:26; Acts 15; Phil. 2:1–2).[35] The Spirit is at work, therefore, in God's world and not

32. See Heaney, *Post-Colonial*, 153.

33. Heaney, *Post-Colonial*, 153.

34. At one level, this was my aim in *Post-Colonial.*

35. Stephen B. Bevans, "God Inside Out: Toward a Missionary Theology of the Holy Spirit," *International Bulletin of Missionary Research* 22, no. 3 (1998): 102–105 at 103.

just in God's Church. Thus, absolution may not be pronounced by those selfsame people who acknowledge historical sin and its ongoing consequences. Rather, those who have been sinned against or those representing them might be discerned as the confessors amidst historical and ongoing sin. In the case of the UCC, this meant that the indigenous leaders embodied the forgiveness of God's grace and the "not yet" of God's final absolution at the end of days. These leaders beyond the Church invited the Church to do better and to, in practice, demonstrate what it means to be the body of Christ living in grace. Bergen sums up the theological significance of such practice:

> The church embodies reconciliation as it hears the cries of the marginalized people, overturns power imbalances and addresses ways to heal individuals and communities, while developing structures to ensure voices are in the future heard and the wrong is not repeated.[36]

The approach to reconciliation laid out in this chapter is practical. It calls the Church toward a just vision and a way of just witness in the world today. Careful readers will have noticed that such a practice seems to be predicated on a view of the Church that, at least in some quarters, would be controversial. That is to say, this practice of reconciliation seems to depend on the notion that the one, holy, catholic, and apostolic Church can sin. This seems to be in stark contrast to dogmatic commitments to a pure church.

Pope Pius XII defined the Church as "definite and perceptible to the senses" but as the mystical body of Christ it is "a perfect society."[37] The Catechism of the Catholic Church teaches that "the Spirit of holiness" gives life to the Church but that it is "the sinless one made up of sinners."[38] Such theologizing is often received in simple dictums such as "its members may sin but the church does not." This view of a sinless church, motivated no doubt by a desire for theological coherency, depends upon an abstraction that lifts the Church out of history.

---

36. Bergen, *Ecclesial*, 286.

37. Pius XII, *Mystici Corporis Christi* (1943), 14, 63.

38. *Catechism of the Catholic Church* (1992), 867.

In more recent years, there is evidence, in Catholic and ecumenical theology, that more nuanced understandings of the holiness of the Church are emerging. The Vatican II document, *Lumen Gentium*, depicts the Church as a pilgrim people that welcomes purification and reform as it journeys toward God's ordained end. That end will be God's work in bringing the Church to "full perfection" in "the glory of heaven."[39] This, along with a range of public statements and confessions, seems to open up an understanding of the holiness of the Church that also makes space for a church that sins. Arguably, the most significant statement in modern times was the Drancy statement (1997) issued by the Roman Catholic Church in France. This statement was a public act of repentance for the Church's complicity in anti-Jewish legislation in Vichy France during World War II.[40] The bishops confessed that anti-Semitism was at work in the Church's teaching and liturgy.[41] The Church had sinned. Given, therefore, the particularities of historical sin and this fresh willingness to confess that sin in practical reconciliation—a renewed understanding of the holiness of the Church seems necessary.

A renewed understanding of holiness, arising from practices of reconciliation, will reject any continuation of an appeal to abstract or ahistorical understandings of ecclesial purity. The holiness of the Church will not be defined or guarded by making a distinction between the children of the Church and a sinless ecclesial mother. Rather, the holiness of the Church will be defined by God's presence. The Church is holy because God is present in her midst. God is present in the historicity of the Church. The Church is holy in her reception of the grace of an eternally loving God. The Church is holy. The Church is becoming holy and this is not despite her historicity but because of her historicity. In her proclamation of Christ's gospel, and in her ongoing formation as a reconciled and reconciling fellowship, God's ordained consummation (Rev. 21) begins to break in even now.

---

39. Vatican II, *Lumen Gentium* (1964), VII:48.

40. See Patrick Henry, "The Art of Christian Apology: Comparing the French Catholic Church's Apology to the Jews and the Vatican's 'We Remember'" *Shofar: An International Journal of Jewish Studies* 26, no. 3 (2008): 87–104.

41. Henry, "Art," 100; Heaney, *Post-Colonial*, 150–151.

The Church depends upon the abiding presence and mission of the Spirit leading it into deeper grace through practical reconciliation.[42] The Church is the fruit of God's mission in Christ. The Church's identity is received from another and in repentance "the church makes clearer what is always the case: the basis of its hope is not itself, certainly not its good efforts or best intentions, but Jesus Christ."[43]

---

42. Heaney, *Post-Colonial*, 155–158.

43. Jeremy M. Bergen, "Whether, and How, a Church Ought to Repent for a Historical Wrong" *Theology Today* 73, no. 2 (2016): 140.

CHAPTER 5

Reconciliation and the Peace Process

Sarah Snyder

Introduction

Perhaps the best place to begin understanding reconciliation is to identify what it is not. Reconciliation does not require agreement or physical proximity. It can apply equally to restoring a relationship between those who continue to hold very different views. It does not require that those being reconciled share the same story. Their narrative of the past—the reasons for the brokenness—can be and often are in sharp contrast to one another. In the West, we have been so inculcated into a binary way of thinking, that we believe if you are right, then I must be wrong. We listen defensively—in fact we don't really listen at all, but are busy preparing our own counterargument. This way of relating is framed by debate, which has its place, of course. But if our listening skills are only trained for such encounters, we are not effective listeners.

Reconciliation: Healing the Broken

A Biblical Vision

Reconciliation, quite simply, means healing what is broken. Biblically, the Greek word is *katallage* (καταλλαγή). The term appears only four times in the New Testament and only in Paul's epistles. It refers to the broken relationship between God and humanity. The break was and is committed by us, while the reconciliation is the work of God. The cross can be seen as a site and symbol of reconciliation. The vertical axis signifies reconciliation between God and all creation and the horizontal axis signifies reconciliation among people:

> So if anyone is in Christ, there is a new creation: everything old has passed away; see, everything has become new! All this is from God, who reconciled us to himself through Christ, and has given us the ministry of reconciliation; that is, in Christ God was reconciling the world to himself, not counting their trespasses against them, and entrusting the message of reconciliation to us.
>
> (2 Cor. 5:17–19)

The end result of reconciliation is resurrection and new life, and it is only in heaven that a perfect reconciliation will be revealed. This does not mean we remain idle in the meantime. As Christians, we have the mandate and the opportunity to seek reconciliation in "the here and not yet." Paul goes on to write,

> So we are ambassadors for Christ, since God is making his appeal through us; we entreat you on behalf of Christ, be reconciled to God. For our sake he made him to be sin who knew no sin, so that in him we might become the righteousness of God.
>
> (2 Cor. 5:20–21)

Deep Listening

While in the West we have been inculcated into binary ways of thinking (I am right, therefore, you are wrong), the call to reconciliation is a call to deep listening. We need to attune ourselves to deep listening which is at the heart of every journey toward reconciliation. Deep listening is to step into the shoes of the other for a little while, to see the world through their eyes, before stepping back into our own familiar shoes. Our aim is not to *become* the other or to necessarily agree with the other. Rather, the aim is to rise above our own limited seeing and hearing. The aim is to take the risk of seeing as our opponents see and hearing as they hear in order to better understand the brokenness of our relationship. Such listening dismantles some of the high walls we have built around us or between us and our enemies. Such listening and seeing can be the hardest challenge we will ever face. Yet, hearing the stories of others, though difficult, is critical to moving forward on the path toward reconciliation.

As human beings, we naturally try to make sense of the present through referencing the past and anticipating a future of some kind. From a reconciliation perspective, the difficulty comes when another's story of my past is not a story I recognize—it is not my story. Their stories of the past—my past—do not fit with my remembering. They are simply not true. Part of reconciliation is coming to terms with and understanding the differences that arise as a matter of perspective. Deep listening, along with the following elements of reconciliation, are necessary to address disagreements and conflicts that are part of our past and impact greatly our present and our future.

The Three R's of Reconciliation

Re-membering

We attempt to understand the past through *story* and this is usually our own story of what has happened. When we speak of story, we are not talking about made-up narratives or fiction. Story is, rather, the ways in which we piece together the actual milestones of our past to create a meaningful narrative about what happened. We include other characters in our story—good and bad. We tell their stories for them in ways that fit with our own perspectives. All of this is vital to our making sense of the past. We never forget the past and the purpose of reconciliation is not any such forgetting. Reconciliation is a re-membering more honestly.

When we remember the past and tell our own stories, we also tell stories on behalf of others. When we tell stories of people who have hurt or upset us, we often frame our narratives in ways that justify our own status as victim and their role as offender: They did this. It is their fault. They are responsible for all that has gone wrong. There are, of course, times when we *are* an entirely innocent victim. Sometimes the offender is entirely in the wrong. Their story might, however, begin before their encounter with us. Their behavior and attitude might be in light of other parts of their story, including the parts where they are somebody else's victim. That does not change our story. But it might help us to see a bigger picture, one that takes into account some of our offender's story too.

Re-membering is a move away from telling the stories of others. Re-membering our past requires a willingness to hear the story of the other, instead of telling their story on their behalf. Re-membering is the recognition of their right to tell their own story, not only of themselves, but also of us. In listening to their story, we are not indicating agreement. We are not seeking compromise or denying the truth of what has gone wrong in our relationship. Yet, in hearing our offender's story, we sometimes begin to see our own story in a different light.

Re-humanizing

When we tell the stories of our offenders (instead of listening to them), when we stop looking them in the eye and stop seeing their face, we tend to create our own image of them and see that instead. We focus on several aspects of their character or behavior, which eventually becomes our entire picture of them. We forget the full humanity of our offenders. We de-humanize them, and de-face them. We mask their true identity. In cases of extreme conflict or disagreement, we demonize them, and we start to believe our own creations: they hate us; they are out to get us. A tiny illustration of this is the moment a Palestinian Christian came face to face with a member of the Israeli Defense Forces in one of our reconciliation programs. In a moment of reflection during the program, he said that prior to this encounter, he never realized that Israelis smiled. He had only encountered them at checkpoints and other situations where, for understandable reasons, nobody was smiling.

Israelis and Palestinians, Protestants and Catholics in Belfast, and many others have a physical wall separating them much of the time; but most of us create metaphorical walls between ourselves and those we find difficult or different. Sometimes they are necessary walls for our protection, but in every case, they serve to remove the face of those on the other side. This encourages us to build our own replicas of them. We make our enemies according to our image of them. We do not see them as made in the image of God. The fact is, God loves our enemies, just as much as he loves us. In light of that, Jesus gave us that hardest of challenges, "But I say to you, love your enemies and pray for those who persecute you" (Matt. 5:44).

Sometimes the enemy we find hardest to love is the one within. When we think about re-humanizing, we are not only contemplating others. Sometimes the demons we see in others are a reflection of the parts of ourselves we find difficult to love. I wonder if Jesus was on to something when he reminded us not only to love God, love our neighbor and love our enemies—but all along to love ourselves—the enemy within. In my experience, the re-humanizing that is needed at the heart of reconciliation is not only of others. It is also of ourselves and those parts within us we find hardest to love. Our ability to love others is deeply connected to our ability to love ourselves. I have experienced this on many occasions, one of which was with a very senior leader in South Sudan. Faced with his own demons, including participation in bloodshed, he wept, "Why was I born a Dinka?" If only I was somebody less known, less significant, less called on to act on behalf of others. He was traumatized by what he had witnessed and done, and yet at the same time he was the cause of others' trauma. Caught between a rock and a hard place, he felt he had nowhere to turn. No way out of the cycle of violence he was caught within. The one place he could turn was to God. God knew and understood the glimmer of vulnerability expressed at that moment. As we see so often in the journey of reconciliation, vulnerability is a vital but seemingly impossible step. It is the willingness to see and express our own failings and weakness in the midst of chaos and conflict. Vulnerability is vital. It opens the door to imagining a different future—one in which we can begin to dismantle the walls we have built and look beyond.

Re-imagining

Re-membering and re-humanizing encompass the willingness to reframe our own stories in the light of the stories of other people. This might mean starting the story earlier or filling it in with previously unknown or overlooked milestones. It could mean seeing a different end point, or re-imagining a different outcome. Re-imagining means recognizing shared elements between our story and another's, rather than limiting the story through our own narrow lens. It allows us to relinquish the desire for revenge and retaliation that perpetuate broken relationships in a never-ending cycle. We seek a different way forward. This is a way that turns us outward to those around us whose lives are also impacted by our broken relationships. This is an imagined future in which we find the strength to seek the flourishing of everyone—ourselves, those who have offended us, those we have offended, and anyone else impacted by the conflict we have lived out for so long.

This may seem humanly impossible much of the time, but as Christians we are not alone in facing the challenge. We are reconciled reconcilers. Former enemies ourselves, we have already been reconciled to God in Christ. It is from this reality that we in turn are asked to serve as ministers of reconciliation—ambassadors of Christ—his hands and feet. It is by the power of the Holy Spirit that we find the strength to act, day by day, in the smallest encounters of our lives as well as those more significant. By cultivating mini habits of reconciliation every day, we prepare for those moments when a much "bigger ask" is made of us.

Jesus set us a perfect example in crossing boundaries to see and hear those his contemporaries overlooked, often meeting with those considered "unclean" or enemy to his own community. He healed the man by the Bethesda pool who could not walk or reach the healing waters without help (John 5:2–9). He revealed himself to the Samaritan woman who visited the well at midday because she was shunned by her peers (John 4:7–26). He welcomed the despised tax collector, Zaccheus (Luke 19:1–10). He accepted the offering of a "sinful" woman's tears at Simon the Pharisee's dinner party (Luke 7:36–50). Christ recognized, engaged, and transformed the lives of those considered outsiders and enemies. We are called to cultivate lives shaped by the example of Jesus. What might be the characteristics one needs to develop in this important work of reconciliation?

Habits of Reconcilers

Those who wish to enter deeper into the work of reconciliation can develop habits that serve the work: hospitality, curiosity, generosity, empathy, vulnerability, humility and lament, forgiveness, gratitude, hope, stewardship, and creativity. We call these *habits* because they are not inborn dispositions. Developing a reconciling spirit is something that brings peace to the world around us—our homes, workplaces, houses of worship, local communities, and nations. While many of us might find that some of these characteristics come more naturally than others, all are habits that anyone can choose to foster and develop. No one practices these habits perfectly, and yet no one is incapable of growing into these habits.

Hospitality

We in the West often have a skewed view of what hospitality is about. We equate hospitality with the actions and materials of the host: who the host invites, what food the host serves, what accommodations the host provides. This view creates a problem. It causes us to focus on things, rather than the single most important component of hospitality: the guest. The Latin root of the word hospitality is *hospes*, which means guest, and this guest-centric view of hospitality shows itself repeatedly in scripture. As reconcilers, we are challenged to take the risk of being another's guest—to meet them in their own spaces rather than always expecting them to come to ours; to move beyond our own familiar, comfortable place, and sit with them, in theirs. By doing this, we live out a mutual form of hospitality—one in which we are sometimes host, and sometimes guest.

The book of Genesis illustrates the idea of hospitality in the story of three guests hosted by Abraham and Sarah, and as the Bible often does, it turns the idea of hospitality on its head. At first glance, this is a story about Abraham and Sarah hosting three strangers and providing them with refreshment and rest. As we read deeper into the story, we realize that it is the three strangers who are the real host, and they provide Abraham and Sarah with the miraculous news that Sarah will bear a son.

Curiosity

Curiosity or a sense of wonder is crucial to the work of reconciliation. In our current world of social media and news feeds, it is easy to isolate ourselves into self-affirming bubbles. Faith calls us to move beyond the bubbles and beyond our comfort zone. We are called to wonder and wrestle with those questions that challenge our beliefs. In the words of the late Rabbi Jonathan Sachs,

> Faith is not opposed to questions, but it is opposed to the shallow certainty that what we understand is all there is . . . Far from faith excluding questions, questions testify to faith—that

> history is not random, that the universe is not impervious to our understanding, that what happens to us is not blind chance. We ask, not because we doubt, but because we believe.[1]

Curiosity and wonder require us to listen deeply. We are required to focus on what others are saying rather than simply focusing on our own position and how we are going to adapt or challenge what is being said in an attempt to mold it to our preconceived notions. Doing this draws us deeper into reflection where we allow ourselves to be surprised, which in turn gives rise to greater curiosity and wonder, and more questions. In many respects, curiosity is an important element of hospitality because it enables us to tear down the walls that separate us from the "other," from an "us versus them" mindset. It invites others into our space and draws us into their space and their worldview.

Generosity

If curiosity allows us to enter into the space of the other, generosity allows us to enter into the space of the divine. Generosity is the act of giving of ourselves without expecting anything in return. For people of faith, this is in imitation of the blessings that God bestows on us. While we cannot do or say anything that can even begin to return divine generosity—God calls us to cultivate a spirit of generosity. We hear this divine call set forth for Moses, a prophet familiar to Jews, Muslims, and Christians alike. The laws set aside portions of the harvest for the poor and allowed for periodic forgiveness of all debt, freeing of slaves, and the return of ancestral land to those who had lost it through debt. There is an awesome work of generosity in these texts and they in turn call God's people toward deep generosity. You may not be in a position to offer such monetary generosity but generosity in reconciliation remains important—words of encouragement and a smile can make a profound difference to the recipient and open up a pathway to reconciliation that might not have been obvious before.

---

1. Jonathan Sacks, *The Chief Rabbi's Haggadah: Hebrew and English Text with New Essays and Commentary* (New York: HarperCollins, 2007), 106.

Empathy

Empathy grows out of curiosity and generosity. In order to understand another's pain or suffering, one needs to first possess curiosity that enables one to ask questions that seek to understand what the other's experience is about. Empathy also stems from the habit of generosity. Giving the other person our time, attentiveness, understanding, and concern is a tremendous gift. So many of us go through life feeling that nobody is listening or bothering to understand what it is like to be us. To give another person the opportunity to feel understood is a liberating and affirming experience. It is also a gift that we give ourselves because when we show empathy to another, it often enables us to move beyond our own pain and distress. Like generosity and curiosity, deep listening is a crucial element of empathy. It is important not to rush in to attempting to "solve" the other person's problem or project our own preconceived ideas upon them. To be empathetic, one needs to temporarily put aside self and step into the experience of others.

All of these habits provide us with ways of opening ourselves up to others—inviting them into our world and daring, when invited, to enter into theirs. Implicit in such habits is the practice of vulnerability.

Vulnerability

Vulnerability is opening ourselves up emotionally and spiritually to relationship. When we are vulnerable we are open to love and to joy, but also to the risk of being hurt, disappointed, or rejected. As risky as that sounds, the alternative to choosing vulnerability is to close ourselves off to others. It is to wrap ourselves up in busyness and creature comforts. It is to insulate ourselves against this risk of being hurt. However, it also renders us stagnate and frozen. For Christians, the ultimate model of vulnerability is Jesus:

> Christ Jesus . . . though he was in the form of God, did not regard equality with God as something to be exploited, but emptied himself, taking the form of a slave, being born in human likeness. And being found in human form, he humbled himself and became obedient to the point of death—even death on a cross.
>
> (Phil. 2:5–8)

God, the Creator of the whole world, came to visit us in human form: Jesus Christ. The word became flesh. God Himself experienced human life and human suffering. This gospel of divine love for humanity was and is the model of human vulnerability in its perfected state. True vulnerability is a tall order, but helping on that journey is the habit of humility.

Humility and Lament

Humility is not about debasing ourselves or setting ourselves up to be victims of abuse. Neither is it about ostentatious displays of faux humility in order to garner the praise of others. A critical element of this habit is striving toward a right relationship with God. It calls us to cease competing and measuring ourselves against others and orienting ourselves to serving God. Thinking of ourselves less, rather than thinking less of ourselves.[2] When we focus on this vertical relationship with the divine, it enables us to no longer see our horizontal relationships with our fellow human beings as threats or competition. It calls us into an understanding that we are both wonderfully unique and beloved by God, and in turn, so too are all others that we encounter.

If humility is a product of being in right relationship with God, acknowledging simultaneously our value and limitations as well as that of others, lament is one way in which humility manifests itself. In the words of Jo Bailey Wells,

> To lament is to name the ruptures of this world so truthfully that we move beyond the point where any explanation or action is adequate, to the space where the only way forward is the desperate anguished cry directly to God.[3]

The Psalms frequently express songs of lament of crying out to God in anguish and pain at the suffering and injustice of the world. When we are suffering hurt or injustice, a rupture occurs within ourselves as well. It is natural that we lash out or perhaps behave irrationally. It is vitally necessary that we be able to name and mourn these ruptures, both in the world and in ourselves. This is not done so that we will be provided with

---

2. Clive Staples Lewis, *Mere Christianity*, rev. ed. (New York: HarperCollins, 1996).

3. Jo Bailey Wells, Lecture, Coventry Cathedral, Coventry, United Kingdom, February 2013.

neat simple answers or fixes. Often there may not be any viable solution. Like Jacob, confronted by the loss of his beloved son Joseph, we are left in God's presence with only grief and questions. Allowing space for lament, both our own and others, requires that we sit with the pain of rupture and unanswered questions without rushing in to "fix" the problem.

Forgiveness

Perhaps the hardest of all these habits is forgiveness. Forgiveness is messy and difficult because the boundary between victim and offender can be blurred. It is important to note that forgiveness does not entail ignoring or glossing over a particular offense. Rather than forgetting or pushing it under the carpet, forgiveness recognizes and names the fact that something is wrong. Furthermore, it asks us to forgo the just retribution that is in fact deserved. When we have been injured or when we have injured another, the absence of forgiveness means that the event continues to own us and define us. Forgiveness requires us to let go of our offender's hold over us. Letting go of an offense is extremely difficult. However, if we do not forgive, our wounds go untreated, they fester, and we become sick with the hold that our injuries have over us.

Forgiveness is rarely a one-time act, but something that we must revisit over and over again. Frequently working through forgiveness may require that we seek the help of a professional. It is important to understand that forgiveness does not always result in reconciliation. There are instances in which the best outcome is for the parties involved to go their separate ways. The amazing thing about forgiveness is that we are not asked to forgive in our own strength. Forgiveness is only fully possible through God, the source of all forgiveness. We can find the grace to forgive because God forgives us. This means that we can forgive someone even if they refuse to acknowledge their wrongdoing, and we can offer an apology even when the injured party refuses to accept it. One way that often helps those who are struggling with forgiveness is simply to commend the other person to God's mercy and justice, trusting our broken relationship to his wisdom.

Gratitude

Supporting us in our efforts to forgive and to receive forgiveness is the habit of gratitude. Gratitude, like forgiveness, builds on humility. It begins with the acknowledgment that we are not the sole authors of the good things in our lives. Every "generous act of giving, with every perfect gift, is from above, coming down from the Father of lights, with whom there is no variation of shadow due to change" (James 1:17; also see 1 Chron. 16:11–12). We are dependent on God and on one another. Gratitude is one of the most powerful habits that we have at our disposal and supports reconciliation and healing in so many ways. To dwell in a spirit of gratitude often opens us up to possibilities and the blessing that even our most challenging situations can prompt. Gratitude requires that we allow ourselves to receive from others (not always easy) and to recognize and name the giftedness that they bring. This can be especially helpful to members of society who are on the margins or who rarely feel seen or heard. Sincere and genuine thankfulness to those in our lives who bless us with their presence is the foundation of healthy and lasting relationships.

Hope

Hope is the ability to see beyond the current constraints and limitations of a situation. Like lamentation, it requires that we name and recognize the brokenness that is in the world. It often puts us in opposition to the majority who see the situation as hopeless or unsolvable. Hope is not about naivete or being unrealistic. It is about waiting and watching for signs that a given situation can change, can be improved, and the world made better by it. In the Christian scripture, Simeon and Anna were both very old by the time Jesus was born. Simeon spent much of his life praying and teaching in the temple. Anna likewise had devoted herself to praying in the temple in watchful hopefulness. Both were hoping in the promise of the Lord through the prophets, that the anointed one would come. Imagine devoting your life to waiting, watching, and hoping. Yet it was that hopefulness that enabled them to immediately recognize that the little infant carried by his seemingly unremarkable parents, too poor to even bring the customary offering for the first born, was the salvation of the world (Luke 2:25–35).

Stewardship and Creativity

If we live in a state of expectant hope, we also understand that to recognize and act on those signs of hope, we must use what we have been given wisely. Islam, Judaism, and Christianity all acknowledge that we humans are stewards of God's creation. A steward is a servant to a master. A steward is not the owner. We are not the owners of creation: God is. In the words of the Prophet Muhammad, "The world is beautiful and verdant, and verily God, the Exalted, has made you His stewards in it" (Hadith, Saheeh Muslim). In the Jewish tradition, there is a midrash that God takes Adam to show him the Garden of Eden and says, "Look at my works! See how beautiful they are—how excellent! For your sake I created them all. See to it that you do not spoil and destroy My world; for if you do, there will be no one else to repair it" (Midrash Ecclesiastes Rabbah 7:13). Good stewardship recognizes that we are servants, and the bounty of creation must be cared for wisely and to the benefit of everyone.

We must also be good stewards of our own person and ask ourselves frequently how are we choosing to spend our time, our personal resources, and our passions? We too do not belong to ourselves but to God, and as such, we must allocate our very lives in service to his purposes.

Good stewardship coupled with hope for the possibilities of what can be leads us down paths of creativity. If we are dwelling in a spirit of hope, seeing new ways beyond the status quo, and if we are mindful of our obligation to use all that we have to the benefit of others, a desire to create and construct something better will inevitably erupt from within. Creativity is, above all, an act of love. When we create, we are acting out of that divine imprint that dwells within all of us. We, like little children, imitate the actions of our divine Creator parent.

Anglicanism and Reconciliation

There exists in Anglican Christianity an instinct for holding things together in creative tension. Our own genesis occurred in a country teetering on the edge of civil war, and the Elizabethan Settlement, which many regard as the foundational moment in Anglican Christianity, was just that. It was a settlement, a compromise between two opposing religious movements. A state of creative tension is not always comfortable. The natural human impulse is a desire to resolve conflict. It is much easier to resolve the tension in one direction or the other, but that often means one side "winning" and the other "losing." Genuine reconciliation frequently looks for ways in which two sides can live with their tensions. It seeks a way that is not destructive, nor which capitulates to one side or the other. While resolution might result in some cases, the goal of reconciliation is to channel conflict constructively, not destructively, often leading to healthy innovation. Archbishop Justin Welby describes reconciliation as "the transformation of violent or destructive conflict into non-violent and creative disagreement."[4] Alexander Roper Vidler, an Anglican theologian and Dean of Christchurch Oxford during the 1950s and 1960s, expressed it thus:

> Anglican theology is true to its genius when it is seeking to reconcile opposing systems, rejecting them as exclusive systems, but showing that the principle for which each stands has its place within the total orbit of Christian truth, and in the long run is secure only within that orbit . . . when it is held in tension with other apparently opposed, but really complimentary principles.[5]

Anglicanism has a few tools at its disposal that can facilitate reconciliation. An integral part of our common worship incorporates the need to both seek and grant forgiveness. Like our Roman Catholic brothers and sisters, we recognize the centrality of sacraments. A sacrament is a ritual through which we recognize and appropriate truth regarding ourselves, others, and God. We not only recognize the sacramental nature of reconciliation through the option of ritual confession of our sins, but we also repent and ask forgiveness every time we engage in Morning Prayer and Evening Prayer from the Book of Common Prayer. Reconciliation, like other important facets of life, needs rituals. It needs these traditional sacramental and liturgical moments, but it also needs the more recent "ritual" innovations such as Truth and Reconciliation Tribunals. These commissions create space for the important work of lamentation. We need space and rituals to lament—not only for our own circumstances but also for others. In ritual we express our longing for healing in the midst of chaos, broken relationship, and violence. Robert Schreiter recognizes the significance of sacrament and ritual: "[The church] can make use of its space for important ritual moments that reach beyond the life of the

4. Coventry Cathedral, "Four Reflections on Reconciliation," 3:57, trailer about reconciliation, https://youtu.be/FBYtcFSMNIU.

5. Alexander Roper Vidler, *Essays in Liberality* (London: SCM Press, 1957), 166.

church to seal apologies, hear declarations of forgiveness, and celebrate movements into new places."[6]

We cannot overlook the significance of reconciliation in the celebration of the Eucharist, the central sacrament of the Church. The objective of reconciliation as a key feature of sacraments is rooted in the universal acknowledgment that we all need reconciling to God. This is an aspect that all groups, all societies, have in common. In the words of Emmanuel Katongole, "The social imagination which the Eucharist performs is not a church of the 'pure' or of the 'holy' but one of forgiven sinners."[7] The Eucharistic feast is a place for the forgiven forgivers. Together we gather round the Lord's table, equal as sinners in God's sight:

> Therefore, my dear friends, flee from the worship of idols. I speak as to sensible people; judge for yourselves what I say. The cup of blessing that we bless, is it not a sharing in the blood of Christ? The bread that we break, is it not a sharing in the body of Christ? Because there is one bread, we who are many are one body, for we all partake of the one bread.
>
> (1 Cor. 10:14–17)

The role of sacrament and sacredness is vital to reconciliation because we must always bear in mind that it is only in God, by the power of the Holy Spirit, that reconciliation (*katallage*) is accomplished. Yet, there needs to be consent on our part. There needs to be a willingness to show up and do the difficult work of deep listening, of recognizing our own part in brokenness, and being willing to expand our own narrow view of the issues. There needs to be an openness to the creative work of the Holy Spirit to paint a picture of a new and reimagined future.

Lastly, as a key peacekeeping tool we, as Anglicans, have our sacred scripture. It is not just our own Bible that resources our practices of reconciliation. Through the shared practice of Scriptural Reasoning, a deeper practice of reconciliation, within and across different faiths,

6. Robert J. Schreiter, *The Ministry of Reconciliation: Spirituality & Strategies* (Maryknoll, NY: Orbis Books, 1998), 129.

7. Emmanuel Katongole, *A Future for Africa: Critical Essays in Christian Social Imagination* (Scranton, PA: University of Scranton Press, 2005), 21.

can emerge. In Scriptural Reasoning, people of different traditions and faiths come together to share and reflect on their respective sacred texts. The goal of this practice is not to convince others of the "rightness" of our own beliefs. It is to share from our own deeply formed scriptural tradition, and to listen to others with very different questions and perspectives, as we address contemporary societal challenges together. By listening to others' interpretation and practice of faith, we find that our own understanding is enriched and expanded, and we gain so many instances of "I never thought of it that way . . ." or "I never asked myself that question before . . . ." By conversing and discussing our sacred texts side by side, not always agreeing and certainly not compromising on truth, we develop a deeper and richer understanding of the divine call to reconciliation.

Conclusion

The DNA of reconciliation is seeing and hearing—seeing and hearing those we place behind our metaphorical walls. Perhaps we do this because they are different to us, or difficult or simply distant—those we overlook, ignore, or walk past every day. The L'Arche movement forms intentional communities in which those with profound disabilities live alongside others who are able-bodied, learning from one another in the process. This philosophy applies to so many situations involving those whose gaze we rarely see or return. When whole segments of society isolate, shun, or ignore another group, we see the fallout of misunderstanding, loneliness, and eventually violence, in word and action. Just as an individual is moved to despair, so too collective isolation and dehumanization result in similar ends.

Re-membering, re-humanizing, and re-imagining require seeing the face of the other. This requires hearing their story even when it does not fit neatly with our own. Reconciliation is one of the hardest challenges of all. It is a long and arduous journey—rarely linear, but full of setbacks and repeats. Yet it is, I believe, a journey every Christian is called to embark on.

SECTION B

Peacebuilding in Context

CHAPTER 6

Peace and Practice

Priorities Amidst Conflict

Fuad S. Dagher

Introduction

Upon receiving a peace prize from his local authorities, one of the members of a regional peacekeeping group wrote, "I had never understood the search for peace as the avoidance of conflict, that we are able to avoid war by being nonviolent is achieving peace." To achieve this peace the Church has a role to play. The Church has a mission, as well as a message, not only to its members, but also to the world at large. Our Lord Jesus is, was, and always will be the perfection of God's will for human reaction to violence. His reaction to the conflict that he experienced in his own life, in the horrible violence of the Passion and Crucifixion, is the ideal model for the Church in how we are to react to conflict and violence in our times. When Jesus was brought before the Sanhedrin and eventually Pilate, one would have expected him to react defensively to the accusations and resist or rebel against the violence of his persecutors. In the culture of the Roman Empire, just like our modern age, his seemingly passive behavior might have been interpreted as a sign of his weakness, submission, and disability. This is wrong. I see in Jesus' silent reaction a sign of strength, love, and peace, because Jesus' silence was his love reaction. It takes far greater measure of restraint and strength of willpower to remain silent when your enemies are circling around you. The Great Mahatma Gandhi of India said:

> To refuse to struggle against the evil of the world is to surrender your humanity, to struggle against the evil of the world with the weapons of the evil-doer is to enter into your humanity, to struggle against the evil of the world with the weapons of God is to enter into your divinity.[1]

Peace in Context

Peace Amidst Conflict

Peace is not only the absence of war, nor is peace an outcome of oppression; we have seen and witnessed how false such peace is in so many places in our world. I would say that peace and prudent national security measures can coexist, but peace and fear cannot. Justice is not the opposite of peace; it is a vital component part of peace, and a vital one at that. Peace can never be achieved by obscuring the truth. In his work with South Africa's Truth and Reconciliation Commission, Desmond Tutu writes of the dangers of trying to achieve peace by denying reality:

> It was pointed out that none of us possess a kind of fiat by which we can say, "Let bygones be bygones" and, hey presto, they then become bygones. Our common experience in fact is the opposite—that the past, far from disappearing or lying down and being quiet, has an embarrassing and persistent way of returning and haunting us unless it has in fact been dealt with adequately. Unless we look the beast in the eye, we find it has an uncanny habit of returning to hold us hostage.[2]

To achieve peace in God's Kingdom, we need to be just with our neighbors and ourselves in speaking our truth. We also need to deal with them as our fellow human beings no matter their religion, race, or ethnicity.

Our calling in the Middle East, not dissimilar to the peace wished for after the fall of apartheid, is to be an instrument of peace and love

1. Cited in Neil Paynter ed., *Lent and Easter Readings from Iona* (Glasgow: Wild Goose Publications, 2008 [2002]), 22.

2. Desmond Tutu, *No Future Without Forgiveness* (New York: Doubleday, 1999), 28.

in a world of violence and hatred, despair, and injustice. Our calling is to respect people of other faith affiliations, striving to build bridges to reach the other. It is not to build faith ghettos or walls which will separate us from the other. We are called to be a prophetic voice in the wilderness of our wounded world. As Christians in the Land of the Holy One, we are ideally placed to reach out with a message of peace, love, and reconciliation to the east and to the west. Therefore, we must seek to know the truth, to speak the truth, and to live out the truth. On the foundation of this truth, we must all strive for justice and love through which we are able to achieve an everlasting peace.

It was the Palestinians who first heard the call of Jesus on the Sea of Galilee. The fishermen Jesus called were Palestinians. It was these people of the land, centuries before Jesus arrived, that accepted the call into a covenantal relationship with God through Father Abraham and were the first witnesses to Jesus' work and message. Jesus' message of love and peace especially echoes in the ear of Palestinians. Arab Christian Palestinians, therefore, feel a special call to be peacemakers in their own land and, in so doing, to be a model for the world.

Archbishop Elias Chacour, retired Archbishop in the Galilee Melkite Greek Catholic Church, is a Palestinian Arab. The ethos of the culture Chacour perpetuated during his tenure was that the Palestinian loss of land and homes should be a kind of victorious story. This story challenges the Palestinian people to rise from all the damages they have and are suffering from others today and turn their story into a story of reconciliation. Chacour described this as "stretching out our arms to others." Bishop Chacour sought to build bridges, not walls, around the other. We continue today to respond to Chacour's challenge to organize multiethnic and religious youth camps, schools, and summer camps as building blocks to peaceful coexistence rather than violence and division.[3]

For me, Chacour is a prophet. If I think, as a Palestinian, that my Jewish neighbor is not an occupier, I can begin to see him as a person. As an Arab Palestinian, this does not mean that I give up my story. It does mean that we need to be partners with the Jewish Israelis to make a real and just peace. There needs to be a new way of looking at each other. We are each

3. See Elias Chacour and David Hazard, *Blood Brothers: The Dramatic Story of a Palestinian Christian Working for Peace in Israel* (Ada, MI: Baker Books, 2013).

other's neighbor; we are people, not the oppressor or the oppressed. We can do this reorientation by teaching the new generation that their neighbor is not their enemy but a human being capable of being a partner to bring peace. We cannot see each other as people if we do not interact with each other. We need to be in a relationship to accomplish this.

Christ was and is many things. Most notably, Christ is reconciler. It is through the paschal mystery, the passion, death, and resurrection of Christ, that we are reconciled to God. We all possess the imprint of our divine Creator, and so we too have this spark of the divine that enables us to be reconcilers as well. How are we to share in God's divinity by bringing peace to our wounded world? It cannot be accomplished by staying in our faith ghettos. We need not forget the words of Jesus who challenges us saying: "Blessed are the peace makers for they shall be called the children of God" (Matt. 5:9). In this chapter, I will try to lay the foundation for peacebuilding and the practice of it in pluralistic communities out of my own experience especially in times of conflict.

Peace Amidst Conflict Defined

To build peace, we need to be in a relationship with each other. One of the most fundamental steps that needs to occur for personal growth, advancing peace and coexistence, is community building. We need to begin by defining peace on an individual level. Individual peace may start with having calmness within oneself. We can do this through prayer, and through contemplating sacred scripture, especially the gospels where we can ponder on the peace of Christ and what that means. How did Jesus engage with those who were other? How did Jesus handle those who opposed him and those who attacked him? Are there ways we might emulate his example in our own lives, families, and communities? Expanding outwardly, peace entails agreement and harmony among people. At its largest scale, peace is to live without violence, conflict, or war. Peace is not easy, but it underlies our quality of life.

Many spiritual traditions and teachings throughout history have emphasized peace, both as an inner journey and as an outward commitment to living in mutual benefit with our families, our communities, and in the world at large. Other ingredients essential to the creation of peace are fairness, justice, inclusiveness, and human rights. These must be embedded into the community to foster agreement and harmony.

Chacour related a moment of reconciliation between a group of Muslims and Christians in the village of Ibillin in the Galilee. As vicar of the Church, he scolded his parishioners:

> "Sitting in this building does not make you a Christian," I began awkwardly. My voice seemed to echo too loudly in the shocked silence . . . "You are a people divided. You argue and hate each other - gossip and spread malicious lies. What do the Moslems and the unbelievers think when they see you? Surely, that your religion is false. If you can't love your brother that you see, how can you say you love God who is invisible? You have allowed the body of Christ to be disgraced."[4]

Peace then is the coexistence of diverse peoples achieved by recognizing each other as children of God.

Peacebuilding in Community

Steps Toward Peacebuilding

Peace enriches our communities and individual lives, as it directs us to embrace diversity and to fully support one another as much as possible. Through caring, generosity, and fairness, we provide a cornerstone for attaining a sustainable, just, meaningful, vibrant, and fulfilling personal and community life. To bring home this point, we all need to consider the following questions:

- Can our families and communities thrive without mutual support and peace with our neighbors?
- Can peaceful communities exist without attention to justice and equity?
- What would be the prospects of a world without peace?

Promoting peace requires valuing and considering both oneself and others. As such, peace is central to every situation throughout our lives. Just as a child is enriched as he or she learns to take on more responsibilities, the meaning in our lives grows as we learn to recognize

4. Chacour and Hazard, *Blood Brothers*, 173.

and take more responsibility for one another and the world. While such a broad application is encouraged, individuals and communities can enhance their impact by strategically focusing on these efforts in an intentional and deliberate way. In community organizing, promoting peace is in many ways like other areas of strategic planning. One of the models that I have found helpful is the peacebuilding work accomplished by Parents Circle. It is an organization that merits mention here as a group that promotes peace against the backdrop of tragedy and shared loss. It was started by a Jewish father and a Muslim father who both lost children due to the Israeli–Palestinian conflict. Parents of all ethnicities, Arab and Jew, Muslim, Christian, meet regularly to share stories of their lost children who were killed by war. Their different family structures and their different practices of faith no longer act as walls of hatred and distaste. Instead, the parent's grief unites them, and their shared pain allows them to coexist. From this difficult work, I identify four steps toward peacebuilding in community. They can be summed up as: discover and assess; focus and commit; build and launch; and evaluate and maintain.

First, *discover and assess.* This means learning more about the issues and assets that affect peace in the community. A quick snapshot of concerns can be identified through statistics on criminal activities, hate crimes, and school incidents. More in-depth information may be gained from discussions with residents and local human rights commissions. The cultural and spiritual organizations in an area can also be valuable in engaging diverse residents to share their cultures and to promote learning about current efforts devoted to harmony and cross-cultural/interfaith understanding.

Second, *focus and commit.* With this information in hand, the most important issues to the community can be ascertained, particularly those specific to promoting peace. This might involve, for example, arts, music, and cultural programs that promote peace; peace and interfaith collaborations, events, vigils; restorative justice programs in schools and community settings that focus on healing rather than punishment; formation of local peace commissions; and instituting community by-laws and other policies that foster peace and justice.

Third, *build and launch.* One does not have to start building from scratch. Peace seekers can join with others already active in a community to pursue common goals for peacebuilding. It is worth finding out if your town has a peace commission or similar organization. If not, the *Charter for Compassion* can be a helpful resource.[5] The Charter is an international network for communities, churches, and other organizations to connect with and support each other. It has many useful materials on its website and also lists many communities that have committed to the principles of compassion and are mobilized to take action. If your community does not have local groups that are connected with the Charter, their website offers ideas and resources to reach out to local organizers to form such a group.

Fourth, *evaluate and maintain*. Evaluating peacebuilding efforts can help ensure they are effective and sustained. Setting clear and measurable objectives can pave the way for progress that can easily be monitored transparently. It is vital to be inclusive and listen to the voices of the entire community through development, implementation, and evaluation, as well as to celebrate the success of these phases.

Local Peacebuilding

Initially, it is useful for peacebuilding actions to start among neighbors. Peace with neighbors starts with a broader understanding. Simple actions can further such understanding. These can include holding interfaith discussions, organizing films or guest speakers to display approaches to peacebuilding, and gathering with neighbors to identify local issues and opportunities.

Residents in local peace groups, whether organized independently or through schools or faith-based organizations, magnify individual efforts by identifying local issues in their community and tying these to an understanding of national and global issues of peace and justice. The phrase "Think globally, act locally!" applies here in constructing these efforts.

In a small village west of Nazareth, Shefa-Amr or Shfar'am, we have gathered Jewish choirs and actors to perform at the Anglican Church on multiple occasions. As this custom started during the Christmas season, word spread and what developed overtime was an annual concert of Jewish players performing during the Christian high holy season. Imagine! This

5. See "Charter for Compassion," https://charterforcompassion.org, accessed February 22, 2022.

was birthed by the simple gesture of building a friendship over coffee and sharing the mutual language of music. When the COVID-19 pandemic grew in the region, the local musicians met over Zoom, and this resulted in a Palestinian singing at Notre Dame alongside a 48 person Jewish orchestra, led by a Muslim conductor. The language of music bridged all differences and transcended conflict toward peace.

In addition, we have hosted, at the Episcopal cultural center in Shfar'am, courses for children ages four to twelve years of all faiths in painting, craft creations, cooking classes for "young chefs," and lab practices for "young scientists." Just as with the music program, we used the common language of the arts to bridge the gap between Jewish, Druze, Christian, and Muslim children living in the town and surrounding villages. Again, just through the simple act of establishing an initial connection, any connection, between our young people, we are supporting their ability to see each other's common humanity. The child can look at the other and realize that although there are many differences, this other boy or girl likes to dance or sing or paint just like I do. Our songs and stories may be different but together we are singers of songs and tellers of stories.

The reason why these arts-based children's programs and other initiatives can be so powerful is because they strike at the very root causes that are obstacles to peacebuilding. They remedy those deeply rooted patterns of behavior that stand in the way of achieving peace in our communities.

Critical Benchmarks in Peacebuilding

I recommend establishing benchmarks to evaluate programs. This is especially important as organizers need to be alert to damaging behavior patterns that need to be changed. In my experience, organizers need to be alert to key areas of harmful attitudes and actions.

First, fear causes us to look at others as primarily a source of harm. Being insular may be a protective impulse but it also causes an unwillingness to risk reaching out to others. This is difficult to combat because it is such a basic human instinct. In designing a program, how can we gently encourage the children and adults to intermix with each other and not stick just with their friends? This can be as simple as establishing a seating arrangement for activities or in some cases intermixing can happen naturally. If you decide to start an interfaith choir, the altos will naturally have to sit with the other altos, and the other sections likewise, regardless of ethnicity or faith background. The nature and function of the group that is coming together can naturally help intermix diverse people and perspectives. It is through this intermixing, through giving participants a chance to see the humanity of one another that gradually we can chip away at fear.

Second, strong adherence to one's own faith may cause an intolerance to the faith and tradition of others. This is an area in which the institutional church both locally and globally can lead by example. We do not need to all agree with everyone on all matters of faith. This does not mean that we deny or ignore the importance of our faith tradition or that we gloss over and pretend that there are not significant differences. It does mean that we do not allow these differences to be used as an excuse to harm or slander someone else because of their beliefs. Local church leaders, both lay and ordained, need to be attentive and intentional about embodying mutual respect and promoting a worldview where religious diversity exists as a gift and not a threat.

Third, violence and division cause hatred. Tragically, this is our day-to-day reality as those who live in the Land of the Holy One. Deeply seeded fear and mistrust is a tremendous obstacle and eradicating it is no simple task. How do you tell a parent whose child was killed that they need to forgive and trust and have a relationship with someone from the group that was responsible? How do we work with those who feel that their own value depends upon diminishing another person? How do we build peace with those who confuse retribution with justice?

These challenges and obstacles may seem insurmountable. We are easily tempted to toss up our hands in defeat and tell ourselves that the problem is too big for us to make any measurable difference. However, we must always remember that bringing about God's peace is just that: *God's* peace, not ours. God is the source of the peace that surpasses understanding. We have a choice as to whether or not we wish to work with God in bringing about the peaceable kingdom. Whatever our response to God's call, we must never assume we are the sole architects of peace. God is architect and peacebuilder. Such realization is both humbling yet also hopeful because the burden is not solely on us. We can take courage in the words of a prayer written in honor of Oscar Romero, a Salvadoran bishop and martyr, who lived and died amidst horrendous violence:

It helps, now and then, to step back and take a long view.
The Kingdom is not only beyond our efforts,
it is even beyond our vision.
We accomplish in our lifetime only a tiny fraction
of the magnificent enterprise that is God's work.
Nothing we do is complete,
which is a way of saying that the Kingdom always lies beyond us.
No statement says all that could be said.
No prayer fully expresses our faith.
No confession brings perfection.
No pastoral visit brings wholeness.
No program accomplishes the Church's mission.
No set of goals and objectives includes everything.
This is what we are about.
We plant the seeds that one day will grow.
We water seeds already planted,
knowing that they hold future promise.
We lay foundations that will need further development.
We provide yeast that produces effects far beyond our capabilities.
We cannot do everything,
and there is a sense of liberation in realizing that.
This enables us to do something,
and to do it very well.
It may be incomplete, but it is a beginning, a step along the way,
an opportunity for the Lord's grace to enter and do the rest.
We may never see the end results,
but that is the difference between the master builder and the worker.
We are workers, not master builders;
ministers, not messiahs.
We are prophets of a future that is not our own.
Amen.[6]

---

6. Cited by the United States Conference of Bishops, www.usccb.org/prayer-and-worship/prayers-and-devotions/prayers/prophets-of-a-future-not-our-own, accessed April 22, 2022.

Critical benchmarks that alert the peacebuilder to the dangers of fear, intolerance, and hatred are vital to the success of any program. Alongside these critical benchmarks a number of planning benchmarks are also critical. Although the Romero prayer teaches us that there is no final endpoint—at least not in this life—there are real and tangible ways that we can understand whether we are making progress toward our goals. This needs to happen not just in our final assessment stage, but it needs to be a key ingredient in our planning phase.

Planning Benchmarks in Peacebuilding

When we go on a journey, we need to know where it is that we are going so we can chart our course. Peacebuilding and community organizing are not any different. We need to know where we are trying to get to if we want to be able to plan how to get there. Here are some questions and corresponding assessment measures that can help assess whether a community is following the principles of peace and advancing mutual respect and love:

- Planning question: is everyone in the affected community represented?

  Assessment: who participated in the planning and designing of the program? What was the breakdown between ethnic and religious groups, men and women, and any other delineation that is a source of division.
- Planning question: who drives decisions?

  Assessment: keep a log of what decisions were made both in the planning and execution of the project. Consider what were the various viewpoints discussed. Was the final decision reached by consensus or was it a majority decision? How did this happen and why? It is not necessarily wrong to make decisions by majority rather than reaching consensus as long as the outcome does not repeatedly only represent one perspective. This is why it is useful to keep track of the details.
- Planning question: is the decision-making process just?

  In the previous question, we were looking at who is involved in the decision. In this question, we are looking at the how, when, and what of decision-making, that is, the structural mechanism of how the group functions.

Assessment: based on your decision-making log, you can assess your actual structure. How are topics brought to the group for decision? How does the group decide the priority addressing decisions?

- Planning question: what is/are the desired outcome(s) of your efforts?

  Is there a particular end goal that you have in mind? Will it be a finite or ongoing activity? For instance, if the goal is to organize an interfaith children's choir, you may have a specific one-time concert event as your initial end goal. If it is an ongoing project, think about what a successful ongoing project will look like.

  Assessment: it may be that an ongoing activity is the result of a successful one-time event. For a newly formed organization, this can be an especially good preliminary first step in engaging in community building activity. Often it is hard to generate participation when there is an indefinite commitment, so this may be a good way to start.

- Planning question: does the program benefit the greatest possible number of people?

  In planning, it is important to consider how to reach the greatest number of people.

  Assessment: this question is easily assessed by simply keeping track of how many participants are involved. It is also important to assess which people are participating. If the goal is to bring together diverse groups, how diverse is the composition of attendees?

- Planning question: are connections being fostered?

  In bringing together groups of people for community building, it is important to have built into the program time and space for participants to interact and get to know each other. This is a subtle art form. When people are going into a situation that is unfamiliar or alien, formal structure to a program can give participants a certain sense of security. Perhaps in planning a program, it is useful to have more structured programs early on and as people become more comfortable to allow for increasingly more unstructured time for fellowship.

  Assessment: this dimension is not something that lends itself easily to objective measures, but that does not mean that it cannot be assessed. It can be useful for the organizers to meet immediately after each session to talk about their observations and impressions of how effective the program is in fostering connections. This also provides an opportunity to assess which elements are working and which might need to be modified. This assessment also needs to extend beyond the program itself. Organizers should make an effort to observe how they see the results manifesting in the community and ask does the program lead toward peace and better quality of life?

This detailed planning is meant to be a starting point. It is important not to become too tied to our own expectations and planned agendas. As peacebuilders, we need to be open to the movement of the Holy Spirit. There may be hopes and visions that we have for a program that will not turn out the way we want, but we should not necessarily see this as a failure but rather that God has other plans for how this is to unfold. Throughout the whole endeavor one needs to remember that we are serving God and God's mission, so it is important that those engaged in this work maintain an active and vibrant prayer life.

Conclusion

While many peacebuilding strategies have been discussed, on an individual level much of the work of promoting peace comes down to focusing on the following:

- Bring people together, even those who have traditionally been at odds.
- Consider how to extend efforts even further to engage new partnerships, collaborative efforts, and populations.
- View all persons as potential assets that can enrich the community.
- Tie local work to the larger world community, taking advantage of the increasing ability to connect with communities across the globe.

In our small communities, as well as the larger world, people emphasize schism and violence. This can feed personal dislike, anger, or even hatred for groups of people whom we may hear are taking our jobs, corrupting communities, or threatening us with destruction. We can feel helpless. Yet, God invites us to God's peace. We are invited to listen to the voices of peace. Here we can find hope through the simple act of extending a hand in friendship.

Promoting peace is not a solitary activity. We are joined in the effort by most people in the world who yearn for peace and work to live with each other. We are all called as people of faith, nongovernmental organizations, political societies, and social groups to work for one aim: to accept and respect everyone for who they are regardless of nationality, faith, or manner of worship. We, the three monotheistic religions in the Land of the Holy One, are called to come together and reconcile on faith-based claims. We are called to reconciliation within and then we are called to reconciliation with others. We are called away from misusing holy books as weapons or tools of division. We are called rather to analyze through common study that we might obtain deeper understanding of how the monotheistic texts call for fairness, dignity, and peace. If all monotheistic religions believe in one God, we all should come together to form one body looking for tools and instruments aimed at achieving justice, reconciliation, and peace for all.

It is the right time for the Church to unite and work cooperatively with the mosque and the synagogue, where the small identities melt within the collective vision that sees everybody and represents everybody on equal terms for the sake of peacebuilding. Together we will carve out the path toward that peace dreamed of by the Rev. Dr. Martin Luther King Jr., alongside so many others.

It is our task to develop and support religious, social, as well as political leaders that work to achieve peace, and help to reconcile their communities with the ultimate goals, by creating the vision and allowing everyone to follow. It is also our task to create opportunities for everyone to participate in creating a vision for the whole community, a vision of peace and mutual understanding.

As we look at the recent developments in Palestine and Israel, we see continued death and bloodshed. We see the loss of hope for a lasting solution. We see the failure of the international community to apply international law that allows the peoples of the land to avoid conflict and despair. All this has reached a stage where we witness more extremism and discrimination. Even those mediators who once stood as protectors of democracy and peacemaking have become a biased force and a party to the conflict.

All this has led many to wonder whether international efforts to achieve peacekeeping are based on justice and sound intentions. Many in Palestine and Israel feel that their lives have become unbearable and worse as a result of the peace process. Many have emigrated as a result and others contemplate immigration. Some have resorted to violence. Some have died. Others have lost faith and hope. So, when we look back on the so-called decades of peace process and reconciliation, we have received more hatred and injustice, corruption, and schism. It is time for churches and spiritual leaders to show a different path and to affirm that everyone—Israelis and Palestinians—are brothers and sisters in one wide human family. It is time to say that we can love each other and live together in mutual respect and equality of rights and duties in the same land. This is not a dream. This is the vision that inspired our ancestors, the prophets.

Peace based on dignity, mutual respect, and equality is the only thing that can save us and allow us to live in the land that our ancestors and prophets have sanctified, and which we continue to sanctify with our pursuit of justice and our thirst for peace and mutual love. We need a new direction, a new education, a new vision for this land and the people who live in it. We, Christians, Muslims, and Jews in the Holy Land, must stand with each other to sustain human dignity. Accordingly, we need to point a way out of the status of permanent war, hatred, and death. We need to point out a new way of life in this land built on equality and love. We all need to affirm that every solution must be the goal of all those living in this land without distinction, building bridges of mutual respect and love.

That is why we offer this vision and our experience in working to build peace here in the Land of the Holy One. Our vision allows everyone here to enjoy the equality that God has given us by creating all of us in God's image. We all must believe that equality is the cornerstone of a just and lasting peace, whatever the political solutions propose. We lived together in the past in this land. Why not live together in the future?

CHAPTER 7

An Account of a Palestinian Christian Woman in Peacebuilding

Shadia Qubti

Introduction

In a context of an intractable conflict, I would like to present my experiences as a practitioner in peacebuilding and conflict transformation. First, I will reflect on my own personal perspective especially as it relates to my theological upbringing as a Palestinian evangelical and how that identity and understanding has shifted within that context. Second, I will consider peacebuilding between Israelis and Palestinians from a general perspective. Third, I will examine the particular perspective of Christian Palestinians and Israelis engaged in peacebuilding. Fourth, I will embark on an exhortational perspective, drawing on the need to elevate the voices of Palestinian Christian women as a form of righting epistemic injustice in the field of peacebuilding and as an example of new ways of engagement by indigenous Palestinian Christians.

Conflict: A Personal Account

One hundred years ago, Palestinian Christians comprised nearly 10 percent of the entire population of Mandatory Palestine.[1] Today, there are 180,000 Palestinian Christians in Israel and 50,000 in Palestine. This comprises 2 and 1 percent of the total population, respectively.[2]

Nazareth as Home

I grew up in the Baptist Church in Nazareth, proud to walk the paths Jesus walked, see the views of the mountains and hills he held so dear, knowing that I was part of the small community still bearing witness to Jesus' message in the city closely associated with his name. Growing up Baptist, I was taught to personalize my relationship with God and others, and from a young age, I learned that Jesus' vocation as a peacemaker between God and humankind was a path I should follow. The need for peacebuilding in Israel and Palestine is great, and perhaps my zealous twenty-year-old self jumped at the opportunity to see this as my vocation in God's mission. I would work for the practical reconciliation between Israeli and Palestinian believers because they had already been reconciled to God. It seemed like the right thing to do and a very noble cause. My work in peacebuilding was very rewarding. I gained extensive knowledge and skills in that work, be it in facilitation, coordination, public speaking, theology, and political science.

I was a minority within a minority—a Palestinian among a majority of Israeli Jews; a Christian among the more populous Muslim Palestinians; and an evangelical among the more prevalent Catholic and Greek Orthodox Christian denominations. One of the moments of realizing my double minority was in my first year at an Israeli University. The class had around 600 students, and the overwhelming majority of them were Jewish. Among them, a total of 15 Arab students were in this class and only two from this number were Christians. I was the only female.

---

1. "Report by his Majesty's Government in the United Kingdom of Great Britain and Northern Ireland to the Council of the League of Nations on the Administration of Palestine and Trans-Jordan for the Year 1937." *Mandate for Palestine – Report of the Mandatory to the LoN (31 December 1937)*, web.archive.org/web/20130923061547/http://unispal.un.org/UNISPAL.NSF/0/7BDD2C11C15B54C2052565D10057251E.

2. This is based on the Christmas 2020 population report by the Israeli Statistical Burearu. See www.cbs.gov.il/he/mediarelease/DocLib/2020/419/11_20_419b.pdf, accessed June 12, 2021.

The evangelical community numbers around 15,000 in both Israel and Palestine. The Baptist Church, one of the primary evangelical churches there, has its roots in the Southern Baptist Church in the United States of America. They too wanted to have a home base in the Holy Land and have been able to sustain a presence since the 1940s. My parents were drawn into the Baptist Church primarily due to the positive influence the missionaries had in their personal lives. They became part of the first generation of Baptists in Nazareth. My father received an education through the Baptist School, and my mother was raised in a Baptist orphanage as a result of Israel's war of independence, which Palestinians call the *Nakba*, or catastrophe, marking the beginning of our diaspora and national fragmentation. Through the Baptists, my mother had an opportunity to further her education in North America. The theology that I was brought up with helped us cope with the chaos around us. It turned us inward by focusing on our individual salvation and the individual salvation of those around us. This theology centered on being socially and politically impartial, as the most important cause of our mission and our lives should be nothing short of caring for people's souls and salvation. We believed through their peace with God, and through drawing people to God, they would ultimately become reconciled to one another. I did not learn anything about my people's history or suffering in the Church, but rather how to overcome any suffering through the love of Christ. What good is history and politics and social justice when it just distracts us from our main cause—eternal salvation?

During my upbringing, when political events happened, the Church did not have the tools to address them with a communal theological lens. Once again, the impetus was left to the individual—to feel guilty for experiencing hate or injustice, to ignore injustice in the name of a greater cause, because after all I am to "love my enemies." As you can imagine, this push left me and many others feeling very isolated and alone, unable to articulate, much less understand, what a Christian perspective on the conflict should be. However, this situation was to change.

Shifting Engagements in Palestinian Evangelicalism

In more recent years, we have seen a stream of theology from within and without the evangelical church resource a new way of thinking.

The Palestinian church has an impressive variety of indigenous theologians that includes Naim Ateek, Munther Isaac, Azar Ajaj, and Yohana Katanacho. The indigenous church has made significant progress in reclaiming its own theology and applying it to our unique social and political context. They have been pivotal in elevating our cry as Palestinians. They are engaged in the important work of contextual theology. They foreground how our suffering shapes our reading and they provide Christian Palestinian response to our suffering. However, while their lived experiences and articulations of action and engagement have been informative and healing to me, they build their experiences on their position *as men*. They reproduce a platform of engagement *for* men, and they overlook the particular lived experiences and engagement of women.

Women's voices and perspectives are important for several reasons. Not only are we half of the population, those filling the seats in churches and working alongside Palestinian men in theological and social engagement, but we also bring a different perspective to the conflict. It is women who are politically and socially marginalized from making influential decisions about peace in Israel–Palestine. It is women who bear the brunt of the frustration when Palestinian men return home from a day of humiliation at the hands of the Israeli occupation. It is women who permeate nearly all aspects of concern for care in education and charity work. They know the needs and actions necessary to improve the situation. It is women who teach our children in children's programs in churches, who sister and mother the next generation and seek to instill in them self-love and dignity in the context of unending oppression. It is women who are living the theology they do not always have the training to articulate. Women turn the other cheek. Women shepherd the next generation. Women bear witness to the injustice perpetrated on themselves and their loved ones. They do this just as Mary, Mother of Jesus, bore witness to the injustices perpetrated against her son. These are some of the reasons I strive to center the marginalized voices of women in my context, especially in the field of peacebuilding and the role of the Church. I believe this takes us a step closer to developing a Palestinian theology where women's particular lived experiences and perspectives contribute to our readings and interpretations of scripture.

Peacebuilding Between Israelis and Palestinians

Across formal peacebuilding efforts, most of the practitioners and fieldworkers I have come across are women. However, when it comes to decision-making, women's insights on engagement are not represented, even less so for female Palestinian theologians. The scarce and infrequent peace conferences focusing on Israeli and Palestinian relations are almost exclusively dominated by men. They have dedicated their lives and careers to get to where they are, and that is certainly commendable. As Palestinian Christians, we are thankful merely to be invited to speak, and therefore, the gender of the speaker can be treated as an irrelevance. We are fighting for our self-determination and right to exist as a free people in their homeland, and from that perspective, gender seemingly has no standing. However, the exclusion of women from these forums does a disservice to our communal efforts to survive and thrive.

The political, social, and economic imbalance of power puts Palestinians at a disadvantage in day-to-day life, all the more so in peacebuilding. The social price Palestinian Christians pay to participate in peacebuilding with Israelis is high. We are going against the threat of being labeled as collaborators and normalizers. In our context, to "normalize" has a particular meaning. In Palestinian society, normalization is viewed as any participation in any

> project or initiative or activity, local or international, specifically designed for gathering Palestinians and Israelis, whether individuals or institutions; that does not explicitly aim to expose and resist the occupation and all forms of discrimination and oppression against the Palestinian people.[3]

Merely having hopeful expectations that participation will bring a change in our situation is a risky endeavor.

Grassroots peacebuilding efforts have been going on for decades. Yet, peace seems farther away than ever before. The occupation is choking my people's ability to live in freedom and dignity. Despite this, over the past thirteen years of work in peacebuilding I have built relationships

---

3. Rifat Odeh Kassis, "Thoughts on Normalisation in the Israel-Palestine Conflict," No2BrandIsrael.org, June 3, 2015, accessed August 31, 2019, www.no2brandisrael.org/thoughts-on-normalisation-in-the-israel-palestine-conflict.

with Israelis on an individual basis based on common interests and a shared belief in a more just future, based on the willingness to take sacrificial steps and concrete action to better our context. These handful of relationships become transformational, but they have failed to reach a critical mass to see a successful grassroots movement for collective change. The Israeli political left, since the Oslo agreements, has been on the margins of the larger Israeli society and therefore is politically weak.

As Palestinians, we all share similar experiences of injustice in my context—be it as second-class citizens of Israel or as Palestinians in the occupied Palestinian Territories. This geographical and political fragmentation of us as a people—be it refugees, East Jerusalemites, Gazans, West Bankers, Israeli citizens, and those in the diaspora—mirrors the ongoing sense of displacement imposed on us. In my own research on majority–minority relations in Israel, I was able to account for many different terms relating to my particular demographic among Palestinians—Palestinian who hold Israeli citizenship—including Israeli Arabs, Israeli Palestinians, Arab citizens of Israel, 1948 Palestinians. Regardless of our naming, we are a part of the Palestinian people. The attempts to separate our historic ethnic identity from who we are today are ongoing. My engagement in peacebuilding raised my social and political consciousness. As I widened my Palestinian network of relationships beyond my immediate context, I realized the extent to which my people were fragmented and the underlying historic causes. It also helped me see that in Israel, although I am a citizen, I am not a welcomed part of Israeli society. The superiority of the Jewish homeland supersedes its own democratic values, and as of last year, with the passing of the Nation State Law, people like me, who comprise 23.4 percent of Israel's population, were relegated to second class citizens, not only in practice but also in legal terms.[4]

A Particular View of Peacebuilding: Christian Palestinians and Messianic Jews

While I have engaged in far-reaching peace work among various Israeli and Palestinian communities, the place I thought I would find most

4. Central Bureau of Israel, "Population of Israel on the Eve of 2021—9.3 Million," www.cbs.gov.il/he/mediarelease/DocLib/2020/438/11_20_438e.pdf. Accessed June 12, 2020.

common ground would be among those who are followers of Jesus Christ. It was my conviction that the gospel unites disparate peoples. Throughout my work, I participated in numerous activities with Palestinian Christians and Messianic Jews. Yet my hopes to find common ground around shared beliefs fell flat. I realized theology can divide as much as it can unify.

Messianic Jewish theology in Israel is intertwined with challenging assumptions about the role of modern-day Israel. A view exists that assesses the current conflict as irreconcilable. This view is, at times, supported by a particular biblical reading that depicts an inevitable conflict between the descendants of Jacob and the descendants of Esau. This theology is used to justify injustice as part of God's plan. It subjugates the Palestinian people. Here, the message is acquiescence: Palestinians need to accept their God-given fate and let God's chosen people rule over them. This theology has been passed on by some missionaries who desired a home base in the Holy Land. When Messianic Jewish participants listened to how Palestinian Christians suffered from the political implications of their theology, they withdrew from the engagement. They realized that many young Palestinian Christians have not only a theological consciousness but also a political consciousness calling for justice. Faced with the implications of Palestinian theology, the Messianic Jews retreated to their own communities.

The price required in truly transformative peacebuilding is a shift in one's identity. One is called to a wider vision. We are not simply members of a national group for whom justice is shared. We are part of a larger international collective for whom justice should be a shared endeavor. This idea is most threatening to those in the majority, those who hold power. As my own experience in peacebuilding deepened, I realized that one of the largest obstacles was theological. This obstacle was particularly evident among followers of Jesus across national groups. The longer I worked in the field, the more disillusioned I became. If we followers of Christ could not reconcile around our shared beliefs, there was little hope for inter-religious reconciliation. This was the logical social and political conclusion I had come to because of the narrow formation I received in an evangelical community. Consequently, I stepped away from dialogue groups' peacebuilding. While there are positive outcomes of peacebuilding in the form of dialogue groups, I think the more important need currently is to center marginalized voices and to engage them socially, politically, and theologically. If we seek a more holistic and inclusive approach to peace as well as social and political engagement, it is critical to engage women and bring their voices to the center. These voices are increasingly coming to the center, and it is my goal to bring them to greater prominence. My goal is to seek them out and to have their voices heard locally, nationally, and internationally.

Our willingness to participate in peace efforts—whether dialogue groups or other forms of joint social, political, or theological activism—is driven by our faith. We are called to be peacemakers to ourselves and those around us, not only to reconcile humans to their God but humans to each other. Today, more than ever, we are in dire need of divine intervention toward different ways of engagement. My journey so far has brought me to promote the voices of Palestinian Christian women in the discourse of peacebuilding and the Church. I see a clear role for us to play alongside my fellow Palestinian Christian men. Our experiences as women—mothers, daughters, sisters, grandmothers—and as practitioner-theologians are needed alongside those of our colleagues.

Two years ago, to create a platform to elevate the voices of women, I was part of an initiative called "Women Behind the Wall" podcast. The podcast features stories of nine Palestinian Christian women who share their experiences of living in conflict and how their faith helps them deal with their situation. The stories they share need to be heard. They articulate how politics penetrates the personal lives of individuals. Their narratives give names and voices to the cold, harsh headlines that do no justice to what is happening to our people.

Women often believe their stories are not important and they believe their stories are often not heard. Women rarely have the platform to get these stories to a wider audience. Again and again, in spite of our efforts, we are pushed aside, if not by our local male colleagues, then by our foreign counterparts. I remember when we launched the podcast—I approached several Christian outlets, including a contact who worked with one of the largest Christian publications. I pitched the podcast to see if he would be interested in featuring us. He said, "My feeling is that it is too small to bring to [us] by itself but may work well as an item in future reporting." I wrote him back and said that women have always been part of peacebuilding initiatives, and that it is a shame such a premier Christian publication only seeks quotes and stories when they need a token Palestinian representative. When we locals articulate an important need and seek a platform, our engagement is "too small." The podcast was embraced by a secular independent news magazine called *+972Magazine*, comprised of Israeli and Palestinian journalists bringing alternative perspectives on the conflict to audiences abroad.[5] In an article entitled "This Palestinian Life—Uncovering Stories of Women Behind the Wall," they discussed the podcast at length, centering the voices of Palestinian Christian women where Christian publications would not. Imagine that! Why are we too small a story for a Christian news site but not so small for a secular one? How does one obtain a platform among Christian circles?

An Exhortation: Hear the Voice of the Women

Our stories as women are painful but they are also meaningful, hopeful, and transformative. In conclusion, then, hear the witness of the women. Together they share and navigate the complicated realities we live as young women, old women, single women, and mothers. The stories present each woman's particular situation and how their faith plays a role in them. To me, these are examples of a theology in practice. Thus, I offer no analysis of the words here. The podcast was tailored for an international audience, and so far the responses to it are positive and welcoming. My hope is that this project can be used as a point of reference for anyone interested in the context and experience of Palestinian Christians. Here are a few examples of stories you can hear on *Women Behind the Wall.*

Shireen personifies how politics impacts personal choices of love and relationships. She is a Palestinian from Israel who married a Palestinian man from the West Bank. Falling in love and committing to a shared life impacts a whole range of issues: citizenship, where they might live, and access to health care are determined by their choice to love one another. In order to ensure her children have the same rights as she had as an Israeli citizen, Shireen found unimaginable strength to drive through a checkpoint during contractions. Then she drove all the way to the Galilee so that the baby was registered in Israel, which is about two hours' drive. Through her story, we are introduced to the macro issues of the conflict.

5. Hanriette Chacar, "This Palestinian Life: Uncovering the Stories of Women Behind the Wall." *972 Magazine*, August 30, 2018, accessed August 31, 2019, 972mag.com/this-palestinian-life-uncovering-what-life-is-like-for-women-behind-the-wall/137531/.

Amira is a young woman who challenges the binary view of this conflict through a religious lens. Being a Christian Palestinian, with a strong theological position for justice, she challenges any simple reading of religious texts or historical realities between Jews, Christians, and Muslims:

> I thought this at the time, if this God that I am believing in . . . wants to give a land to his people who are the Israelis over my people's dead bodies, over my people's destroyed houses over our trees our uprooted olive trees I really don't want this God. I really don't want to deal with him. I don't want to talk about him. I don't want to have anything to do with this God if this is really the truth...I started to learn that no, Jesus is a very just man. A man who talked against injustice. He really has something to do with my conflict with my hard situation.[6]

Hanan was converted from Islam and became a Christian at age twenty three. While she acknowledges that she is a Christian culturally, she still identifies as Muslim. In the Middle East, the religion of one's family and ancestors play a major role in determining a person's self-identification. Most of Hanan's social interactions, such as weddings and other gatherings, are with other Muslims. Growing up in the Galilee, she experienced an environment of tolerance between Muslims and Christians. While there were obvious differences, the two groups had much in common as people of faith and celebrated together those things that the two traditions have in common. However, this toleration did not translate into her family's acceptance of her conversion. In Islamic culture, renouncing one's faith is not merely a personal decision. It impacts the reputation and social standing of the whole family for generations. She had paid a high personal price to become a Christian, and because of family persecution she moved to Jerusalem from the Galilee. Although she has since rebuilt her relationship with her family, this took many years and was a painful process. Once in Jerusalem, she started meeting with fellow Christians and to her shock, she found Christians taking sides in

---

6. Shadia Oubti, "Amira's Story: Challenging Western Christian Justification of the Occupation," June 3, 2018, in *Women Behind the Wall*, Podcast, Episode 3, www.womenbehindthewall.com/blog/2018/6/3episode-3-amiras-story-challenging-western-christian-justification-of-the-occupation, accessed September 10, 2021.

the conflict. She was especially shocked to find that there were Zionist Christians. Once when she introduced herself as a Palestinian, a woman asked her, "Aren't you shy to say that you are Palestinian?" Compared to the Galilee, people in Jerusalem are much more overtly religious and the various faiths are much more segregated than they are in the villages. Moving to Jerusalem also meant that, for the first time in her life, she had to contend with passing through a checkpoint. Because she is an Israeli citizen and speaks Hebrew, she was generally not harassed but she has witnessed many instances of the Israel Defense Forces (IDF) soldiers insulting and menacing elderly citizens and children. Today Hanan works for a Christian agency with women and children who have converted from Islam to Christianity. Some of her projects involve helping with financial difficulties, health care, and aiding victims of domestic violence.

Eilda was born in Jordan and her family worshipped in the Greek Orthodox Church. They are Palestinian refugees who had been displaced from their home. It took many years, and wading through much red tape, for them to be allowed to return to the Palestinian territories. In Eilda's story, she emphasizes the tremendous impact that trauma has had on her people. She is a yoga instructor who, along with another Palestinian woman, has started a yoga studio called Beit Ashams (House of the Sun) as a safe place for women. It is a safe space to practice yoga, meditate, and engage in fellowship.[7] The work, however, was to extend far beyond catering just to women.

Her focus on yoga stems from her belief that the impact of intergenerational trauma that most Palestinians bear resides primarily in the body and for healing to take place, they must first deal with the physical manifestations of the trauma. As she says in her interview, "Trauma is constant when one lives in occupied Palestine; trauma disconnects one from their body." She has, in recent years, worked with young Muslim men who are activists in Hebron, who on a daily basis are confronted with physical danger from harassment by Israeli soldiers as well as the psychological damage inflicted by living in fear. One young man spoke about the ceaseless fear of walking alone because of the risk of

7. Shadia Qubti, "Eilda's Story: Holistic Healing for a Community in Ongoing Trauma," June 10, 2019, in *Women Behind the Wall*, Podcast, Episode 4, www.womenbehindthewall.com/blog/2018/6/3/episode-4-eildas-story-holistic-healing-for-a-community-in-ongoing-trauma, accessed September 10, 2021.

detainment, imprisonment, and possible death. Her work with these men has put them in touch with their need for self-care of the body, mind, and spirit in order to be able to survive in this environment.

Eilda extended her work to children. In particular, she and her partner work with children who have been imprisoned by the occupying forces. Each year 500 to 700 children between the ages of twelve and seventeen are arrested and taken into military or police custody. There have been individual cases of children as young as six being detained. These children are usually arrested for throwing rocks. In these cases, the whole family suffers from trauma—the children from the experience of being incarcerated and the parents when confronting their powerlessness to protect their children. One group that she worked with were girls ranging in age from twelve to sixteen. In many cases, the girls did not actually do anything; they were simply suspected of something. This creates a profound sense of mistrust of the world. It disabuses these young people of any notion that the world is a safe place. For children such realizations can be extremely damaging. Eilda relates the story that on the first day of the workshop she was taking these girls through a guided meditation. Normally, she summons participants out of meditation by ringing a bell. However, when she rang the bell, the girls did not stir, and she realized that they were all sound asleep. She came to realize that for many of these girls, their ability to sleep had been severely compromised. This was the first time, in a long time, that their bodies felt safe and secure enough to fall into a deep sleep.

All of these stories identify common obstacles that these women must face each day. Amira and Eilda both speak extensively about what it means to be living under the permit system. This system not only restricts their ability to travel to Israel but also to travel within their own communities. Some roads are designated "forbidden roads" and are closed to Palestinians. In Amira's case, if she has to travel internationally she cannot simply go to the airport in Tel Aviv. She has the added expense of having to travel through Jordan to get an international flight. The permit system is capricious at best. For Eilda it has been very rare that both she and her husband have been able to enter Israel together. When Palestinians enter Israel, they are not allowed to take their own cars. They must take public transportation. These restrictions are not merely inconveniences—they are deeply demoralizing. Amira recounts her father being bullied and harassed by young Israeli soldiers, and later telling his daughter that there is nothing they can do about it—the soldiers have guns.

Conclusion

Our right and claim for self-identity and self-determination as Palestinians continues. Palestinian Christians are an integral part of the Palestinian people. In the interlocking dimensions of the personal, political, and religious, we have a role to play in peacebuilding. Others have paved the way, but our lived theology as Palestinian Christian women has yet to be heard. These stories of women in this chapter are but a small sampling of the many unheard voices in Israel and the Palestinian territories. It is time for this testimony to be heard in our national and international communities. We seek a seat at the table. We need your help to get there.

CHAPTER 8

Building Dialogue in Small Groups

Practical-Reflective Peacebuilding

Jean Cotting

For many years before enrolling as a student at the Virginia Theological Seminary and subsequently being ordained to the priesthood in the Episcopal Church, I worked in the corporate world, mostly in banking and insurance. Frequently, I had the opportunity to attend various conferences and training sessions. It was good stuff. Whether it focused on learning new tricks in Excel spreadsheets or how to improve communications with customers or other departments, I would walk away from these sessions excited and eager to try out what I learned. Often though, once I returned to my office, real life would start creeping in. If you have never worked in an office setting, emergencies and disasters are routine occurrences. Computer systems crash, the state insurance examiners show up unexpectedly, a valuable employee gets seriously ill, and their duties need to be redeployed. Simply being away from the office for a few days to attend a training class causes much work to pile up. That pile up itself can become a small-scale emergency.

The work or business side of doing church is not very different. There are times when I will hear a colleague give an especially inspiring sermon, attend a lecture, or read a book, or listen to a podcast, and I say to myself, "Wow! That's excellent! I want to try to do that!" And just like my days back in the wonderful world of corporate accounting, once I get back, the everyday business of pastoring and teaching sets in and takes over. Despite my best intentions, I fall back on the familiar and comfortable ways of doing things. My grand plans to revolutionize my congregation or classroom fall by the wayside.

Being a church leader is often challenging. It is not for the fainthearted. Whether you are a lay leader or ordained clergy, you know how much of your heart and soul you are pouring into your congregation or faith community every day. Being a leader in a situation where there is conflict and strife, either internally in your congregation or externally in the wider community, working through the challenges this presents can be overwhelming. It can be exhausting, frustrating, and draining. Yet, as Christians we are called to be witnesses of God's reconciliation even amidst conflict (2 Cor. 5:11–21). In this chapter, two issues will be considered. First, how might we connect the Christian vision of peacebuilding with Christian practice? How might we build a bridge between the theoretical and the practical? Second, and more specifically, how might you find touch points in both sections of this book that can help you relate the material to your own situation?

The overriding purpose of this book is to help you find ways to encourage constructive dialogue in specific situations of conflict. This book has three major sections. In sections A and B, authors address peacebuilding dialogue from theological and/or conceptual perspectives. These authors are taking their area of expertise (both academic and practical) and boiling it down to its basic essence to create more general concepts, principles, or practices that might be applied in a variety of settings. This is not to say that those who have written these first chapters are simply ivory tower theoreticians. In distinct ways, they are on the front lines of helping to heal conflict by building dialogue.

Section C of this book examines specific contexts where people of faith are working through situations of conflict in their own communities. As with the early chapters, the work of the regional team authors is a combination of theological vision and contextual reflection and practice. Further, many of the authors in sections A and B were also part of the regional teams in section C. Some team members like myself were students; others are church or seminary employees. Some of us are ordained; others are lay leaders, but without exception all of us who participated in this project were acutely aware of our own weaknesses and limited vision.

My goal here is to bridge the first two sections with the third section so that you can begin your own work of connecting theological vision and general guidance to the specificities of your own context. I will suggest that a practical-reflective approach to this material is characterized by hospitality, intentional reflection, identifying major themes, and considering primary questions. It is hoped that such an approach serves both the material of this book and other material you might be considering in your context and community.

Practice Hospitality

Whether you are reading this book as part of a group effort or reading it on your own, there are some basic things I think you will find helpful in gaining a more robust experience as you work your way through it.

Make room for prayer. You will notice that most of the chapters in the third section include an element of prayer. This is one of the most necessary ingredients for fruitful dialogue. We begin by being open or hospitable to the Spirit of God. Such a beginning need not be marked by a formal prayer, although it could be. It need not be particularly religious, although it might be. Regardless of your views on organized religion, striving to create peacebuilding dialogue is sacred work. Obviously, if you are reading this book as part of an interfaith dialogue group, you will want to be sensitive to the beliefs of others in selecting how you will pray. Whether you are working in a group or reading on your own, take a few minutes before you dive in and invite the God of your understanding into guiding your efforts.

Make room for informal conversation. You will notice that just about all the groups in section C and some of the authors in sections A and B include practices of hospitality. Food and drink, even if it is simple, is an act of welcome. Indeed, such informal fellowship aided by refreshments can be some of the most constructive time that your group will spend together. Make sure you are giving your group a space to simply chat and enjoy getting to know each other and being together. As with prayer, if you are working with other faiths, you need to be sensitive to dietary restrictions, but that too—learning about the practice of someone else's faith—can be a grace-filled opportunity to connect with others. The nonverbal acts of hospitality can be some of the most important statements that we make in dialogue with one another.

Make space for different personality types. If you are working in a group, it is always worthwhile to consider structuring discussion time to allow for different personality types and communication modes. Some people are comfortable talking in larger group, some in smaller groups, some prefer one-on-one conversation, and some need time to reflect and process ideas on their own. Consider varying the formats that you use throughout your meeting time. Consider also asking all members to bring a journal and put aside a little time each session for everyone to record their thoughts and reflections on the session. The more comfortable all members are with format, the more fruitful your discussions will likely be.

Create opportunities to share. If you are reading this book on your own, you too can create hospitality around the experience. Invite a friend or two, perhaps members of your faith community, out for coffee so that you can share with them some of what you are learning from this book. In addition to more firmly fixing the main ideas in your head, talking about them in dialogue with others will open up new questions, thoughts, and inspiration for you. Practicing hospitality is a grace-filled experience.

Practice Intentional Reflection

Hospitality is, at the very least, welcome and openness to God and each other. It is opening our hearts and lives to grace found in an encounter. Hospitality opens the door to reflection. In the next two sections, I invite readers to intentional reflection by making space for new ideas and naming one's location before turning to careful identification of major themes at work in this book.

Make room to struggle with new ideas. When a class, lecture, sermon, article, or book strikes us as brilliant, it may also strike us as a bit overwhelming. This is my experience. I often need to return to material to reread, ponder, and further digest. Readers should not see this as any kind of deficit. It is important information and learning to take care and be open to struggle with ideas is also important. Do not feel self-conscious about struggling with content. There are chapters that you may need to go back and reread a time or two to fully appreciate them. You may need to break certain chapters down into bite-size pieces so that you can more easily digest them. This is normal. Most importantly, when you are confused, do not be intimidated about admitting it to others. They may be experiencing the same confusion, or they may have had some excellent insight that they are just dying to share with someone else. Giving them an opportunity to share is a gift. This experience of intellectual struggle, just like prayer and hospitality, is a grace imbued experience. Think of the story in the Gospel of Luke (2:41–52) that tells us about the boy Jesus wandering off from his family to converse with the Jewish scholars in the temple. Talking, questioning, arguing, and struggling are all part of the wonderful experience of being human in which Christ himself participated.

Name your location. We all approach scripture, theology, and each other from particular places. We are shaped by culture and context. We are located. How might you describe your location, culture, or context? How does this shape your understanding of Christian witness and peacebuilding? Already in sections A and B, you have met a range of leaders from a range of locations.

Shadia Qubti was one of our guest lecturers when all four teams gathered in Jerusalem in the summer of 2019. She writes from a distinct location and perspective. First, she is a female lay leader and comes from a Baptist background. The Palestinian team (chapter 9) was made up mostly of male Anglican clergy. They were writing about the work that they are doing through their parishes in interfacing with their Muslim and Jewish neighbors and how they have gone about doing it. Interestingly though, the Qubti, Dagher, and Palestinian team chapter underscore the importance of identity within that situation and how it plays out. The multidimensional intersectionality of identity can heavily impact how a situation is experienced. Qubti's work emphasizes the unique situation of women, both Christian and Muslim, and how the partitioning has specifically affected them. She brings to the foreground the implications of ignoring the female voice theologically, politically, and spiritually.

For the individual, there are many variable dimensions of identity to consider. Gender, age/generational identity, sexual orientation, occupation, class, access to power, ethnicity, marital status, and personality type will influence perspective. Were that not complicated enough, all of these dimensions of identity can alter depending on how they interact with other dimensions of identity and how they interact with external factors. Certainly, a global pandemic has had an impact on how many of us think about identity, location, and vocation. This pandemic underlines how external factors can impact dimensions of personal and communal identity. Wealth, access to health care, political systems, structures of governance, cultural expectations, historical developments, and relationships to a variety of institutions shape identity and impact how we understand peace. For example, Sarah Snyder (chapter 5) has particular relationships with institutions that shape her perspectives. Her role directing the Rose Castle Foundation and its reconciliation work, as well as being Canon for Reconciliation to the Archbishop of Canterbury, is often that of an outside advisor. It is interesting to put her thoughts and reflections about the work being done through religious institutions in juxtaposition with Robert Heaney's chapter about the sins and offenses committed by Anglican Christianity in both the distant and not so distant past (chapter 4). Institutional affiliation, role within the institution, and historical perspective also define elements of identity that can vary widely and influence interpretation. In all four of the team chapters, you will find there are elements of identity which have an effect on perspective.

Bear in mind that perspective is not merely a concern when considering a writer. As a reader, you are an active participant engaged with the text. Understanding your own particularity—your nationality, race, gender, socioeconomic situation, etc.—will impact how you respond and interpret the chapter. The Palestinian conflict is a situation that many people have strong preexisting opinions about. This may impact how you feel about the perspective of the authors of these chapters. It is not incumbent upon you to agree with them or to change your opinions, but reading will be a far more enriching experience if you are able to take stock of how you feel about the material and question yourself about the origins of your opinions. Practice mindfulness as you are reading the chapters and discussing them with others. Are there certain ideas that upset you or that you strongly disagree with? Why do you feel that way? Are there significant elements that you believe the author has overlooked or ignored? Taking the time to examine your own reactions will not only enrich your reading of this book but also will enable you to better understand your own feelings, behaviors, and reactions to conflict.

Now that you have prayed, spent some fellowship time together, assured yourself that struggling with theological material is demanding, and considered the impact of location—let us reflect on some of the major themes raised in sections A and B that might also arise in section C and might frame how you approach and read section C.

Identify Major Themes

At least three major themes run throughout sections A and B and will also impact analyses of conflict and visions of peacebuilding in section C. These themes are the presence of history, the depths of trauma, and the witness of the Church.

First, in analyses of conflict and in envisioning peace, history is always at work and deeply entrenched. Speaking on institutional sin, I was part of the U.S. team based at the Virginia Theological Seminary. We wrote about racism with a particular focus on the institutional racism of the school where we worked and studied. As you can observe from the U.S. team (chapter 12), the 200-year-old seminary bears the shame and scars of long-stranding racism woven into the very fabric of the nation. We live in a country with a highly glorified sense of history. It often ignores the cost, the pain and suffering, that came at the expense of those who have never benefited from the derived wealth. During one of our small group discussions at the Jerusalem meeting, when we were discussing the U.S. team's project, one of the Liberians turned to me and said, "I do not understand your problem. If you people know what the problem of racism is, why do you not simply fix it?" I was at a loss to provide her with a satisfactory answer and have been haunted since by the question. Why are we not able to fix this problem? The United States of America was not the only location that has been embroiled in longstanding disputes. The conflict in the Palestinian territories is rooted in religious, racial, and ethnic divisions across generations. The Tanzanian team (chapter 11) discusses some of the challenges to evangelization in the form of longstanding ethnic/tribal prejudices and conflict. In all these cases, the Church is not immune to these divisions. As you will have seen in the Heaney chapter, reconciliation consists of far more than simply acknowledging historic wrongs and saying "sorry."

In all these contexts, land disputes are crucial to historical understandings and conflict. One cannot ignore that deeply entrenched historical patterns are often caused or at least exacerbated by greed for material wealth and possessions. Racism in the United States of America has its roots in obtaining and maintaining wealth and riches for the European settlers who came as colonialists. As alluded to in Heaney's chapter, the United States of America was not the only western power guilty of this behavior. The imposition of western culture on other nations via missionary efforts was to varying degrees influenced by a desire to enhance commercial opportunity for empire. The acquisition of land and the defense of boundaries is a historical and contemporary issue and it is a cause of conflict internationally and locally.

The Tanzanian chapter centers on contemporary controversies around land disputes. The land conflicts in Tanzania that the Church is trying to mediate were caused by increased land scarcity and the inflation of land values that have occurred since the shift of the national capital. The disputes are between competing groups who do not want to miss out on the economic benefits of holding land or holding rights to land. The right to use and own land is further complicated by cultural practices developed over centuries. The Tanzanian situation includes long-held cultural traditions around family inheritance, the rights of daughters vs. sons, and a way of doing things that were firmly set in place long before the introduction of a more formal bureaucracy. It is difficult and challenging to persuade people to reform practices and laws established over a long span of history. This is seen in a range of contexts including in the United States of America where white privilege remains entrenched alongside concerted efforts to deny its existence or make space for any meaningful reform. The Palestinian conflict, though complex, also centers on the use of land and entrenched attitudes toward land use. Everyday conflict arises from unjust practice and laws that govern who is allowed to occupy, travel between, and reside in which area of the land. Young Palestinians struggle to see a future in their own land. The partitioning of the land has put community cohesion under extreme stress, all but destroyed the local economy, and the prospects for employment. Many are seeking a better life elsewhere.

Second, peacebuilding must come to terms with trauma. When the normal development and progress of a human being is disrupted in a jarring destructive manner, the result is trauma. This can happen on an individual level in instances such as disruptions caused by divorce, domestic violence, an alcoholic parent, or other calamitous circumstances or events that derail normal life. It is especially damaging when suffered by children. However, it can also occur at a collective level, affecting whole groups of people. War, racism, discrimination, displacement, oppression can traumatize an entire community or nation.

Trauma figures prominently in a number of this book's chapters. Torn apart by years of war and civil unrest, the Liberian people are struggling to find their way out of collective trauma. A whole generation of children has grown up amidst violence and conflict. We learn about the *Zogos*; children left to fend for themselves because of the ongoing war. An entire generation of children have been robbed of the basic emotional care and support of family that are needed to grow toward maturity. On top of that, they have suffered the ravages of war and have been forced into the unimaginable horror of living on the streets and in many cases engaging in criminal activity, prostitution, and drug use in order to survive. The damage done to these children is carried forward. It damages their mental health. In most cases, they have been deprived of the educational opportunities that they need to lift themselves out of poverty, and the important sense of self-esteem that goes along with that. It hampers their ability to form the sort of healthy supportive relationships that they need to heal. Furthermore, when they become parents themselves in most cases, they simply have not had the sort of role models they need to effectively parent their own children, and so the trauma has been passed on to the next generation.

The issue of trauma also arises in Qubti's chapter. One of the most moving and disturbing images portrayed is the experience of children who have been taken into police custody. Experiences of trauma do not merely affect the immediate victims. As Qubti explains, they are absorbed by communities and families. This is a different sort of trauma than that suffered by the *Zogos*, but these situations too develop into intergenerational traumas that damage the children and subsequent descendants.

The damage wrought by U.S. racism has left many wounds that have not even begun to start healing. Any conflict involving acts of violence or oppression, if it is allowed to continue long enough, will result in intergenerational trauma. The U.S. chapter focuses on the damage done to Black Americans through systemic racism. The stress and burden of being part of a marginalized group creates traumatic damage, not unlike that suffered by victims of war. Though not covered in this book, systemic racism and its damage can also be seen in the United States and Canada by the damage done to Native Americans through the residential schools. Children were torn away from their families and were victims of forced assimilation to conform to Euro-American cultural norms. In addition to being stripped of their own cultural identity, in many cases the children were victims of violence, abuse, and perilous living conditions. They were malnourished, overworked, and lived in unsanitary and inadequate housing. The mortality rates due to illness were appalling. Tragically many white Christians thought that these institutions were helping the plight of Native Americans and were supported by the churches. The resulting intergeneration trauma is one that continues to plague its victims.[1]

Third, the witness of the Church amidst conflict and in peacebuilding is crucial. It may seem at times, especially in the West where the Church seems to have declining influence and resources, that we have very little to offer. In all parts of the world, it may seem that the problems faced are so overwhelming that we have little power to change things. However, as most of our chapters demonstrate, our strength is not the strength of military, political, or economic might. Our strength is given to us by a God who chose to come into this world as a helpless infant born into a poor family, a member of an oppressed and disenfranchised people.

As one who preaches the gospel weekly, I never cease to be amazed by what a living, vibrant, relevant resource our ancient texts provide to the modern world. It is only natural that we have given over a couple of chapters entirely devoted to exploring these themes (see chapters 1 and 2) and hopefully you will notice the appearance of scripture elsewhere throughout the book. In both cases, these authors focus on the peace of God. Dickson Chilongani focuses on the Hebrew scriptures and John Yieh on the Christian scripture (the Old and New Testaments, respectively). Although the language and the narratives vary significantly, these two chapters demonstrate the unity of scripture.

Both Herman Browne and Sarah Snyder consider the power and impact of liturgy and sacrament. Robert Heaney does as well, although less directly. If you are coming from a faith tradition that does not engage in the liturgical or the sacramental, please do not ignore or dismiss these chapters as irrelevant. The textbook definition of a sacrament is "an efficacious sign of grace instituted by Christ" also sometimes called "an outward sign of an interior grace." These are fancy ways of saying that these are things we do to connect to the reality of what God's grace through Jesus Christ is doing in our lives. Liturgy is simply an organized way of us being together to come and worship God. In both cases, we are

1. For more details about this tragedy see Jean A. Cotting, "The Episcopal Church Involvement in Native American Boarding Schools (1862–1905)" (MDiv Thesis, Virginia Theological Seminary, 2020).

talking about formalized rituals. Though you may not use these specific rituals to feel closer to God, you will have things in your own faith tradition—rituals or set ways of doing things—that help to center you and focus on God's presence in God's world.

Reflect on Primary Questions

I have suggested that an intentional approach to reflection will require intention. This means, at least in part, being hospitable to new ideas and being cognizant of one's cultural location. Given such intention, major themes might be explored fruitfully. I have identified three major themes at work in sections A and B that you will also find at work in section C. The issues of history, trauma, and the witness of the Church are by no means exhaustive of themes in this book or conflict analysis more generally. Nonetheless, they point to the importance of identifying major themes and illustrate some of the themes at work in this book as authors consider both the nature of conflict and Christian visions of dialogue and peacebuilding. You will likely spot other major themes and convergences of ideas on your own (also see the concluding chapter in this volume). In light of major themes, this final section will identify some primary questions you might find helpful in group or individual reflection. The wording of these primary questions is geared toward those working in groups, but as an individual reader you can adapt at least some of them to your own experience, reflection, and practice.

Begin with intention and location. All or some of these questions might be used to invite people into considering intention and location in theological reflection:

1. As you review a single chapter or group of chapters, what new ideas or practices did you discover? What ideas or practices did you struggle to understand?
2. As you think about your own context, are there issues raised that do not seem to relate to your setting? Why is this the case?
3. Think more about your own location and identity: if you are in a group where you all know each other and feel comfortable doing so, create a wall chart with "spheres of identity." This is done by drawing big circles that indicate various dimensions of identity. These can be general classifications such as some of the delineations

discussed in this book: race, religion, ethnicity, nation of origin, or gender, but they can also be categories that have significance to your own setting—political party, denomination of one's family of origin, educational background, profession, or whatever may cause individuals in your group to have varying perspectives. Once these circles are drawn, have everyone go around and put their initials on any circle they see as applying to their location and identity. In discussion, explore how your elements of identity and location differ from the authors of chapters and members of your discussion group.

4. How does your identity, both individual and collective, serve you (what do you gain from it and to what extent is it a source of pride)? To what extent is your identity ever a hindrance? To what extent does the identity of others threaten your identity?
5. How is your identity related to institutions in your context? For example, are all members of your discussion group affiliated with the same institution, denomination, or faith tradition? To what extent do institutions inform, limit, or challenge your identity as a faith community or follower of Jesus Christ?
6. Reconsider the "spheres of identity" you outlined in question 3. How do you think your identity and location might shape your understanding of conflict and the nature of religious dialogue and Christian peacebuilding?

   Explore the major themes: history is always present, conflict involves trauma, the Church is called to witness to peace.

7. As you think about your community's history, who has been marginalized? How far back does such marginalization go?
8. What motivations are at work when one group marginalizes another? Can you think of examples of how scripture names such motivation and how such motivation is explained or even justified in your own context?
9. What is gained or lost when justice is given to the marginalized in scripture and in your context?
10. To what extent does ongoing trauma impact how people understand conflict in your context? Returning to the above discussion of trauma, who are the direct victims involved and how does this

trauma affect others around them. How is it absorbed or reacted to by the community? What are generational ramifications? How does it play out as intergenerational trauma?

11. What support can your community and the Church offer to support healing? Where might you find resources for the healing of trauma in your context (what professional bodies might offer methods and training on trauma and grief? What organizations are at work in your context with a focus on peace and reconciliation?)?
12. Consider Chilongani and Yieh's descriptions of God's peace in chapters 1 and 2. What is holding your community back from delving further into the possibilities that can come from true *shalom* and where do you see signs of true *shalom*?
13. Consider the four phases of repentance that are expressed in the Heaney chapter (chapter 4): contrition, confession, penance, and absolution. Where are you and your group on this journey? Have you confessed but not shown contrition? What has occurred in terms of penance? Have there been any premature claims to absolution by the offender?
14. To what extent does this chapter (or these chapters) resource or refresh your understanding of God or the gospel?

Hospitality means, in part, to begin in prayer, to make room for refreshment and informal conversation, to make space for different personality types, and to nurture an atmosphere where all can share their views. Intentional reflection emerges from such hospitality and centers on exploring and struggling with new ideas cognizant of one's own location. Reflection is aided by clearly identifying major themes that groups can explore more deeply. For the purpose of this chapter, I identified three major themes at work in all sections of the book—the ongoing impact of history, trauma as part of conflict, and the witness of the Church to peacebuilding. As you reflect on the chapters in sections A and B and turn to the contextual chapters in section C, to what extent do these major themes help you frame your own reading not only of this book but how conflict and peacebuilding might be understood in your own context? As an individual reader or as a group of readers pray, reflect, and discern the peace of God amidst worlds of conflict, it is always good to end by reaffirming a humble confidence in the presence and work of God in our midst. You might find it useful to return to the Oscar Romero prayer as a helpful way to end times of reflection:

> It helps, now and then, to step back and take the long view.
>
> The Kingdom is not only beyond our efforts; it is even beyond our vision.
>
> We accomplish in our lifetime only a fraction of the magnificent enterprise that is God's work.
>
> Nothing we do is complete, which is another way of saying that the kingdom always lies beyond us.
>
> No statement says all that could be said. No prayer fully expresses our faith. No confession brings perfection. No pastoral visit brings wholeness. No program accomplishes the church's mission. No set of goals and objectives includes everything.
>
> This is what we are about.
>
> We plant the seeds that one day will grow. We water the seeds already planted, knowing that they hold future promise. We lay foundations that will need further development. We provide yeast that produces effects far beyond our capabilities.
>
> We cannot do everything and there is a sense of liberation in realizing that. This enables us to do something and to do it well. It may be incomplete, but it is a beginning, a step along the way, an opportunity for the Lord's grace to enter and do the rest. We may never see the end results, but that is the difference between the master builder and the worker.
>
> We are workers, not master builders; ministers, not messiahs.
>
> We are prophets of a future not our own. [2]

---

2. The prayer was written by Bishop Ken Untener in commemoration of Archbishop Romero. More information can be found on the Archbishop Romero Trust website, www.romerotrust.org.uk/romero-prayer, accessed December 31, 2021.

SECTION C

Peacebuilding as Christian Practice

CHAPTER 9

Palestine

Building Dialogue in the Holy Land

Wadie N. Far, Jamil Khadir, Susan Ackley Lukens, Fares Naoum, and Nael Abu Rahmoun

Our identity as people is what brings us together. People might be forced to leave their homes or countries, but their country of origin will always be part of their identity. Christians in the Holy Land are facing a deepening crisis and conflict because of the 2017 Identity Law in Israel. This chapter will, first, outline how Christians understand their identity in the midst of conflict and how this is being threatened. Second, in turning to the Old and New Testaments, we reflect on the challenges of identity in a context of conflict and invite you to biblical reflection from your own context. Third, we identify a guiding principle in our peacebuilding and provide examples of how we seek to live out such a principle in our lives and ministries.

Our Conflict

The word "identity" is defined by the Cambridge dictionary as "who a person is, or the qualities of a person or group that make them different from others." The identity of a people is important because it serves to unify a community; it is something passed down through generations. This identity is a continuation of the people. Going back to the Ottoman Empire, we Palestinian Christians in the Holy Land have learned that contending for our identity would be vitally important. For the displaced, who have lost both their land and their family home, maintaining their identity as Palestinians has gained added importance. Our identity preserves our connection to one another, to history, and to the land.[1]

Palestinian Identity

Each group of people has different factors that compromise their identity. For all Palestinians, these factors are ethnicity, religion, nationality, citizenship, and for some, denomination is a factor as well. In the Holy Land, there are people with a range of factors that combine to make up their identity. The different peoples in the Holy Land will share some of the factors but not all of them. Among the various religious groups, there are Samaritans, Druze, Jews, Muslims, Christians, and Bahá'í.

Arab Christians in the Holy Land might identify as Palestinian, Israeli, and Anglican. They are ethnically Arab Palestinians, they are citizens of Israel, their religion is Christianity, and they practice their faith in the Anglican tradition. Each one of these factors of identity is vitally important and adds a different layer to who a person is. It is through understanding how all these dimensions come together that it is possible to understand the identity of Christians living in the Holy Land. Before we explain how these factors come together, we would invite you to think about the factors that compromise your identity. Who are you? How do your religion, ethnicity, and nationality shape your understanding of who you are and how you view the world around you? Why are these factors important to you?

Let us start with the religious factor. We are Christians. For some, religion might be seen as a personal matter that only affects the identity of the individual. In the Middle East, however, religion takes on added significance in our identity as a group. Even if a person is not active in the practice of their faith, their identification as a Christian or Muslim or Jew remains a critical element of their identity. It determines belonging. As Anglican Christians, we are taught to always remember our baptismal vows and their importance in how we live our lives. The effect of baptism as marking us as belonging to God is a significant factor of our identity.

---

1. See Kabahā Mustafá, *The Palestinian People: Seeking Sovereignty and State* (Boulder: Lynne Rienner, 2013); Naim Stifan Ateek, *A Palestinian Theology of Liberation: The Bible, Justice, and the Palestine-Israel Conflict* (Maryknoll: Orbis Press, 2017); Munther Isaac, *The Other Side of the Wall: A Palestinian Christian Narrative of Lament and Hope* (Downers Grove: IVP, 2020), 23–46.

Ethnicity is another major factor. To many people around the world, the words "Arab" and "Christian" do not go together. Sadly, many people mistakenly think that all Arabs are Muslims. This is wrong. There are Arabs who are not Muslims, just as there are Muslims who are not Arabs. Arab as an ethnicity existed before the beginning of both Islam and Christianity. The Arab ethnicity existed long before the times of Christ. The Book of Nehemiah mentions Geshem the Arabian (2:19, 6:1). The second chapter of Acts mentions the presence of Arab Jews among the disciples (2:11). Arab Christians are not a foreign group that immigrated to the Middle East after Islam was established. Christians were present about 620 years before Islam. There have been Arab Christians in the region ever since the day of Pentecost.

Not all Arab Christians in the Holy Land have the same nationality and citizenship. Some of us are Palestinians in both nationality and citizenship. Others living in the state of Israel might identify as Palestinian as their nationality but hold Israeli citizenship. This does not mean one has greater importance than the other; both are a part of identity, equally important to who we are as people.

Threats to Palestinian Identity

Palestinian identity is under threat from within and from without. The younger generation is in fact losing their sense of Palestinian identity because they are not concerned with the history of their own people in the land. They are more concerned with prosperity. They move their family to another country where jobs and opportunities are more plentiful. Many of our children under the age of twenty do not know how to describe themselves. A civics teacher came to our youth camp in the Galilee to teach about the Palestinian culture. For some of the young people they overlook their Palestinian history and heritage and identify simply as Israelis. For identity to remain across the generations, we need to focus on teaching our youth our long history and the real story. They are too confused about the history to articulate their story and be confident in their identity. In Ramleh, for example, many Palestinian young people do not identify as Palestinian. They go to Hebrew school and do not speak Arabic. They are losing their identity or their identity is being stolen. The story of the Palestinian people is being killed from within and from without.

We Palestinian Christian are not only facing a problem with our young people losing a sense of their identity, but recent legislation poses a further threat to our identity. Unlike other countries, Israel does not have a constitution; it rather has a group of basic laws. From each one of these basic laws, new laws can be written. The newest of these laws is the Identity Law which was adopted in July of 2017. Since this law is one of the basic laws, then further laws can be born out of it in the future.[2]

From the name of this basic law, we can understand the objective of the law: "Israel as the National State of the Jewish People." This law is essentially stating that Israel is a place for the Jews regardless of whether they are citizens or not, thus relegating all other people in Israel to second-rate citizens. Given our understanding of our identity, we suddenly find ourselves not welcomed in our own country. If Israel is a Jewish state, then all Samaritans, Druze, Muslims, Christians, and Bahá'í are outsiders, regardless of how long their ancestors have lived in the country or how they have served the State of Israel. There is no equality between the citizens of the same country.

This law also rejects the historical presence of Palestinians in their land. We feel we are no longer protected by law. The new legislation defends Jews only in the State of Israel. It also states that only Jews have an exclusive right to come back to the country. The law makes no provisions for all the non-Jews who have been displaced and wish to come back to their native land. This law has also encouraged the building of settlements on Palestinian land that is under the authority of the Palestinian National Authorities. In effect, the new law declares the Palestinian presence in the West Bank and Gaza illegitimate. The land has become the property of the State of Israel. This law deepens the conflict in our context. It appears non-Jews no longer have a place in Israel. Even the Druze, who serve in the armed forces, are no longer a priority for the Israeli government. The state has become a place for the Jewish people and no one else.

---

2. A full copy of this law can be found on the Knesset website. Knesset, "Full text of Basic Law: Israel as the Nation State of the Jewish People," July 19, 2018, Knesset News, accessed February 22, 2022, https://main.knesset.gov.il/EN/News/PressReleases/Pages/Pr13978_pg.aspx.

Our Conflict in Light of Scripture

Amidst the challenge and conflict the Palestinian people face, two voices from scripture remain particularly pertinent for us—the story of Ruth and Naomi and Jesus' power to calm the storm (Mark 4).

The biblical story of Ruth and Naomi is a perfect illustration of the challenge and conflict the Palestinian people face. In the story of Naomi and Ruth, two characteristics stand out—identity and dignity. When the story begins, Naomi, an Israelite, and her husband are living in a foreign land, Moab, for socioeconomic reasons. They fled because of famine in their own land. Naomi's sons married Moabite women. Both her sons and her husband die. She must return to her native land. Moab is not her community and she has no one to turn to for aid. Her daughter-in-law Ruth, out of loyalty and compassion, chooses to return with Naomi. Now it is Ruth who is the foreigner in a foreign land. In the case of both women, their charity and devotion to each other and those they encounter transform their situation. They not only survive but also prosper. These women are especially important to us as Christians not only because they are examples of loyalty and compassion but because they are direct ancestors of Jesus.

The story of Ruth is a story of hope. Naomi had lost her voice. An alien in Moab, with the death of her husband and sons, she had lost her identity and her land. This is an important lesson for Arab Palestinians living in Israel. If we lose our identity, we lose everything. Naomi had not, however, lost her hope. She decided to make the long and dangerous journey home to the fields of her native land and her people in Bethlehem. When her kinsman Boaz saw her, he recognized her as a member of his tribe. This provided Naomi with hope for a future among her own people and in her homeland. This same hope that Naomi has for her future is a critical life-sustaining vision for Palestinians present in Israel today. Like Naomi, we will go back to our homes someday. This is our hope. It nourishes us in times of conflict, challenge, and suffering. Just as Mary and Joseph traveled to their home village for the census (Luke 2:1–5), we Palestinians are tied to our land as our origin. We consider ourselves the first mothers of Christianity in this land. Even though some of our homes and lands have been confiscated by the Israeli government, we keep our house keys. Like Naomi and Ruth, we maintain our identity which ensures our dignity. Storms may rage, but we maintain our hope.

As Christians, hope is nurtured when we turn to Christ. Particularly important to us is the scene in Mark 4 where Jesus stills a storm. We invite you to reflect on that passage with us and, if possible, do so with a group. Take a moment to read Mark 4:35–41. After you finish reading the text for the first time, we suggest taking a few minutes to meditate on Sadao Watanabe's depiction of Jesus calming the storm.[3] Now, read the text a second time, ask a different person from the group to read the text this time or if you are alone read the text in a different translation. In a group, if a man read it the first time, have a woman read it the second time. Or if an older person read it the first time, have a young person read it the second time.

After reading the passage, and meditating on the icon, consider the following questions:

1. Why were the disciples afraid? Certainly, they were afraid of the storm but what else underlies that? Try to dig deep into identifying the source of their fears.
2. How did the disciples interpret the fact that Jesus was sleeping? In our lives, do we feel the same as the disciples when we lose our sense of peace?
3. After Jesus calmed the sea, he asked the disciples about their faith. How is faith a prerequisite for God's peace in our lives?

After you have finished reflecting on these questions, find a quiet place and reflect on the prompts below. Be innovative in responding to the prompts. You may wish to reflect in a journal, write poetry, author a story, or draw an image in response to the prompts:

4. From your own life experience, describe a time when you felt that you had lost peace in your life. It could be a time when you feared for your life, or when you felt uncertain about the future, or when you were dragged into a conflict.
5. How were you able to regain control of your feelings? How were you able to find your faith and to use that to find God's peace? Were you able to do that by yourself, or did you need the help of others?

---

3. Sadao Watnabe, *Boat in a Storm (Mark 4: 35–41)*, 1967, print on *momigami*, www.sarugallery.com/default.php?L=4&NR=466, accessed February 22, 2022.

If you are reflecting in a group setting, have the group split into pairs and have each pair share their reflection with their partner before returning to the larger discussion group. Ask for volunteers to share their own reflections with the group. Be respectful that each one of these reflections is personal. Give room for discussion after each reflection. Take time to read the Palestinian reflection below. How does it compare and differ from your reflection on scripture? What explains the similarities and dissimilarities?

A Palestinian Reflection on Mark 4

When we live with conflict, regardless of what that conflict is, it is easy for us to feel like we are in the midst of a storm at sea. This metaphor becomes much stronger when the conflict is about understanding our personal identity. When people are confused about their identity, they do not know where they have come from and where they are going. Identity is like an anchor and identification with a community is like a safe harbor. Without some sense of attachment and shelter, a person loses their sense of control over their life and suddenly fear and desperation set in. This is similar to the feelings the disciples had during the storm. They felt they were in mortal danger. They felt they were losing control of their lives. They were not in control of the future. Have you ever allowed a conflict to fill you with such paralyzing fear? Have you experienced fear that drains hope from your existence?

As with the disciples in the storm, if we concentrate only on our problems and our fears we will miss the fact that Jesus is present. Jesus is present in our conflict as surely as he was present to the disciples on the boat that evening. Although the disciples knew that Jesus was with them, they did not understand what that really meant. They thought that he did not care. When they woke him up, they were in awe when he calmed the storm. Where do you see God's presence in conflicts you face? Do you rely on God to fill you with peace in the middle of your conflict?

The disciples underestimated the power of Jesus. Although they had traveled with Jesus for some time and seen him work miracles, they did not trust that Jesus could calm the storm and lead them through this conflict unharmed. This text invites us all to recognize that our God, the God who created this universe, is in control. If we truly believe in God, we will find peace in our lives. Such peace may not come because all our problems are fixed. Such peace does not depend on a miraculous resolution to the conflict. Rather, this peace will come from knowing that with God all things are possible. We, therefore, fear nothing. Amidst the conflict, we need to switch our attention to God's gift of peace. Without such connection to peace, we will not be able to work toward reconciliation. Do you underestimate the power of God in your life? Are you willing to hand over your life to God and trust God to give you peace in the middle of the storm? The work of peacebuilding is built upon such a spiritual foundation.

Resourcing Peacbuilding Amidst Conflict

For us, the fundamental commitment in peacebuilding is service to all. In this section, we explain this commitment and give examples of how it is grounded in practice.

Peacebuilding as Service to All

The work of reconciliation is not easy. The witness of Archbishop Desmond Tutu reminded us of our shared humanity. In both Israel and Palestine, there is fragility and goodness. Tutu reflected on the journey of reconciliation after the restrictions of the Apartheid government were eliminated in South Africa:

> I know that, were I born a member of the white ruling class at that time in South Africa's past, I might easily have treated someone with the same dismissive disdain with which I was treated. I know, given the same pressures and circumstances, I am capable of the same monstrous acts as any other human on this achingly beautiful planet. It is the knowledge of my own frailty that helps me find compassion, my empathy, similarity, and my forgiveness for the frailty and cruelty of others. We have seen that in order to forgive, it is important we accept the facts of what happened and the feelings we felt about what happened. We have accepted our own human vulnerability and frailty. Now we must accept the vulnerability and frailty of the one who harmed us.[4]

---

4. Desmond Tutu and Mpho Tutu, *The Book of Forgiving: The Fourfold Path for Healing Ourselves and Our World* (New York: HarperOne, 2014), 127.

As Palestinians, we welcome dialogue. We are open to hear the suffering of others and we welcome vision that can enable all of us to share this ancient land of the Holy One. God's Church must be a witness to such peace. We, in the Episcopal Diocese of Jerusalem, strive to be witnesses of God's peace through our lives and ministries. We witness to peace in our churches. We witness to peace through our institutions spread throughout the five countries that compose our diocese. We witness to peace through our work in local communities. It is our firm belief that we are here to serve all regardless of religion, nationality, or financial ability. We seek to serve all people even in the midst of conflict. We are witnesses to Christ calming the storm.

Recently, retired Archbishop Suheil Dawani, the former Primate of the Province of Jerusalem and the Middle East and the Episcopal Bishop in Jerusalem, reminded his clergy that the Episcopal churches exist not only to serve Episcopalians, the clergy are present to serve all regardless of their faith tradition or denomination. Some of our churches have more people from other Christian denominations than parishioners of our own Episcopal denomination. That is one of the ways we live the peace of Christ. All are welcomed into God's house. We believe that it is through sharing God's peace with others, in teaching and in parish activities, that peace is spread. This is God's mission into which we are invited to participate.

As a guiding light to our work in the Diocese of Jerusalem, we have sought to establish a vision for how to live as witnesses to God's peace. We have set the following goals:

- Build institutions for the education of our children.
- Provide places of worship for all who live in this land and all who visit it.
- Gather for celebration in each other's faith tradition, knowing that we worship the same God.
- Seek to understand the value of water and land so that a shared land can be envisioned for all.
- Become good listeners so that new understandings can lead to forgiveness and reconciliation.

These are the principles that guide us in deciding what project we will undertake and how we will carry it out. The projects that emerge from these principles of peacebuilding vary according to the needs of particular communities. We have hospitals, schools, a boarding school for orphans, a boarding school for the deaf and deaf-blind, a house for the elderly, and many more institutions. The doors of these institutions are open to all regardless of their religion, nationality, cultural background, ethnicity, or financial situation. If a person comes knocking on the door, the only question we ask ourselves is if we can help this person. If the answer is yes, then that is all we need to know.

Some people think that spreading the peace of God can only be achieved by preaching or lecturing people on the gospel. We believe this is false. We believe that the gospel can be articulated without words. The gospel is heard in the way we interact with the people who come to our institutions looking for aid. The gospel is heard when we treat people with respect, care, and love (John 13:34–35).

Peacebuilding in Action

In 2008, 120 deaf and blind students made up the Holy Land Institute for the Deaf and Deaf-Blind in Salt, Jordan. Only one of the students was a Christian. For over fifty years, our vision has been that students will experience full inclusion in society and be part of a movement that shapes a better Middle East.[5] In short, we share Jesus through the way of love. Just as we realize how important it is for our young people to hold onto and retain their sense of identity and connection to community, we respect and encourage that same vital connection for others.

The Cultural Center in Shefa-'Amr, Israel, is a place where all people of all backgrounds are welcomed to share the rich heritage and culture of this land. One of the best ways that we can preserve and maintain our own cultural identity is to share it with others and, by the same token, learn about and appreciate the culture and identity of others. A range of activities and events are arranged at the Cultural Center—music recitals, choir singing, educational and medical workshops, art exhibitions, and ecumenical and interreligious dialogues.[6] We celebrate and honor the

---

5. See "Holy Land Institute for the Deaf," www.holyland-deaf.org, accessed January 7, 2022.

6. See Pat McCaughan, "Toward a Cultural Center in Jerusalem," *Mission: The Church's Heartbeat* (blog), *ECF Vital Practices*, November, 2011, www.ecfvp.org/vestry-papers/article/241/toward-a-cultural-center-in-jerusalem, accessed January 7, 2022.

richness that diversity brings. As Christians, we do not see diversity as the enemy of peace. The enemy of peace is fear and it is ignorance.

Having learned something about how our diocese and communities are working to spread God's peace, we would like you to think about your own faith community's work and context:

1. How does your church understand its responsibility in spreading God's Peace? What are the needs of your region?
2. Is your church active in responding to these needs?
3. How might your church improve the way it is spreading God's peace?

Peacebuilding as Art

As a Christian minority, living amidst conflict, there is an "art" to how we are present and how we witness to the living Christ in our context. It is hoped that you have already discerned this as we have sought to describe our conflict, reflect on scripture, and define our approach to peacebuilding. We also make a direct appeal to artistic works as a means of peacebuilding. For God speaks to us through many different means. We believe that the one who created all has put a spirit of creativity and it is through this spirit of creativity that we can deepen our relationship with the divine.

The well-known poet, Mahmoud Darwish (شيورد دومحم), wrote "The Speech of Peace" (مالسلا باطخ).[7] Darwish was known as the Palestinian National poet. The poem asserts that the price for this peace might be high, but it is worth it. It encourages people to adapt to a new vision for peace. This piece of cultural heritage invites us to seek genuine peace regardless of the cost. The peace to which the poem is inviting us requires the entire world to change, and so it is a peace that will only come to pass after a long time. Such a vision of peace may reflect the peace that God offers his creation. It is a peace that can change the heart now and a peace that we can but glimpse in art and in history.

In your culture, what cultural resources talk about peace and might help people envision peacebuilding? How do these resources reflect or

7. Mahmoud Darwish, "The Speech of Peace" *Index on Censorship: A Voice for the Persecuted* 23, no. 6 (1994): 181–183.

compare to your understanding of peace as a Christian? How does an artistic vision of peace compare or contrast to your earlier reflections on the biblical text?

Conclusion

In this chapter, we have shared with you the struggles that we Christians face in the Land of the Holy One. We are faced with deepening conflict because of the introduction of the Identity Law (2017) that segregates us and serves to threaten our religious, ethnic, and cultural identity. We live in an environment threatened by violence. Yet, in the face of all of this we turn to scripture for understanding and inspiration and we turn in service to all the people of this land.

> Pray for us. Pray with us:
> Our gracious Lord,
> you are the source of true and everlasting peace.
> Grant us faith that we might keep our eyes on you as we journey on the troubled waters of this world.
> Help us to remember, always, that you are present with us in our voyage.
> We ask you to fill us with your peace in the midst of the storm.
> Give us the strength to surrender the rudder of life to you,
> so that you can guide us through the conflict.
> Give us the strength to share your peace on earth,
> so that all your children might flourish.
> This we ask in the name of your Son our Lord Jesus Christ,
> who calmed the storm with the strength of his word. Amen.

CHAPTER 10

Liberia

Building Dialogue Amidst Civil Unrest

Anne Fredericks Cooper, Kofi Ankrah, Herman B. Browne, C. Patrick Burrowes, Julia Duncan Cassell, Allen V. Gaye, and A. Siede Williams

This chapter seeks to provide a historical account of the conflicts and divides that plagued the people of Liberia for twenty-four long years and how that has impacted the Church and her witness. As members of the Cuttington University community, we will reflect on the sources of civil wars, the ongoing damage to our society (especially our young people), and reflect on what scripture may teach us in understanding and confronting these challenges. We will explore how the Christian churches may contribute or facilitate national healing.

Our Conflict

Liberia's civil unrest began in 1979 with the so-called Rice Riots. The fighting was temporarily suspended in 1993 with the signing of the Accra Peace Accord. Full cessation of fighting did not occur until 2003.[1] A civil war, which began as a conflict between the government and an insurgency, evolved into eleven armed factions jockeying for power. The Accord

1. On April 14, 1979, a rice riot began as a result of the increase in the price of rice from $22 per 100 pound bag to $26 per 100 pound bag. For the Accra Peace Accord see: Government of Liberia, Liberians United for Reconciliation and Democracy, the Movement for Democracy in Liberia, and the Political Parties, *Peace Agreement Between The Government of Liberia (GOL), The Liberians United for Reconciliation and Democracy (LURD), The Movement for Democracy in Liberia (MODEL) and The Political Parties*, Accra, Ghana, 2013, https://2001-2009.state.gov/p/af/rls/24149.htm.

brought together all warring factions under agreed-upon guidelines to cease fighting. As John Paul Lederach observed, "Most peace accords are not solutions in content but proposed negotiated processes, which if followed, will change the expression of the conflict and provide avenues for redefining relationships."[2] This has been the Liberian experience.

Prior to the signing of the second Accra Peace Accord, Liberia experienced two civil wars that caused destruction at all levels of society. Between 1989 and 2003, 150,000–300,000 people were killed, 1.2 million were internally displaced, and 235,000 persons were driven into exile. Women were raped, children were drugged and armed, religious shrines were burned, and hundreds of civilians were massacred in the sanctuary of a church. These acts of violence deeply wounded the soul of Liberia. The nation's social fabric was torn and the body politic maimed. Although the healing process is underway, these deep wounds have left deep scars, and heart-wrenching pain continues to impact daily life.

The Conflict in Historical Perspective

The idea of our nation began in 1816 through the establishment of the American Society for the Colonization of the Free People of Color (commonly referred to as the American Colonization Society or ACS), which was led by white Americans. The ACS raised funds to relocate free blacks who lived in the United States of America during the era of race-based enslavement. These freed Black people were Christians who brought their religion with them when they returned to a foreign ancestral home. Between 1820 and 1840, about 3,000 people of African descent returned to live in eleven towns along the west coast of Africa. The residents of those towns, which included indigenous Africans who were already living in the region, formed an independent republic called Liberia, meaning "land of the free." By 1900 another 16,000 Blacks immigrated from the Americas.

Over the years, Liberia would expand to encompass its current 43,000 square miles with four million people grouped into four language families and subdivided into over seventeen ethnic groups. Its expansion intensified after the Berlin Conference (1884–1885), when European nations

2. John Paul Lederach, *The Moral Imagination: The Art and Soul of Building Peace* (Oxford: Oxford University Press, 2005), 46.

colonized and divided Africa. As Liberia became more diverse, descendants of the American repatriates, known as Americo-Liberians, continued to be disproportionately represented in senior government positions. This led to a government that did not reflect the diversity of all its people.

Tensions continued to mount over the ensuing decades. The Rubicon was crossed in 1979 when a mass demonstration opposed to a proposal to increase the price of rice, the country's staple food, degenerated into rioting and lawless behavior by civilians, police, and soldiers. Facing a breakdown in military command, the government invited troops from neighboring Guinea to restore order, a move that angered rank-and-file Liberian soldiers. Approximately one year later, on April 12, 1980 seventeen noncommissioned soldiers, led by Master Sergeant Samuel K. Doe, seized power and murdered President William R. Tolbert. Ten days later, on April 22, thirteen government officials were executed by firing squad. The coup ended 133 years of Americo-Liberian dominated civilian rule.

Due to internal and external pressures, elections were held in 1985. As the acting head of state, Doe ran for the presidency. He lost and then nullified the results, which led to splits within his governing body, the People's Redemption Council (PRC). This resulted in the embrace of violent methods by some in the previously peaceful opposition. Competition for power among members of the PRC soon led to a series of clashes that culminated in extrajudicial killings. Those clashes took a dramatic turn in 1985, with a failed coup d'état attempt by the former commanding general of the PRC government, Thomas Quiwonkpa. The aftermath of the failed coup led to violent attacks against ethnic groups from Quiwonkpa's home county of Nimba. Particularly atrocious was the massacre of nearly a thousand Dan and Ma civilians who had fled to what they hoped was a sanctuary in St. Peter's Lutheran Church, Monrovia. Such violence only deepened ethnic divisions and animosity.

In 1989, an armed insurrection was launched from neighboring Cote d'Ivoire by Charles Taylor. The National Patriotic Front of Liberia (NPFL) drew upon deep longings for redress among the heavily repressed citizens of Nimba County. Alienated from his former civilian and PRC allies, Doe turned to wealthy members of the predominantly Muslim Mandingo ethnic group for financial backing. In response, rebels began indiscriminately attacking Mandingos. After the murder of Doe in 1990, his supporters formed an armed faction of their own, which three years later split into the ULIMO-J, led by a Krahn Christian, and the ULIMO-K, led by a Mandingo Muslim. The conflict now took on a religious dimension. After having peacefully coexisted for over a century, Liberian neighbors of different religious backgrounds suddenly became bitter enemies. From a conflict between the PRC and NPFL, the Liberian war developed into a conflict between a multiplicity of armed factions. Such circumstances led the nation into a period of intense civil war from the late 1980s until the early 2000s. The nation and its people have yet to recover.[3]

The Ongoing Impact of Conflict on Our Youth

The effects of the war remain evident among today's youth who tend to live their lives as products of a fractured environment. The youth learned right from wrong from those eager to control their young minds. Many young people were traumatized by the war and forced into acts against their will. Young girls became sexually active at nine or ten years old either by rape, drugs, or as a means of survival. For some, their lives were irreparably damaged by the sale of their bodies to support themselves and their families. These young girls became what is generally referred to as "girl mothers." Boys were also traumatized, abused, and terrorized into becoming murderers. Many of them were forced into taking drugs as a means of numbing their feelings so that they might carry out the atrocities that defined the Liberian conflict. These young children became pawns in the execution of evil by adults.

Today, the effects of the war are visible among many young people who have become drug addicts, referred to as *Zogos*. The *Zogos* (male) and *Zogees* (female) continue to complain about feeling abandoned by their leaders. For them, drugs have become an escape from hardship and pain. Even when provided with aid and support, finding God's peace often eludes these young people. They find themselves unable to obtain employment because of their drug addictions or fractured schooling. To support themselves, they turn to violence and theft. No adequate rehabilitative systems exist to serve them. Our faith community has striven to work with these young

---

3. See also George Kieh and Eric Paterson, *Liberia: Religious Leaders, Peacemaking, and the First Liberian War* (Washington, DC: Berkley Center for Religion, Peace and World Affairs, 2013), https://s3.amazonaws.com/berkley-center/130801BCLiberiaReligiousLeadersPeacemakingFirstLiberianCivilWar.pdf, accessed February 22, 2022.

people. One young *Zogo* who frequently worshipped at Trinity Cathedral was welcomed and supported by parishioners. They even provided means for him to start a small retail business. Unfortunately, after a few months he had used the profits from the business to purchase drugs. He returned to the streets along with other *Zogos.*

Another *Zogo* came to worship. He sat and participated in the service. When it was time for the Eucharist, he remarked that he could not take Communion because he had done too many evil things. He wanted to be rehabilitated and was given funds to enroll in a rehabilitation program. Our hope is that he stays in the program and becomes clean. Many of the affected youth hope for better lives. They want to unshackle their bodies from addictive drugs.

Some of the children who grew up in the war are now parents and are passing on the trauma of the war to their children. This intergenerational trauma means that physical and psychological repercussions, in compromised health and chemical imbalances, are being passed on to the next generation. Extreme violence impaired parental ability to nurture their children and frequent eruptions of child abuse resulted. Parental stories of painful experiences further influence children by stimulating a desire for revenge. Psychiatrist Dr. Edward Grant maintained that "These children are the most dangerous segments of the fighting machine. They are accustomed to committing atrocities while under the influence of drugs."[4] This is the plight in which Dukuly Togah found himself. What is remarkably different about Dukuly is that during his most trying times, he relied on God. He recounted:

> Sometimes Iron Jacket would give me some kind of white chalk to rub on my body so the bullets can't touch me . . . but I never used to like it. When I go on the battlefront, front-line troop, I can pray to God. When I come back, I can tell God thank you. I had my Bible in my pocket. I don't know how to read. But every time I go on the front line, I would knock it on my forehead, put it in my pocket, and go.[5]

4. Tim Weiner, "At 14, a Liberian War Veteran Dreams of Finding a Way Home," *New York Times,* August 25, 2013, www.nytimes.com/2003/08/25/world/at-14-a-liberian-war-veteran-dreams-of-finding-a-way-home.html, accessed January 8, 2022.

5. Weiner, "At 14."

Our Conflict in Light of Scripture

In the Old Testament, the sons of Isaac, Jacob and Esau, were constantly vying for their birthright. This birthright was the basis of status and power. Birthed from the same womb, born from the same flesh, Jacob and Esau's envy of each other and their focus on their own self-interest blinded them from what bound them together—love. Their story was one of deception, revenge, guilt, and reconciliation. Like Jacob and Esau, Liberia's conflict was rooted in competition over a birthright, the birthright of a nation.

Take a moment to read and reflect on Genesis 32:3–12. Read the text again and write down the words from the passage that describe how Jacob was feeling? What other words, not in the text, would you choose to describe Jacob's feelings in this scene? What causes such feelings in your own life, the life of your community, and in the life of your nation? Can you identify fractured relations in your family and community where betrayal, fear, and guilt were underlying factors?

As is often the case in the aftermath of conflict, Jacob was afraid to be reunited with his brother. He was afraid that Esau had not forgiven him. Similarly, there is fear and suspicion among Liberians. There remains much forgiveness yet to be granted. When Esau ran to meet his brother, he embraced him with love (Gen. 33:1–4). To embrace, it was necessary for Jacob to recognize and face his fears. That embrace is the essence of reconciliation.[6] What images from this text, from other biblical texts, or from other sources do you envisage when you hear the word "reconciliation"? Why do these images speak to you about the nature of reconciliation? How might the witness of the Church promote and support such visions of repentance and reconciliation?

From the New Testament, the example of the paralyzed man at the pool of Bethesda is important in our context (John 5:1–9). Take a moment to read that passage. The paralyzed man laid on his mat for thirty-eight years waiting for someone to place him in the pool to be healed. As time passed, discontent, self-pity, and jealousy seeped in and his faith was shaken. In your context, to what extent do longstanding and intergenerational problems cause you to question, doubt, or lose hope?

---

6. See Miroslav Volf, *Exclusion and Embrace: A Theological Exploration of Identity, Otherness, and Reconciliation* (Nashville: Abingdon Press, 1996).

Like the paralyzed man, Liberians remain paralyzed by our generational divisions. In his article about the First Liberian Civil War, George Klay Kieh calls on religious leaders and peacemakers to address the lack of support from the Christian community:

> Despite the hegemony of Christianity in the Liberian polity, the church, with few exceptions, has historically been a defender of the status quo. That is, with the exception of a few Christian leaders, such as the late Bishop George D. Browne of the Episcopal Church of Liberia, the late Bishop Roland J. Payne of the Lutheran Church, and Archbishop Michael K. Francis of the Catholic Church, the church has not been an advocate of social justice and human development.[7]

It is easier to remain on the mat surrounded by those paralyzed than to believe healing is possible. We have become comfortable on our mats surrounded by those we consider like-minded. We have become complacent in offering healing to our brothers and sisters. If we desire true healing in our land we must, like the paralyzed man, follow Jesus' commandment and stand up and walk together as a community. In your context, where do you see complacency in the life of the Church? What might be done to stir the Church out of such complacency in your community?

It is Jesus who is the ideal and perfection of reconciliation toward which we strive. According to the Gospels, Jesus knew Judas would betray Him (Matt. 26:24–25; Mark 14:18–21; Luke 22:21–23; John 13:21–30). It may be that Jesus knew this when He called Judas to be His disciple. Jesus knew it as He knelt and lovingly washed His feet (John 13). Jesus sowed the seeds of reconciliation in His daily walk. We are called to do the same. This level of sanctity seems beyond us as human beings. We are not Jesus. Yet, we have many ordinary human examples we may follow. There remain testimonies of everyday men and women who repented

---

7. George Klay Kieh Jr., "Religious Leaders, Peacemaking and the First Liberian Civil War," *Journal of Religion, Conflict and Peace* 5, no. 2 (2012), 8, www.manchester.edu/docs/default-source/academics/by-major/philosophy-and-religious-studies/journal/volume-5-issue-1-2-fall-2011-spring-2012/religious-leaders-peacemaking-and-the-first-liberian-civil-war.pdf?sfvrsn=70668962_2, accessed January 7, 2022. See also George Klay Kieh Jr., "The Roots of the Second Liberian Civil War," *International Journal on World Peace* 26, no. 1 (2009): 7–30.

and rose to the sort of holiness to which the gospel calls us. This is one of our prayers about the fifth-century saint, Moses the Black:

> God of transforming power and transfiguring mercy: Listen to the prayers of all who, like Abba Moses, cry to you: "O God whom we do not know, let us know you!" Draw them and all of us from unbelief to faith and from violence into your peace, through the cross of Jesus our Savior; who lives and reigns with you, in the unity of the Holy Spirit, one God, now and forever. Amen.

Moses the Black was transformed from a life of violence to one of compassion and peace after being convicted by the work of Jesus' Gospel of peace. He was a former slave and a violent career criminal who was reformed and became a member of a monastic community.[8] As the patron saint of nonviolence, the story of Moses the Black is an important example for followers of Christ. We must continue to witness to each other. We must continue to share these testimonies from our tradition.

In your context, who is it that you look to as an example of what it means to be a peacebuilder? How can you find out about other peacemakers in your setting and beyond? How might you teach your friends and community about these leaders in peace? How might the lessons they learned resource a ministry of reconciliation in your context?

Resourcing Peacebuilding Amidst Conflict

In our context, peacebuilding is resourced by traditional practices, ecumenical and interreligious cooperation, the witness of women, and dialogue across ethnic diversity. These resources are drawn upon as peacebuilding is understood as constructive social change. For John Lederach, this means:

> the pursuit of moving relationships from those denied by fear, mutual recriminations, and violence towards those characterized by love, mutual respect and proactive engagement. Constructive

8. "Moses the Black, Saint," *Claremont Coptic Encyclopedia* (1991), http://search.ebscohost.com.libproxy.udayton.edu/login.aspx?direct=true&db=edsoai&AN=edsoai.ocn759741319&site=eds-live, accessed January 2, 2021.

> social change seeks to change the flow of human interaction in social conflict from cycles of destructive relational violence towards cycles of relational dignity and respectful engagement. The flows of fear destroy. Those of love edify. That is the challenge: how to move from that which destroys towards that which builds.[9]

In the traditional Liberian setting whenever there is a misunderstanding, the community gathers in the *palava* hut to solve the problem. In the *palava* hut, the community gathers to relax with friends and family, sort out differences, and seek ways to reconcile. The *palava* hut is a traditional building usually constructed with mud, sticks, and thatch. The hut has a round base with open sides and a thatch roof that is held in place by sticks. It may be seen in many towns and villages. In his article, "Mending Broken Relations After Civil War: The Palava Hut and the Prospects for Lasting Peace in Liberia," Kwaku Dansu describes the Palava Hut as:

> a gathering place, usually a *round* thatched hut symbolizing the sustained relationship that is the essence of the process . . . Palava Hut gatherings are usually convened and presided over by a respected Elder or a panel of Elders within the community or the town chief, playing a mediatory role. The process is based on consensus in most communities and usually seeks for permanent resolution of disputes. The Palava Hut process has many dimensions that may include truth-telling and acknowledgment of responsibility by the offender, forgiveness by the victim (and the Elder(s)) . . . The Palava Hut is also thought of as a concept, and not a specific place . . . There is no homogeneous Palava Hut system practiced by all the ethnic groups in Liberia . . . Since the individual is considered a part of the community, justice for the community will translate into justice for the individual. Given the magnitude of atrocities committed during the civil war, and considering the centrality of justice and reconciliation under the Palava Hut, there can be no doubt that the Palava Hut has relevance for the ongoing transitional processes taking place

9. Lederach, *Moral Imagination*, 42.

> in Liberia. There exist formidable obstacles at the same time, however.[10]

We see from the example of the Palava Hut that there are aspects of our culture already in place that naturally lend themselves to facilitating the reconciliation process. In concert with a theology of reconciliation, traditional modes such as this can be leveraged to promote healing and peace.

As political leaders seek to address the truth and seek reconciliation, the Church has a responsibility to make its voice heard and heed Jesus' call to be peacemakers (Matt. 5:9). Unfortunately, the Church has not always lived up to this responsibility of speaking truth in the face of adversity. During the decades of sorrow, toil, and pain, few Church leaders spoke out against the atrocities for fear of being persecuted. Some faith leaders compromised their beliefs by prioritizing the norms of their political parties over their priestly vows. In contrast, the responsibility of the Christian community is to be

> doers of the Word, and not hearers only, deceiving ourselves. For if anyone is a hearer of the word and not a doer, he is like a man observing his natural face in a mirror; for he observes himself, goes away, and immediately forgets his own face.
>
> (James 1:22–24)

Reconciliation is, then, an ecclesial or community responsibility. Reconciliation, by definition, does not happen in isolation. In 1982, the Liberian Council of Churches (LCC) was established. Membership was open to any church that confessed faith in the blessed Trinity, faith in Jesus Christ as Lord and Savior, and faith in the Bible as the inspired word of God. The LCC set its mission on uniting, empowering, reconciling, and grouping its constituencies through strategic networks and cooperation with national and international ecumenical bodies and governments.

---

10. Kwaku Dansu, "Mending Broken Relations after Civil War: The 'Palava Hut' and the Prospects for Lasting Peace in Liberia," *Kofi Annan International Peacekeeping Training Center*, Policy Brief 2 (May 2016): 1–6 at 2–3, https://media.africaportal.org/documents/KAIPTC-Policy-Brief---The-Palava-Hut-in-Liberia.pdf, accessed February 22, 2022.

In 1989, when civil war broke out in Liberia, the LCC realized the myriad challenges required a multipronged solution. The LCC could not engage all the significant parties alone. Neither did it enjoy the confidence of all parties. Acting alone, it could not be effective as an agent of peace in the crisis. The LCC engaged with leaders of the National Muslim Council of Liberia and they both agreed that neither group could succeed alone. These Christian and Islamic leaders collaborated together in the national interest of community. They established an interfaith group called the Interfaith Mediation Committee to engage the warlords and the government to begin talks that would yield a ceasefire.

In 1995, the group changed its name to the Inter-Religious Council of Liberia. They envisioned a tolerant Liberian society "peacefully coexisting where [our] differences are being used for the best interest of humanity."[11] Toward this end, they set objectives that remain important for ongoing peacebuilding in our context. The principles include:

1. Dialogue among various faith communities for peaceful coexistence, understanding, and religious tolerance;
2. Advocate for human rights and justice for all irrespective of creed, religious affiliation, and ethnicity;
3. Promote the prevention, management and/or resolution of conflict through peaceful means;
4. Mobilize collective assets and resources to address issues of common concern that affect common humanity at local, national, regional, and international levels;
5. Serve as mediators in local, national, subregional, regional, and international conflicts/crises by helping to make peace, reconcile, heal the wounds of conflicts, and unite all affected communities.

This collaboration between the two leading organized religions in Liberia was viewed as a positive act. They resolved, in interreligious cooperation, to influence adherents of both religions who were members of the various factions. The opposing sides saw their religious leaders unite and deliver a common message of peace, *shalom*, or *asalamalakum*. With that

11. Zoe Horace, "Inter Religious Council Refutes Being Opposition," *Liberia Public Radio*, April 25, 2019, https://liberiapublicradio.com/2019/04/25/inter-religious-council-refutes-being-opposition/.

coordinated approach, opportunities for reconciliation were enhanced. Indeed, these efforts were recognized when the Interfaith Council was awarded the Desmond Tutu Peace Award in 1990.[12]

Without a doubt, the civil crisis impacted all persons in or associated with Liberia. Thus, reconciliation demanded the participation of all segments of society. Religious leaders were in the vanguard of such reconciliation efforts. They worked for peace inspired by the vision of God found in the holy books of both Christianity and Islam. From an Anglican perspective, we were particularly influenced by an understanding of witness that was defined, in part, by Anglicanism's fourth mark of mission. This understanding of mission calls us to "transform unjust structures, challenge violence of every kind, and . . . pursue peace and reconciliation."[13] It is to this end of seeking peace and reconciliation that Liberians continue to reach across divisions of religion, ethnicity, and gender. Particular progress has been made, as has been seen, between Christians and Muslims. A relationship of enmity has been transformed into a relationship that Bishop Bill Musk refers to as "kissing cousins." Musk writes,

> After the birth of Ishmael, and for thirteen years, the patriarch evidently lavished his love upon this boy whose sex, character, and name an angel had predicted. There developed a strong bond between father and son as witnessed by Abram's plea to the Lord, "Can Ishmael be the one?"[14]

If Abram loved Ishmael as he loved Isaac, maybe it is time that we become "kissing cousins."

There have been many hopeful examples in the last two decades in Liberia. In 2009, during the *Id-el Fitr* celebrated at the end of Ramadan, Christians participated in the breaking of the fast together with Muslims as one people. Sando Moore of *The Daily Observer*, a leading Liberian newspaper, reported:

---

12. See, "Inter-Religious Council of Liberia, *African Council of Religious Leaders*, www.acrl-rfp.org/networks-affliliates/west-africa/inter-religious-council-of-liberia/, accessed January 7, 2022.

13. Anglican Communion, "Marks of Mission," www.anglicancommunion.org/mission/marks-of-mission.aspx, accessed August 31, 2019.

14. Bill Musk, *Kissing Cousins? Christians and Muslims Face to Face* (Oxford: Monarch Books, 2005), 43.

> Yesterday, I observed this "unity in diversity" at the highest level when Muslims gathered at former Associate Justice of the Supreme Court, Karmo Soko Sackor's compound on Duport Road to celebrate the end of the holy Month of Ramadan. At the occasion, there were many high-profile Liberians from the Christian community including former Interim President of Liberia, Dr. C. Amos Sawyer; Justice Minister and Attorney General, Cllr. Christiana Tah, and Cllr. James A.A. Pierre, Jr., among others. Everyone dined together in an atmosphere of cordiality; and when I saw some of our most prominent and powerful Liberians in a chat, I quickly pulled out my camera to feature these great people on Candid Camera, who have kept our country together to remind our younger folks that we may differ in opinions, but indeed in diversity, there is unity.[15]

This dream of God, as discerned by Archbishop Desmond Tutu, is desired by the people of Liberia:

> How I pray that we will open our eyes and see the real, true identity of each one of us, that is one and is not white or black, Hindu, Buddhist, Christian, Muslim, or Jew, but a brother, a sister, and treat each other as such. If we could but recognize our common humanity, that we do belong together, that our destinies are bound up in one another's, that we can be free only together, that we can survive only together, that we can be human only together, then a glorious world would come into being where all of us live in harmony together as members of one family, the human family. God's family. In truth a transfiguration would take place. God's dream would become a reality.[16]

Religious tolerance has come a long way in Liberia. Although there are still divisions, the situation has improved. Indeed, relations have improved not only in terms of formal cooperation but also at local community and family levels. Christians and Muslims now intermarry.

---

15. Sando Moore, "Liberia: CWA Alumni Announces Diversity Symposium," *The Daily Observer*, February 5, 2022, www.liberianobserver.com/node/1727.

16. Desmond Tutu, *God Has a Dream: A Vision of Hope for Our Time* (New York: Image-Doubleday, 2004), 24.

Muslim children attend Christian schools. At our own Episcopal Bravid Washington Harris Episcopal School, about 30 percent of the student body is Muslim. They learn all of the doctrine of the Episcopal Church. The high school valedictorians for the last two years were Muslim and their Muslim relatives attended the commencement exercises, which were held at Trinity Cathedral.

The women of Liberia, both Christian and Muslim, have been instrumental in the peace process. There are rays of hope coming from the activities of dedicated women of Liberia who have formed an activist group called the Women in Peacebuilding Network (WIPNET).[17] Realizing the damage wrought by the war on their sons, husbands, brothers, and daughters, these women decided to come together, from all denominations, to see how their corporate witness could end the war that was tearing families apart. After a series of meetings, the women decided to meet every day at the same time and location to pray for the nation. They avoided cooking, washing, or even having sexual activity with their partners as a form of protest. They demanded a seat at the negotiation table with warring factions and foreign intervenors. Such solidarity, across ethnic, religious, age, and class lines, was a powerful expression of a common agenda for peace. These women dressed in uniforms: white head ties and white t-shirts, with blue and white *lappas*. They prostrated themselves on the ground. They prayed for peace in Liberia. They host workshops. They act as intermediaries. WIPNET continues to be one of Liberia's most enduring and committed peace organizations.

Peacebuilding across ethnic divides remains vital. This should be done with an understanding that the focus of our togetherness is beneficial to all communities. Today the nation is haunted by the absence of authentic community, communication, and communion. These words share the same root in *communis*, which suggests a common public shared by all. The absence of communal sharing is one of the most marked and lingering effects of the war. Disagreements are settled by dictatorial commands and "ma cussing" rather than by thoughtful deliberation. Empathy, the Holy Communion of any society, is rarely shared across ethnic, gender, and religious lines.

---

17. See Dorina Bekoe and Christina Parajon, "Women's Role in Liberia's Reconstruction," *United States Institute of Peace*, May 1, 2007, www.usip.org/publications/2007/05/womens-role-liberias-reconstruction, accessed January 8, 2022.

Liberia has seventeen different ethnic groups and each one has its own traditions, dialect, and customs. Every tribe has its heroines and heroes. Each has its own chief. Besides the Americo-Liberian/Indigenous divide, there exist divisions among the tribes. Some tribes feel superior to others. An African proverb continues to guide the peacebuilders: "when the elephants fight, the grass suffers." Who truly suffers during conflict? Combatants, civilians, and ecosystems suffer. All suffer during conflict. Indeed, those generally impacted by fighting typically have no say in the fighting. Their homes are turned into battlefields. Their lives are disrupted and uprooted. The grass reminds us of the human heart. Long after an event has occurred, a smell or memory can transport one back to that moment of suffering. Conflict is complex because it can take root in the heart. The scripture attests to such struggle, "We as humans remain in conflict between the flesh and the Holy Spirit. The mind governed by the Spirit is life and peace." (Rom. 8:6). For healing to occur, hearts need to be open to others. Change requires careful listening to the voices of people who have suffered greatly.[18] We must allow those who have suffered to bear witness to their experience and allow space and room for their voices to be heard. Equally, the voice of the perpetrators must be heard. Such people are likely to be tempted to hide from past actions. We see this in our country when, for example, politicians run for office and try to conceal past wrongdoing. When taken before the court of justice, warlords deny their past atrocities to protect their freedom. They may even claim they were liberators.

> Peacebuilding requires both condemning human rights violations and, at the same time, acknowledging that human rights violators perceive they are fighting for justice. Regardless of whether their perceptions are justified, they must be acknowledged because to ignore their concerns or needs leaves the possibility of ongoing violence as they seek to pursue a solution that they see as just.[19]

These situations are often not clear cut. In cases of prolonged and destructive violence, such as occur during war, it is possible for an

18. Lederach, *Moral Imagination*, 43.

19. Julie Mertus and Jeffrey W. Helsing, *Human Rights and Conflict: Exploring the Links Between Rights, Law and Peacebuilding* (Washington, DC: United States Institute of Peace, 2006), 80.

individual or group to have been *both* perpetrator and victim. Deep listening and discernment are needed. As the African proverb says, "He who listens, understands." David Spangler describes deep listening as the "act of entering the skin of the other and wearing it for a time as if it were our own."[20] This we see in the life and ministry of Jesus. He listened to those who came for healing. So too must the Church listen and support its community.

Jesus came into the world to bring peace, to bring all people together in one body wherein each person has a place. But we human beings have turned our world into a place of competition, rivalry, conflict and war between races, religions, social classes, and countries. The world has become a place in which each person feels (s)he has to protect and defend her or his own family, own country, own class, own religion.[21] In contrast, the Christian vision of peace is that it is an abundant gift from God. Jesus said, "My Peace I leave with you. My peace I give to you; not as the world gives do I give to you. Let not your heart be troubled, neither let it be afraid" (John 14:27). An old African American spiritual exhorts us to "walk together and not get weary. We must walk and never tire." Christians are sustained for the journey because they are fed by an abundance of peace that is the gift of God in Christ.

Conclusion

In 2013, President Ellen Johnson Sirleaf passionately captured the deep impact of conflict and the deep need for healing when she said:

> The cleavages that led to decades of war still run deep, but so too does the longing for a reconciliation defined by equal opportunity and a better future for all Liberians. True reconciliation means a process of national healing, and learning the lessons of the past to perfect our democracy.[22]

---

20. David Spangler, *Parent as Mystic, Mystic as Parent* (New York: Riverhead Trade, 2000), 70.

21. Jean Vanier, *Befriending the Stranger* (Grand Rapids: William B. Eerdmans, 2005), vii.

22. Ellen Johnson Sirleaf, "Annual Message to the Second Session of the 53rd National Legislature of the Republic of Liberia, Theme: A Time for Transformation," January 28, 2013, lecture at Capitol Hill, Monrovia, Liberia, www.emansion.gov.lr/doc/2013o128_President_2013_Annual_Message_FINAL.pdf, accessed August 31, 2019.

As a nation and a people, Liberia has come a long way since the end of the civil war. There is much work in healing and reconciliation that remains to be done. We have resumed the work of building better interfaith dialogue between Christians and Muslims. We are beginning the important work of helping young people traumatized by the war to rebuild their lives. We are striving to promote honest and sincere dialogue between groups that have long histories of conflict, so that repentance, forgiveness, and healing can take firmer root.

Three prayers have meant a great deal to us as we journey together toward peace. Pray with us.

> Gracious Father, we pray for thy holy Catholic Church. Fill it with all truth, in all truth with all peace. Where it is corrupt, purify it; where it is in error, direct it; where in anything it is amiss, reform it. Where it is right, strengthen it; where it is in want, provide for it; where it is divided, reunite it; for the sake of Jesus Christ thy Son our Savior. Amen.
>
> (The Book of Common Prayer, 816)

With sincere and repentant hearts, we come before Thy throne of grace to pray for forgiveness and guidance as we seek to walk together in peace and unity as one people:

> Dear Heavenly Father, in gratitude for the gift of our children, we offer fervent supplications for their protection and guidance. Shield them from dishonesty, danger and harm. In Your compassion, heal the lingering wounds of ethnic and cultural divides, and forgive the haunting past evils inflicted by Your children on one another. May those entrusted with their care, teach them to love as Christ loves, so that all may live together in unity and peace. We pray in the name of Jesus, Who is the Prince of Peace. Amen.
>
> (Anne Fredericks Cooper)

> O God, faithful and sure, our ever present help in time of simmering conflict and war, in moments of sickness and distress, and in seasons of disease and drought; look upon us whom, in peace, serve you aright and in our darkest moments abandon

all hope. Inspire within us we pray the courage daily to tend to the brokenness of our world with your balm of peace, so that all creatures may be healed, forgiven and restored to that most excellent life known and loved in your son, Jesus Christ. For you are faithful, O lover of souls, and to you we give glory, Father, Son, and Holy Spirit. Amen.

(Herman B. Browne)

CHAPTER 11

Tanzania

Building Dialogue Amidst Land Disputes

Ernest Godwin Ndahani, Hilda Kedmond Kabia, Pendo Gilberth Magayo, David Wilson Mdabuko, Charles Azariah Mwihambi, and Anna Samweli Yohana

Peace is the essence of a meaningful life. If there is no harmony in society, life becomes miserable, and people are deprived of the joy God intended for them. Peace needs to be cultivated, maintained, and nurtured in order to grow within the boundaries of a specified area of relationships. While Christians have distinct theological understandings of peace (see chapters 1–5), for many people living in contexts of conflict, to wish for peace is to wish for a life without conflict. This desire is reflected in dictionary definitions of peace that stress an absence of conflict between humans or between humans and God. Peace is about states of friendliness, amity, concord (see *The Oxford Dictionary of English*). It is particularly this sense of peace that is in view in this chapter.[1]

Conflict, however, is common. It can be experienced internally at an individual level and also in community, family, or broader society. In excess or to an extreme degree, conflict can rob people of the joy and serenity of life that all human beings long to have. The conflict in view in this chapter, affecting individuals and communities, relates to land disputes in the East African nation of Tanzania. In three main sections, this chapter will, first, narrate conflict in relation to disputes between family members, between the Church and individuals, and between the

1. See also Emmanuel Katongole and Chris Rice, *Reconciling All Things: A Christian Vision for Justice, Peace and Healing* (Downers Grove: IVP, 2009), 98–99.

Church and the government. Second, we provide a biblical reflection on this contextual conflict over land rights especially focusing on the letter to the Ephesians. Third, we invite the reader to an analysis of their own experience of conflict and a discernment of where the Spirit of God is at work through traditional ritual practices.

Our Conflict

Land disputes in Tanzania are complex. For this reason, we present here three narratives that illustrate some of the complexities and upheaval that the Anglican Church in Tanzania is currently facing. The first case demonstrates the strife that land disputes are causing in the family even when the Church acts as a mediator. The second and third cases involve the Church itself as a party directly affected by the problem.

A Family Conflict

This narrative illustrates the severity of land disputes in Dodoma, Tanzania. For in this case, a family was almost torn apart. The dispute was the culmination of a series of conflicts between six siblings that climaxed following the death of their father. At that time, three of the brothers had sizeable plots of land, one brother had a smaller plot, and the two sisters and widow had not been given any plots. There were two key disputes that were causing the conflict.

The first was that their grandfather had acquired a valuable plot of land through the villagization programs decades earlier that was part of an initiative to encourage families to move into centralized locations to facilitate shared services.[2] Although the land was subsequently occupied by another party, two of the brothers worked to reclaim the land for the family. The dispute arose when brother #3 needed to raise funds for himself. His elder brother, who had helped him reclaim the land, agreed

2. See Isaria N. Kimambo, Gregory H. Maddox, and Salvatory S. Nyanto, *A New History of Tanzania* (Dar es Salaam: Mkuki na Nyota, 2017), 183–184; Paul Bjerk, *Building a Peaceful Nation: Julius Nyerere and the Establishment of Sovereignty in Tanzania, 1960–1964* (Rochester: University of Rochester Press, 2015), 109–131; Paul Nugent, *Africa Since Independence: A Comparative Study* (London: Palgrave Macmillan, 2004), 141–166; Roger Nord, Yuri Sobolev, David Dunn, Alejandro Hajdenberg, Niko Hobdari, Samar Maziad, and Stéphane Roudet, *Tanzania: The Story of an African Transition* (Washington, DC: International Monetary Fund, 2009), 2–4.

to sell off a portion of the land. However, brother #3 sold off the entire property and kept the funds for himself. In addition to not sharing the proceeds, an additional problem was created because the family had planned to use part of this land to build a house for their mother.

The second dispute arose because the sisters had been given no land. The brothers justified their position on the traditional Tanzanian practice that daughters do not inherit land. This was wholly unjustified since the law no longer supports this practice.[3] Furthermore, in traditional practice married daughters are to be given land by their father at the time of marriage. In this case, that did not happen. Given the lucrative offers from investors, the sister felt that they too should receive part of the inherited land or the proceeds. One brother did side with his sisters. He was particularly concerned because the government was about to claim the land on which a sister's house was built for road development. Despite his concern, his three brothers ignored him.

Through a mediation process, the brothers came to see that they were misinterpreting both the letter and the spirit of traditional thought and inheritance practices as well as modern thought and practice. They also came to see how their individual greed was tearing the family apart. If they were to remain in relationship with one another, each needed to put their self-interest aside and engage with each other in a spirit of charity and generosity. If they were to move forward as a family, they each needed to acknowledge their part in creating the conflict and to refrain from seeking scapegoats to blame for their problems. In the end, the brother who had secretly sold off the land without sharing the proceeds agreed to sign a promissory note to make restitution to his siblings. All agreed to put these conflicts behind them and start afresh.

Conflict Between the Church and the Individual

Tanzania's first president, Julius Nyerere (1922–1999), chose Dodoma as the capital of the nation. However, Dar es Salaam had been the center of government and trade for decades. It is only since 2017 that the government actually began to move to Dodoma. The relocation of

---

3. Helen Dancer, "An Equal Right to Inherit? Women's Land Rights, Customary Law and Constitutional Reform in Tanzania," *Social & Legal Studies* 26, no. 3 (2017): 291–310; Jan Abbink and Mirjam de Bruijn, *Land, Law and Politics in Africa: Mediating Conflict and Reshaping the State* (Leiden: Brill, 2011).

the nation's capital has not only caused conflicts within families, but it has also caused conflict within the Church and between the Church and individual members of the community. The following two cases will illustrate this.

Before the capital moved to Dodoma, people took a more informal attitude toward land possession and use. Now land is being claimed by the government and bought up by a range of investors including those involved in constructing a new airport in the city. The possibility of financial gain has resulted in much conflict between people and groups who previously had amiable attitudes toward one another. The government's laws and courts have not kept pace with the need for more structured rules and dispute resolution. This next case illustrates how even the Church is not immune to disputes and further underscores the problems created by lack of adequate government regulation and processes of review.

St. Luke's Church is in the village of Msalato and is part of the Diocese of Central Tanganyika. Simon, a former church secretary of St. Luke's, tells how the church obtained the land on which the church now stands. They applied in 1986 to the Village Council to obtain the use of a six-acre plot of land to build their church. The application was approved by the Council Chairman. Once they obtained authorization to use the land, in the 2000s they cleared it, constructed the church building, planted trees, and installed some outdoor beacons to illuminate the site at night.

The church's use of the land has since been disputed by one of the parishioners. A farmer had been using a piece of land adjacent to the church for many years. The farmer claimed that in 1986 he was given an uncultivated forest area by the Village Council and was issued the customary Right of Occupancy. He cleared the land and began farming on it. In 2012 he filed a complaint against the Board of Trustees of the Anglican Church of Msalato with the District Land and Housing Tribunal at Dodoma. He claimed that the church had been illegally constructed on two acres of his land. The church argued that this was not the case. Rather, it was argued that the farmer used his relationships with St. Luke's improperly to gain access to church land and use it for his own agricultural activity. The parish pointed out that the land is not owned by the church Board. It is owned by the Diocese of Tanganyika. Additionally, the Customary Title Deed that was presented by the farmer was not a relevant and legal document. The farmer has since appealed to the Land and Housing Tribunal.

Situations such as this are difficult to negotiate. In the past, when land was not such a valuable commodity, clear and definite claims to land use and ownership were less important. The church had believed that even though there had been a period of inactivity between when they obtained permission to use the land and when the actual construction of the church building took place, they still had a clear claim and right to the land. The parish, it seems, did not take clear and appropriate measures to stop the farmer from using the land. This leaves the question that is now coming up time and again in land disputes—whose land is this?

Conflict Between the Church and the Government

The Capital Development Authority (CDA) started to plan in the Kisasa area of the city in 2002. Many plots were arranged for residences and social services. The Anglican Church at Kisasa was among the religious institutions providing social services in the area. Despite the church's existence at Kisasa since the 1960s, the CDA decided, without consultation, to remove the church. The new location was to be on a smaller plot and far from the community it had served for over four decades. The CDA justified its decision on the basis that the area was to be rezoned as an area for social services. The question became—was the church a social service? Given that the CDA failed to give a clear answer, the church decided to press for its rights. Unfortunately, the CDA had already sold the plot to an investor planning to use the land for the construction of a primary (elementary) school. The church consulted the Deputy Minister of Land and the CDA admitted its mistake. It promised to return the land to the church. Due to political factors, however, this did not happen.

The church continued to press for its rights by next consulting and lobbying the Regional Commissioner. He too failed to find a solution. The parish consulted the Minister of Employment under the Prime Minister. Within four days, the CDA was dissolved by the President. The church returned to the Minister of Local Government. He asked the Director of Dodoma Municipality to solve the issue. Naturally, the new owner of the land did not want to surrender it and, in turn, lobbied for his position and rights. Other leaders in the government offered support to the new owner. At the time of writing, the case is not resolved and, for some, appears irresolvable. The church, however, continues to lobby and hope for a new plot to be found for the school so that the church might return to its home.

Our Conflict in Light of Scripture

The displacement of people, their homes, gathering places, and disruption to traditional life goes deeper than just the question of land rights. The movement of the capital to Dodoma, the increased land values that have led to avarice, and the resulting conflicts within family and church have caused many other disruptions. There are many new people whose language, customs, and ways of doing things are alien to the Dodoma area. There are many disruptions to which we need to adjust. Disruption is not entirely a bad thing. Sometimes the old ways of doing things can and should be challenged and upended. In turning to scripture, we find that land disputes are common in the text.

Land Disputes in the Old Testament

Our ancestors in the faith were no strangers to land disputes. In the very first book of the Bible, we read of conflict between Isaac's workers and the workers of Gerar:

> Isaac . . . camped in the valley of Gerar and settled there. Isaac dug again the wells of water that had been dug in the days of his father Abraham; for the Philistines had stopped them up after the death of Abraham; and he gave them the names that his father had given them. But when Isaac's servants dug in the valley and found there a well of spring water, the herders of Gerar quarrelled with Isaac's herders, saying, "The water is ours." So he called the well Esek, because they contended with him. Then they dug another well, and they quarrelled over that one also; so he called it Sitnah. He moved from there and dug another well, and they did not quarrel over it; so he called it Rehoboth, saying, "Now the Lord has made room for us, and we shall be fruitful in the land."
>
> (Gen. 26:17–22)

Tolerance and the zeal to seek peace led Isaac to adopt his approach to this land dispute. He kept calm and he kept his servant calm. On two occasions, Isaac moved from sites of conflict to new places. The people of Gerar, it appears, were jealous and covetous, but Isaac's willingness to create space for coexistence eventually brought contentment. Reading this text contextually, we recognize Isaac's ability to work for coexistence but also interpret the text as suggesting non-resolution. That is to say, while Isaac creates space for coexistence and contentment, we do not see this as denying a future opportunity for him to press for his rights to the other sites. Isaac may be read as adopting a posture of patience—he is waiting to claim back his lost rights when the right time comes. This, in our context, is seeking justice in God's way.

Not all land disputes in scripture were handled in a righteous manner. King Ahab coveted the land of Naboth the Jezreelite and pleaded with him to sell his vineyard. Naboth had inherited the land from his ancestors and, thus, refused the king's request. In response, Jezebel, Ahab's wife, orchestrated for people to testify falsely against Naboth's character. This led to his execution (1 Kings 21:5–14). The land was acquired deceitfully and violently (1 Kings 21:15–16). The prophet Elijah read God's edict against Ahab:

> You shall say to him, "Thus says the Lord: In the place where dogs licked up the blood of Naboth, dogs will also lick up your blood." . . . concerning Jezebel the Lord said, "The dogs shall eat Jezebel within the bounds of Jezreel." Anyone belonging to Ahab who dies in the city the dogs shall eat; and anyone of his who dies in the open country the birds of the air shall eat.
>
> (1 Kings 21:19, 23–24)

This narrative is especially troubling because as King of Israel, it was Ahab's duty to preserve the rights of the people and ensure that justice is done. Yet, as unfortunately sometimes the case today, government officials can be corrupt and behave in an unrighteous manner. It is the call of followers of God to practice and preach the message of the prophet Micah: "what does the Lord require of you but to do justice, and to love kindness, and to walk humbly with your God?"

The Gospel of Christ and Land Disputes

Let us consider an example of an African man from a rural village who, on hearing the preaching of an evangelist, decided to become a Christian. Going to church for the first time, he was astonished to see someone there from a tribe that his own people despised. He was furious: "What is this 'dog' doing in the church? Don't you understand that this 'pig' has contaminated the church? If you knew where he comes from, you wouldn't have admitted him." The man's prejudice is related to place. Someone from different tribal land was considered unclean and an enemy. That the church could be a different kind of place (or land) had not entered into his thinking despite his conversion.

This kind of prejudicial thinking is not alien to scripture. We can see such thinking addressed in the letter to the Ephesians. The text addresses the conflict between Gentiles and Jews in the early Christian church. Take a moment to read the passage from Ephesians 2:11–22. After you read it, take a quiet moment to think about its main themes and central message. How would you summarize the message of the passage? Now, consider these questions:

1. What examples are there in your local context that resemble the relationship between Jews and Gentiles and where people might feel deep "alienation" (2:12)?
2. What did Jesus Christ achieve through his death on the cross in relation to peacebuilding according to this passage (2:11–16)?
3. According to Ephesians 2:17 what was the mission of Jesus? To what extent does this mission shape your image of Jesus? If this mission was taken more seriously, how would it change your approach to worship and witness?
4. What does the passage tell us about the vision of God's peace or salvation to the world (see 2:18–22)? How should such a vision shape our understanding and priorities in peacebuilding?

Let us return to the example of the new Christian from the village. His attitude to a fellow believer seems to be like that of the Jews toward the Gentiles. The early Church struggled with this issue (see Acts 10). Nonetheless, as Ephesians teaches, the gospel declares that where once Jews and Gentiles had been divided by religion, culture, and race, Jesus

Christ had brought them together to form one community of believers. Through the work of Christ, a renewed space or place opened up grounded on God's grace. Those who were previously hostile toward each other had now found a place and peace in Christ (Eph. 2:11–16).

Reconciliation is spoken of as banishment of hostility, not only between God and humanity but also between Jews and Gentiles. The text addresses the question of establishing peace within the human race and asserts that this reconciliation is attained through the redemptive work of Christ. Jesus Christ is our peace (Eph. 2:14). He made peace and preached peace (Eph. 2:15, 17). As Lord of all and judge of all, he could have come to declare war, but in God's grace, he came with the message of peace and reconciliation. Jews and Gentiles are at peace with each other in Christ, and both have open access to God. Christ's death reconciled them.[4] Jesus Christ's mission was to generate in himself one new humanity out of the two. Jesus had come to make peace for all. Those once alienated from each other now worship the Messiah, the Prince of Peace (Isa. 9:6). He has demolished the dividing wall that separated the Jews from the Gentiles through his death on the cross (Eph. 2:14). We could rightly say that the gospel testifies to a deep cure for the evils of racism, tribalism, and a divided humanity.

Verse 17 teaches that "Jesus came and preached peace to the people who were far away and peace to those who were near." In other words, the Jews were near to God because they already knew God through the covenant with Abraham, through the law, and through the prophets. The Gentiles were far off because they knew little about the one true God. The gospel proclaims that this alienation and division was healed through Christ's work of making peace. We are saved through accepting the work of Christ done for an alienated humanity. The letter ends with these words: "Peace be to the whole community, and love with faith, from God the Father and the Lord Jesus Christ. Grace be with all who have an undying love for our Lord Jesus Christ" (Eph. 6:23). The Church exists in the peace of Christ. The Church is called, in its witness and ministry, to testify to this healing and wholeness.

The reconciliation brought about by Christ's sacrifice is not piecemeal. We cannot be reconciled with God and ignore the need to

---

4. Katongole and Rice, *Reconciling All Things*, 144–146.

be reconciled to each other. Yet, the good news of the gospel assures us that we do not need to do all the work of reconciliation on our own. This fundamental curing of broken relationships within the human family is a gift and our reconciliation with one another comes as a gift through the movement of the Holy Spirit. It is not something that we do, but something that has already been done for us. Christ is our peace.[5]

How does this relate to our context? Dodoma people feel puzzled like the Jews. Newcomers seem to have higher priority on claims to the land over the indigenous people already occupying the land. The testimony of Paul is perhaps more relevant to us today in Tanzania than at any other time in our history. As will be seen further, it is the gospel that changes hearts and it will be changed hearts that transform land disputes in Dodoma.

Resourcing Peacebuilding Amidst Conflict: Traditional and Contemporary Practice

In the past two years, the Dodoma community has experienced huge changes. People are becoming increasingly selfish when it comes to material possessions, especially the possession of land. What used to be a lifestyle based on the often-cited proverbial phrase "I am because we are; and since we are, therefore, I am"[6] is increasingly no longer applicable in the lives of citizens. Ethics and moral reflection tend to focus more on individual benefits. This understanding is working against the African way of living together as a community. A contextual approach to peacebuilding will draw both from tradition and scripture. It is our belief that if we draw from these sources, principles and practices for peacebuilding amidst land disputes come into view. If these practices and principles are upheld, the rights of all may be preserved.

Traditional Practices

At one time, among the Wagogo, in the Dodoma area, the community lived in relative peace and unity. Every family had a responsibility to

5. Claude J. Peifer, "Peace According to St. Paul," *Journal of The Bible Today* 21, no. 3 (May 1983), 174.

6. John S. Mbiti, *African Religions and Philosophy*, 2nd ed. (Oxford: Heinemann, 1989), 141.

maintain peace within the family and the community at large. In this traditional culture, solving disputes among the community was taken seriously. Parties that had a disagreement were called together by the elders. In most cases, people were brought up with a cultural norm that prohibited lying to elders. If lying was discovered, the guilty party was heavily punished and banished, perhaps even cursed. Elders would listen to evidence in a bid to establish the facts and uncover the root cause of the conflict. The offender was strongly warned and a fine was imposed.

A range of public rituals were associated with peacebuilding. The offering of a goat or sheep as part of a ritual of reconciliation is important in the tradition. Damages would be assessed by the elders, and a fine would be accompanied by killing a goat or sheep and then a special meat was prepared. Those in dispute were asked to bite one end of the meat and the eldest of the elders would cut the meat in between so each remained with a piece in their mouth. The two parties then ate the meat immediately as a sign of restored peace between them. Finally, they would shake hands to show that no grudge remained.

In family disagreements between siblings, or close members of kin, water rituals were also part of traditional peacemaking. The exercise involved the head of the family putting water in his or her mouth and spitting it on each of the disputing parties' faces to cleanse them from ritual uncleanness. Sometimes water would be poured on a three-legged stool and the members in dispute would be asked to drink the water. Such rituals would be followed by reconciliatory words from the person playing the role of a priest.

Rituals such as these have power. Physically and publicly acting out the process of reconciliation was a highly effective way of embodying the restoration of peace. Such practices helped people to live in harmony, and, when conflict arose, people sought reconciliation immediately. The community was prompt to dismiss conflicts that were deliberately instigated. The fines charged and the chastisement of the elders to the offender acted as a deterrent against such behaviors. The emphasis was on healing of relationships and restoring harmony. It is believed that when two people are reconciled, the spirits of the ancestors are pleased and can confer blessings. Those who refuse to reconcile or pretend they have been reconciled would face curses from the ancestors that might include the death of their children, loss of flocks, and a bad harvest (see also Deut. 27:16–25; 28:1–6). It is believed, therefore, that feigned reconciliation would only deepen conflict. Further ritual would be inevitable if the power of the curse was to be lessened or overturned.

The story is told of a married and pregnant woman in Dodoma who entered into conflict with her father-in-law. The details of who said what to whom are not significant. The point is that the daughter felt the need to assert herself in some fashion and the father-in-law felt that he had been disrespected. In retaliation, the father-in-law had said harsh words against the woman. After a few days, the woman gave birth to twin babies. Following the harsh exchange of words, the health of one of the babies changed very rapidly and there was a dramatic change in the infant's skin color. Within a short time, the baby died. After the burial, the woman discovered that her second baby was also experiencing the same condition, and it was worse. The woman's mother had observed the situation and stepped in as peacemaker. She wanted something to be done and for peace to be restored. She asked the father-in-law to openly discuss the dispute. The father-in-law entered into sincere dialogue with the woman and her mother, and he confessed. He had cursed the woman for not being respectful.

Healing this rift would also require a reconciliation ritual. The family came together. They used water to sprinkle upon the remaining child while uttering words to remove the curse. After the ritual had taken place, the baby recovered and was in good health. The tradition and traditional practice teach that rituals have power. They bring reconciliation. They are healing. Perhaps the real power of the ritual is in the coming together of the aggrieved parties and talking in an open and respectful manner.

Contemporary Principles

Today government laws seek retribution and punishment while paying little attention to the healing of relationships. Unfortunately, traditional rituals have not been adopted by today's individualistic society. Further, because our nation is made up of many different ethnic groups, we have not yet established shared traditions and rituals that address conflict. The need to find realistic ritual substitutes is of paramount importance. Surely, the Church can lead in this effort. Regardless of what kind of rituals may emerge, they should be based upon shared principles.

1. Land occupancy is a right that all citizens deserve. People should not manipulate others, whether by money or by their position. Government policies regarding land should be clearly published and made available to every citizen.
2. People should understand that some traditional laws and practices are no longer reasonable in our modern world. Hence, where traditional laws contradict current law, as legislated by the parliament, the law of the land should take precedence. All children, regardless of their gender or status, are entitled to share and benefit from the family property.
3. The Church must continue to reflect on scripture teaching equality between men and women and the right use of land and land sharing. The Church should advocate for the rights of the weak and for good governance. The Church is called to be a prophetic voice. We must speak for the weak when their rights are plundered by the strong and thc cunning.

Contemporary Christian Witness

Reconciliation is the work of God (2 Cor. 5:18).[7] Being reconciled to God means sins forgiven and it means restoration. At the heart of the message of reconciliation is the truth that each human being is valuable. The Church is commissioned by Christ to go forth and proclaim this gospel or this peace of God. It is God's peace that sanctifies us and keeps our bodies and souls sound and blameless before Christ (1 Thess. 5:23). This is the gift of God. Yet, without the Church's proclamation Dodoma, and the nation, may not know that this gift is offered to all. As a contextual theological approach to peacebuilding, we sought not only to speak for ourselves but also to testify to the witness of the people in our context. Thus, we conducted interviews in Dodoma, asking Christians how it was they articulated the gospel of peace. We received many more responses than we can share here. The following are particularly representative of the contemporary church's witness in Dodoma.

The Rev. Alexander Malejehe shared with us how he sees peace in relationship to our salvation:

7. See George Eldon Ladd, *A Theology of the New Testament*, rev. ed. (Grand Rapids: Williams B. Eerdmans, 1993), 493.

> Peace . . . means Jesus Christ. The birth and death of Jesus Christ in many Christians' minds is the reason humankind and God have a good relationship. The first couple's disobedience caused humankind to be separated from God. They were called sinners. God in his love and compassion gave to the world his only, beloved son to suffer and die for the world. Through the blood of Jesus, the son of God, we were forgiven and made free from sin. Today we are in peace with God because Christ is our peace.

Joyce William observes that the peace of God is experienced in normal day to day life. For William, God's peace is found in the experience of family and community. In such settings, peace means harmony, a happy life, and love. Most people in Dodoma believe this and try to live their faith. She said that most families in Dodoma are living in an extended family and a community life. Each one is responsible for the happiness and safety of the other. Maintaining peace is the collective responsibility of everyone.

According to Jonathan Mfugwa, God gave our country the gift of peace. Every Tanzanian, to some extent, lives a free and happy life. Tanzanians are free to do what they want so long as they do not break the law. This is the freedom that comes from peace. Mfugwa emphasized that God's gift of peace, even in places riven by violence, remains available. God sent Jesus Christ into the world as a gift, a gift that heals, forgives, and loves. Because of him, God is no longer in conflict with those who receive him.

Ernest Ndahani argues that peace, according to the Christian gospel, is achieved through Christ's sacrifice on the cross (see Eph. 5:1–2). This too can have ethical implications. It might be possible, for example, for some people to relinquish their rights for the sake of maintaining peace. People in our context frequently see justice as nothing if it compromises peace. For them it is only God who has the right to judge. The story of the family conflict over land mentioned earlier in this chapter demonstrates this type of sacrificial peacekeeping. The sisters kept quiet although they had every right to their land inheritance.

Individual Christians can testify to peace found in Jesus Christ. However, the Church as a whole is called to be a witness in Dodoma and to the nation. The Church is called to be a role model in its practices of meditation and reconciliation. It is called to take seriously as part of its formation program to prioritize teaching on theologies of peace and reconciliation. In our context, music and the ministry of choirs is particularly potent. For example, the AIC Chang'ombe choir sings *Usikate Tawi (Amani)*—Don't cut a branch (Peace).[8] The choir demonstrates a person cutting the branch that he is sitting on as a metaphor for those who might destroy the peace. This Tanzanian choir insists that peace means more than wealth, freedom, and good health. We must nurture more comprehensive views of peace. Music will remain an important medium for the promotion of richer and more nuanced understandings of peace.

Alongside music, the Church must continue to equip its teachers and preachers with resources on theologies and practices of reconciliation. The nation's first president, Mwalimu Julius Kambarage Nyerere, insisted on unity above all else. The Church has been active in promoting this unity by modeling tolerance. Through the Christian Council of Tanzania, there have been seminars that call leaders and theologians from many regions, countries, and different faith traditions (especially Islam) to engage in dialogue to promote tolerance and live in peace. It is especially in the production of Kiswahili resources that tolerance and the living out of a peaceful faith will inspire all Tanzanians. The Tanzanian population is composed of more than one hundred ethnic groups, each speaking its own dialect. Yet Kiswahili is the country's common language. If we are not able to speak the same language, how will we be able to promote healing and reconciliation when there is conflict? The language is used as a medium of communication in churches, schools, and local communities. Kiswahili has been instrumental in forging a strong national identity. The Church too honors the language as a means of reconciliation in the land.

Conclusion

Land disputes in Dodoma continue to create conflict among families and between institutions. Both traditional and governmental laws have been applied to bring reconciliation and restore peace among people. Yet, many cases remain unresolved and some that have been resolved legally continue to create conflict. In such circumstances, the Church will honor

---

8. Chang'ombe Choir (CVC), "*Usikate Tawi*," directed by CVC TV, July 25, 2017, music video, www.youtube.com/watch?v=pTd6ZxHiyk4.

the legal process and, when appropriate, uphold traditional ritual and resource ritual for new circumstances. Ultimately, however, the Church will maintain that true reconciliation is theological and evangelical. That is to say, we affirm that God alone, through the ministry of reconciliation embodied in his son Jesus Christ on the cross, can embrace all who are divided.

Reconciliation and restoration are not found in law courts or in rituals alone. Reconciliation is found in Christ and in his atoning sacrifice. Government legislations may compensate us for what we lost, but they cannot heal the wounds of our broken relationship. Traditional laws and rituals seek to reconcile us horizontally but cannot reconcile us with our heavenly Father. Managing conflict requires us to humble ourselves, rid ourselves of prejudice, and discern if Christian witness requires us to lay aside our claims for our rights. May the Holy Spirit heal our wounds, enable us to listen to each other peacefully, and build communities of dialogue.

CHAPTER 12

United States of America

Building Dialogue Amidst Polarization

Ebonee Davis, Jonathan Musser, Chris Cole, Jean Cotting, Stephen Crippen, Vannessa McCormick, and Hartley Wensing

Our team spent considerable time discussing a number of divisive issues at work in our community and in the United States of America more broadly. Given the complexity of conflict at work in our context, we chose *polarization* as a term that best captures the struggles we face in the nation and in our community at Virginia Theological Seminary (VTS). First, we begin with the sin of racism at work in polarized histories and cultures in our own community. Second, in reflecting on polarization as racism we approach scripture as a way to deepen our understanding and direct our practice. Third, we identify principles for an emotionally mature, practically directed, and theologically centered approach to polarization.

Our Conflict

A half century ago, the average level of diversity (ethnic, political, socioeconomic, etc.) within communities in the United States of America was significantly higher and less polarized than it is today. Several recent studies have indicated that within the last two decades, a large majority of communities in the United States of America are becoming increasingly more homogenous in their political ideologies and demographic make-up.[1] As a result of increased homogeneity, an ever-increasing polarization

1. Probably the most famous of these studies was Bill Bishop, *The Big Sort: Why the Clustering of Like-Minded America Is Tearing Us Apart* (Boston: Mariner Books, 2009). Other studies support Bishop's findings, most notably the Pew Research Center study cited below.

of society is taking root. In 2014, the Pew Research Center conducted an exhaustive study of political polarization across the country. They found that individuals of differing political persuasions were not only becoming more internally consistent within their own party they were also viewing opposing perspectives with increasing hostility and contempt. In a number of follow-up studies, Pew has continued to track this polarization as it has grown more pronounced in the intervening years.[2]

As if to illustrate this polarization, our team—made up of U.S. citizens from different communities across the country—was not of one mind on the primary issue that makes polarization manifest in our context. We spent considerable time debating whether the most polarizing issue at work within our country and Church was race or human sexuality. In the end, most members felt racism was the issue that most needed addressed in our context of conflict. Each of the authors of this chapter are members of the VTS community. While VTS is by no means an exhaustive representation of the many ways that polarization impacts our nation—it is a diverse microcosm with some representation of the whole.

On February 24, 2005, the African American Episcopal Historical Collection was officially dedicated and opened at VTS. Established in 2003 as a joint project between the seminary's archives and the Historical Society of the Episcopal Church, the collection preserves and documents the history and experience of African American Episcopalians in the United States of America. While laudable, the irony of such an effort being undertaken at VTS did not go unnoticed. The Right Reverend Herbert Thompson Jr., former Bishop of Southern Ohio, gave the opening remarks and reflected on the memory of his first visit to VTS:

> My first visit to Virginia Theological Seminary was in 1962. A junior at General Theological Seminary [New York], I arrived with my wife by bus with a host of General Seminary students for the annual V.T.S./G.T.S. basketball game. I was the only African American in my class on the trip. Armed with

2. Pew Research Center, *Political Polarization in the American Public: How Increasing Ideological Uniformity and Partisan Antipathy Affect Politics, Compromise, and Everyday Life*, June 2014, www.pewresearch.org/wp-content/uploads/sites/4/2014/06/6-12-2014-Political-Polarization-Release.pdf, accessed October 26, 2018.

> thuribles and incense, cassocks and birettas, and brimming with excitement about the weekend, we pulled to a stop on campus. A Virginia student, and apparent weekend organizer, boarded the bus with a clipboard in hand. He made the necessary introductions and announced that we each would be hosted and housed with V.T.S couples or students who were waiting outside the bus to escort us to dinner, the game, and other events. As he called out our names, G.T.S. students exited and went off with their respective hosts. When he called out "Herbert Thompson, Jr." I raised my hand and said, "Here!" He looked at me, startled and flustered, and said, "I'll get back to you." The bus emptied. Our weekend organizer disappeared. My wife and I sat there for almost two hours with the bus driver. Returning, full of apologies, the organizer informed us that there was a mix-up, and our proposed hosts were not available. He then escorted us to a wing of a dormitory that apparently had been cleared to accommodate us.[3]

Thompson, outraged by the experience, almost left the Episcopal Church. Countervailing influences, however, like the white Dean of General Seminary openly weeping upon hearing about the interaction, helped Thompson resolve to remain in the Church and work for greater inclusivity. Unfortunately, the bishop's story is not unique in the history of the Episcopal Church and the history of VTS. Thompson later recounted that Malcolm X asked him, "What in the world is a black man doing in the Episcopal Church?"[4] Current students of color at VTS acknowledge that such a perception remains even today.

Race has been a polarizing issue in North America at least as far back as the earliest European colonists. VTS was founded in 1823, had slaves present on the campus prior to the Civil War, and continues to struggle to this day with issues of race and racism. In the broader context, the nation has a conflicting and ugly history with race, which over time has contributed to the perpetuation of systemic oppression of people of color. Science has proved that race is nothing more than a social construct

---

3. Herbert Thompson, "A Black Bishop's Journey: To Reconcile. To Heal. To Liberate. To Serve" (Address, Virginia Theological Seminary, Alexandria, VA, February 24, 2005).

4. Thompson, "A Black Bishop's Journey."

based on slight variations of skin color and hair type. Yet, it continues to be one of the most polarizing issues in our context.

The United States of America's history with race can easily be traced back to slavery and the founding of the country. While slavery itself was not a new concept, basing it on race was. The more profitable the slave trade became, the more dependent the country's economy became on it and, thus, the more important it became to stress the inferiority of non-white races.[5] Audrey Smedley observes, "Race and its ideology about human differences arose out of the context of African slavery. But many peoples throughout history have been enslaved without the imposition of racial ideology." She goes on to discuss how the development of race as an ideology created new social identities which, in turn, "created the only slave system in the world that became exclusively 'racial'."[6] The concept of race justified the enslavement, persecution, discrimination, and disenfranchisement of persons of color. Racial ideology and the implied inferiority of non-white races granted society permission to develop a hierarchical structure that preserved whiteness.

Today, race and racial polarization continue to be contested issues within U.S. society as a whole and the VTS community in particular. It serves as a classifier, divider, and unifier all at the same time. In each of these roles, people's experiences and opinions surrounding race vary. For some, race is a privilege, a source of pride and identity. For others, it is a burden, crutch, or tool of divisiveness. In all of this, the presumed superiority of the white race, and the implicit biases attached to this belief, have for generations helped to keep citizens stuck in their theoretical "corners."

VTS has a history of racial divisiveness and polarization that it is working to recognize, reflect upon, and from which it is seeking to repent. The original campus buildings were constructed through the labor of enslaved persons. In the mid-nineteenth century, 83 percent of clergy

---

5. Ira Berlin, "Making Slavery, Making Race," in *Many Thousands Gone: The First Two Centuries of Slavery in North America* (Cambridge: Belknap Press, 1998), 1–14; John Hope Franklin and Evelyn Brooks Higginbotham, *From Slavery to Freedom: A History of African Americans*, 9th ed. (New York: McGraw-Hill, 2021); Charles Johnson and Patricia Smith, *Africans in America: America's Journey through Slavery* (New York: Harcourt Brace, 1998).

6. Audrey Smedley, "Origin of the Idea of Race" *Anthropology Newsletter*, November, 1997, as found on "Race—The Power of an Illusion," PBS.org, www.pbs.org/race/000_About/002_04-background-02-09.htm, accessed February 23, 2022.

in Virginia owned slaves and the seminary had faculty and trustees who had been slave owners. Although some faculty supported the training of a few Liberian Africans for the priesthood in the late 1840s and early 1850s, it was for service in their native country only, not in the United States of America. While some students put pressure on the seminary to support and protect them as they ministered to local Black Christians, their approach was pervaded by paternalism and inequality.[7]

During the so-called Jim Crow era that began in the late 1800s—and was characterized by violence against Black Americans as well as segregation and disenfranchisement laws—the seminary remained mired in endemic racism.[8] This racism was expressed in many ways, from moving the campus post office to the edge of the property, because it was being used by local Black citizens, to the seminary's history of segregation in educating Black seminarians, to the fitful way the seminary began integrating Black students in the 1950s and 1960s. The seminary community still contains vestiges of racism. As late as 2005, a Black seminarian, at a seminary event, was assumed by trustees to be there simply to collect the dirty plates. It is from this context that VTS currently confronts the issue of polarization.

Our Conflict in Light of Scripture

We have chosen two texts as a means to reflect biblically on polarization in our context. Both are from the Book of Genesis and are, therefore, foundational texts in how Christians understand their place in God's creation. As will be seen presently, the story of Cain and Abel provides the first use of *sin* in a biblical text, and it provides a frame for reflection on racial polarization. The story of Jacob's son invites a familial and emotional reckoning with polarization.

Cain and Abel

Take a moment to read the story of Cain and Abel in Genesis 4:1–16. Who are the characters in conflict? What is it they are in conflict about

7. William Archer Rutherfoord Goodwin, *History of the Theological Seminary in Virginia and Its Historical Background*, vol. 2 (New York: Edwin S. Gorham, 1923–1924), 170.

8. See, "Jim Crow Era," Black Civil Rights, Howard University Law Library, https://library.law.howard.edu/civilrightshistory/blackrights/jimcrow, accessed February 23, 2022.

and how do they experience polarization? To what extent is the conflict of polarization resolved in the passage? How can this story help you understand issues of polarization in your own context?

The story of Cain in Abel in Genesis chapter 4 frames the conflict of polarization in three significant ways that relate to the issue of racial polarization in our context. First, the brothers are polarized through their social roles and responsibilities. Cain means "metalworker" and in many traditional societies these workers belonged to marginal ethnic groups and were looked upon with suspicion and disdain. According to the text, Cain was initially a tiller of the ground (Gen. 4:2). Like his father, he would continue the troubled relationship between man (*'adam*) and the ground (*'adamah*). His name and story, therefore, not only reflect an ancient marginalization based on labor and ethnicity, his occupation itself harkens back to the first violation and alienation from God and the land (Gen. 3:23).

Second, the brothers are polarized by the way in which their social roles and labors are rewarded. Abel's work, though presumably easier, is richly rewarded. Cain's toiling is not looked upon as favorably. John Byron notes:

> Cain brought an offering "from the fruit of the earth" and Abel an offering form "the firstlings of his flock and of their fat portions". Though it is not spelled out, the more detailed description of Abel's offering is usually taken by modern commentators to provide the reason God was pleased with his sacrifice. The care used by the author to describe Abel's offering as being from among the choice of his flock echoes biblical mandates for such (Exod. 22:28–29; 34:19–20; Lev. 3:16; Deut. 32:38; Ps. 147:14). A possible conclusion, based on the descriptions offered is that Cain's sacrifice was defective since, unlike Abel, it was not taken from the choicest part of the harvest.[9]

Reread this commentary by Byron. To what extent does it help you understand the story better? What questions are you left with?

We see a twofold implication in Byron's commentary. First, Cain may not have offered all of his labor—or more accurately the best of

9. John Byron, "Cain's Rejected Offering: Interpretive Approaches to a Theological Problem." *Journal for the Study of the Pseudepigrapha* 18, no. (2008): 5.

his labor—to God. Thus, his offering is not considered as favorable as Abel's offering. Second, as is noted, God looks more favorably both upon Abel and his offering. It is possible that Cain's reaction to God's response conflated his brother with his brother's labor. Cain may have been unable to see his brother in his humanity but instead viewed him according to his labor. We might call such a view, *materialist.*[10] Take a moment to reflect on ways you have been treated and ways you treat others. In your context, how does a materialist attitude impact the way people are treated? What other attitudes are present in your context that cause prejudice and polarization?

Third, resulting from this objectification of his brother and his labor, Cain feels alienated and disempowered. Reread the passage. Write a short summary of the story from the perspective of Cain. Pay particular attention to his feelings of alienation.

In his polarization, Cain responds with violence and aggression at the perceived system that values him and his labor less. Interestingly, it is with this story of violence and violation that the language of *sin* enters the biblical text. Ronald Hendel writes, "the first mention of *sin* in the Bible . . . is depicted as a predatory animal, *lurking* at the door . . . ."[11] It is in the context of bloodshed that sin first appears in the biblical text. Scripture teaches that "Blood is sacred, for it is the seat of life (Gen 9.4; Deut. 12:23), and blood of unpunished murders pollutes the ground (Num. 35:30–34)."[12] Adam and Eve's violation of God's command (Gen. 2–3) is widely understood to constitute *The Fall* or the *First Sin*. Yet, it is in this scene of polarization, borne out of conflict, that the presence of sin is depicted first in scripture. The story of Cain and Abel suggests that polarization, and its sinful consequences, is a long-standing reality in human history. Cain's sense of alienation and devaluation puts him into conflict with his brother. This leads him to a polarizing mentality. He comes to see the situation as an either/or extreme where the only way to fix the situation is to deny his brother's humanity and commit an act of retribution to right a perceived wrong. In your context, what are examples

10. See Martin Buber, *I and Thou*, trans. Walter Kaufmann (New York: Touchstone, 1970), 4.

11. Ronald Hendel, "Genesis," in *The HarperCollins Study Bible*, rev. and updated, ed. Harold W. Attridge et al. (San Francisco: HarperSanFrancisco, 2006), 17.

12. Hendel, "Genesis," 17.

of polarization that have led to conflict? To what extent does our reading of the story of Cain and Abel shed light on this conflict?

The Civil War in the United States of America occurred in the middle of the nineteenth century. It was deeply rooted in issues of racism and is often described as a war of brother against brother. Indeed, whole families were torn apart by deep societal polarization. The reality is that these issues of polarization and conflict remain largely unresolved in this country today. While the polarities shift over time the underlying racist realities remain constant. The mark of white supremacy and violence remains.[13] Like Cain, we in the United States of America (and in the Episcopal Church, and at VTS) have never been able to fully acknowledge the wrongness of this polarity. A polarity that is the deep sin of racism and the sin of denying each other's existence even unto death.

Jacob's Sons

Recognizing and redressing issues of polarization is historically significant in our context. It is also psychologically and emotionally demanding. One way to prepare for such work is through considering a family-systems approach to polarization.

Family systems, and the metaphor of family itself, speak to the common predicament shared by everyone in the polarization we are addressing. We are "family" insofar as we are all *caught up in each other*. We operate in emotional force fields that emerge whenever more than one human being is present. "Family," as a concept, is about our interlocking dilemmas. These dilemmas are often seen clearest between couples. John Gottman has studied couples for decades. On the basis of this research, he has developed a particular method of family-systems counseling.[14] He documented in his research that when couples argue, the anger and resentment they express typically mask deeper feelings of longing and sadness. A therapist often must listen to an angry or sarcastic comment and hear beneath that brittle veneer a softer, deeper pain. It can be time-consuming to work with clients to access deeper feelings.

13. See Nyasha Junior, "The Mark of Cain and White Violence," *Journal of Biblical Literature* 139, no. 4 (2020): 661–673; James Baldwin, *The Fire Next Time* (1963; repr., New York: Vintage International, 1993), 40–41.

14. For a brief overview, see "Research," Our Mission, The Gottman Institute, www.gottman.com/about/research/, accessed February 23, 2022.

These patterns of longing and sadness are not merely limited to the dynamics between couples but play out across the full range of human interaction again and again. These relational patterns play out within larger familial structure, and as we shall see these unsatisfied longings and sadnesses can also be considered as possible root cause of the dynamics that result in patterns of polarization. As we grapple with complicated conflicts, we are dealing with misunderstandings, fears, unrecognized longings, and unexpressed affection. Rather than explaining family systems and relational dynamics in abstract terms, we illustrate the analysis this method can provide by applying it to the story of Jacob's family in Genesis 37–50. The story of Jacob's sons reveals highly sophisticated emotional dynamics that closely resemble the layered, complicated emotional dynamics at work even today. The brothers betrayed Joseph and sold him to the Ishmaelites who took him to Egypt (Gen. 37:18–28). Eventually, Joseph rose to power in Egyptian society (Gen. 41:37–45). When famine hit Egypt, the people had provisions because of the wise leadership of Joseph (41:53–57). Indeed, the text tells us that "the world came to Joseph in Egypt to buy grain, because the famine became severe throughout the world" (Gen. 41:57). This included Joseph's brothers who were unaware of his rank in Egypt and did not recognize him when they saw him (42:1–7).

As this well-known story develops, we witness in the back-and-forth a closeness-and-distance churning in the story. Joseph and his brothers slowly gain access to their deeper feelings, their truer, more ultimate desires, their highest priorities and fondest hopes. They subtly communicate information beneath and between their words, signaling to each other how they view their individual and collective relationships with their father, how they make sense of the history of conflict they share, and their readiness to set their relationships on a new footing. Even before they recognize him, Joseph's brothers reflect on their betrayal of him (while he eavesdrops just outside the room), and how this current interaction with an Egyptian official is somehow related to it (Gen. 42:21–24). These characters are developing, and they are doing so by listening to their *feelings*.

Central to Joseph's story is entrapment. Benjamin is a pawn in a drama that is not directly about him. Simeon is in jail (Gen. 42:24). Joseph feels a restrictive impulse to hide his feelings and goes on to plant objects in his brothers' sacks to trap them into a dialogue with him (Gen.

42:26–35; 44:1–13). There are terrible decision points where no option is attractive and there is the restrictive power of the father's grief. Jacob's grief functions to hold the family back, invite the family to stay stuck, drive the family with fear (Gen. 42:36–38). They just cannot get away from each other.

Amidst the polarization and conflict in the story of Jacob's sons, what can we learn? We have developed our understanding of human psychology, emotional family systems, and culture, and these developments invite psychological and emotional analysis of the text in the context of polarization. The characters in this narrative grow in emotional and psychological maturity. Joseph cries three times in the text and in each instance his weeping is more intense than the last (Gen. 42:24; 43:30; 45:2; see also 45:14–15; 46:29; 50:1, 17). Joseph moves from private to public in his emotional expression, finally making it plain for all to see how deeply moved he is by this conflict and the possibility of resolution. When he tests his brothers, it may not be a step too far to interpret this, from our own context, as a test of emotional maturity as much as one of honor or repentance (*t'shuva*). While Joseph is expressing and working through deep feelings of sadness and longing, his brothers are coping with anxiety that could easily undermine their goals and lead their family to ruin. Judah in particular is stressfully balancing competing priorities and needs, and he does so with admirable courage. No one in the story is wallowing.

In this context of familial polarization, in the broader context of societal crisis, we recognize the importance of recognizing the complicated nature of conflict at the emotional and psychological level. Without such recognition, the complex issues at work in polarization will remain unresolved. In this text, conflict is fueled by misunderstandings, fears, unrecognized longings, and unexpressed affection. There is a lurching rhythm we can learn from as—back and forth, back and forth—the brothers draw close and retreat. Joseph can be seen as designing a complicated process for the sake of reconciliation. As the characters move through this complicated family-system dance, they create (intentionally or unintentionally) space for all of them to listen to their deeper feelings and to find God there. In our context of conflict, with deepening polarizations, a family-system approach like this resources a way of reading scripture and our relationships in potentially healing ways. We are to walk *slowly* together, slow enough to listen, slow enough to feel, slow enough to allow our deepest desires to surface. This is difficult work and it is long-term work. We have the example of Joseph who reflects on his whole experience theologically. He proclaims that the will of God is to preserve life. In the process of gaining deeper wisdom about their own emotional maturity, Joseph and his family develop faith in God and God's purpose for them. The brothers gain insight and achieve a hard-won wisdom. "The God who creates also saves."[15]

Resourcing Peace Amidst Conflict

In this final section, we move from considering polarization through historical and exegetical lenses to identifying some resources for deeper Christian witness amidst conflict. These resources relate to principles that arise from a recognition of the principles at work in family systems and the fundamental theological principle that amidst polarizations, God's own witness in Christ is central.

Principles from Family Systems

Arising from this family-systems reading of polarization, three principles can be identified to resource peacebuilding amidst polarization. First, a ministry of *recognition* is the place to begin. When Joseph's brothers encounter him in Egypt, they do not at first recognize him (Gen. 42:8). In situations of polarization, people often fail to recognize the depth of their connections with one another. Polarization around race or sexuality can blind community members to the ways in which they share in history, tradition, and common culture. It is impossible to begin the work of reconciliation until people begin to recognize the other and name their common bonds. The goal is to make visible our essential kinship in community, so that the effects of polarization can also be recognized. To achieve this recognition, perhaps it is possible to offer certain "tests." Whom from the community do we each not see enough and would like to see again? That is, who do we already recognize in love? How might we ask the community to come together, so that we each might seek a reunion with those we already hold in powerful filial love?

---

15. Agnes W. Norfleet, "Genesis 45:1–15," in *The Renovaré Spiritual Formation Bible*, ed. Richard J. Foster et al. (San Francisco: HarperSanFrancisco, 2005), 79.

Second, a ministry of *reflection* is also important. Joseph's brothers were eventually changed as part of the efforts Joseph made to reconcile with them. That reconciliation does not happen immediately. After meeting and failing to recognize Joseph in Egypt, the brothers return home. There, they show that they are still willing to lie and see their family break apart in order to cover up their lies. Further, their father, Jacob, whose selfish love and self-absorption helped create the rift among his children, continues to think only of how events affect him personally. "All this has happened to me!" he proclaims (Gen. 42:36). Joseph, on the other hand, is carefully working with events to bring about the reconciliation of his family. While Jacob lacks real awareness of the other, Joseph demonstrates an intense consciousness of the other and designs events to create a desired end. In our context, a ministry of reflection could encourage community members to identify ways in which they have remained unchanged in their thoughts, words, and deeds toward their neighbor and to recognize their own selfishness and self-involvement. To the extent polarization has been a source of conflict, reflecting on our own unreformed patterns of participation in polarization and noting our tendency to see it only in terms of our own points of view will help to create the prerequisites for reconciliation. There is a call here to be like Joseph who even though he is in pain can see the other and dislike Jacob who feels only for himself.

Third, in facilitating reconciliation, the Church should encourage ministries of *repentance*. A ministry of recognition and reflection allows us to see how we have distanced ourselves from and wounded one another. Confession and repentance can disclose real transformation. Joseph's brothers, through Judah, admit to their role in the conflict that tore their family apart and they resolve not to repeat that pattern again. They are no longer the brothers who will tolerate enslavement or a brother sacrificed for their convenience. No longer will the brothers orient the world only to themselves. Through confession and repentance, the brothers announce that they will live differently. In contexts of polarization, confession and repentance can be transformative and healing. This work is ongoing and always a call to confess to each other and repair the polarization. In our context, part of this work has been undertaken in a reparations program at the seminary. In the era of slavery and Jim Crow, Black Americans were forced to work at VTS. Now, through a process of tracing the descendants, families of those Black workers are receiving reparations payments and learning more about the lives and witness of their ancestors who worked at the seminary. For genealogist, Maddy McCoy, no manual exists for such a project. There will be, she says, "ups and downs and a lot of really, really difficult decisions and difficult conversations, but that's what this work is."[16]

Christ as the Heart of God's Witness Against Polarization

As we have seen, amidst conflict we must resource the witness of the Church with deeper understanding of polarization through coming to terms with its psychological and practical complexities. As we have also seen, for Christians this work is also resourced by historical and biblical awareness. In this final section, we begin to identify a Christological center to the witness and practice of peacemaking.

The Church's belief in seeing God's peace and salvation as restoration and reconciliation is an understanding that runs throughout theology. Karl Barth wrote of the "Divine Yes" as being the participation and assent of God in an active involvement in all that God created. Furthermore, all that God created bears the characteristics of God's grace, compassion, and beauty.[17] It seems, then, that all subsequent interactions of God with humanity, most importantly seen in the incarnation and cross of Christ, are movements back toward the restoration of God's creation. God, in Christ, is present as peacemaker in the deepest of our conflicts. But, how do we understand God's presence and peace in contemporary contexts of human conflict?

There are no segments of society that are immune from the problems that plague all of humanity. It seems all communities struggle to set aside or resolve historical conflicts, cultural biases, and inflexibilities of perspective. As we have seen, polarization occurs when one group chooses to set itself apart from another and cast out the other group through physical or cultural violence. Divisions are then reinforced by

---

16. Will Wright, "Seminary Built on Slavery and Jim Crow Labor Has Begun Paying Reparations," *The New York Times*, May 31, 2021. www.nytimes.com/2021/05/31/us/reparations-virginia-theological-seminary.html, accessed January 10, 2022. See Virginia Theological Seminary, "Reparations," Virginia Theological Seminary, https://vts.edu/mission/multicultural-ministries/reparations/, accessed February 23, 2022.

17. Karl Barth, *Church Dogmatics*, vol. 3: *The Doctrine of Creation*, ed. Geoffrey W. Bromiley and Thomas F. Torrance, trans. J. W. Edwards, O. Bussey, and Harold Knight (Edinburgh: T& TClark, 1958), 330–334.

constructed barriers that determine who is "inside" and acceptable and who is "outside" and marginalized. It is through the breaking down of such constructions that God comes to us in Christ. Jesus Christ is *mediator* and *advocate* amidst circumstances where human life is marked by barriers that define "insiders" and "outsiders." In other words, the Church's understanding of peace is the restoration and salvation achieved through Christ. Christ is the redeemer and restorer of God's *shalom*. Over and over through the movement of the Holy Spirit, this redemption continues to break into the world and manifests itself, drawing the world closer to the final (eschatological) return to peace. Such a vision should not resource passivity. On the contrary, to align one's self with God's peace is to work for truth and peace in history telling, in emotional dynamics, and in reparative practices. Such work is nothing less than a call to be attentive to the movement of the Holy Spirit. This is hard work and we must remain vigilant. We ask God's help to counter ego, bias, and self-interest. In the end, though, it is God's peace and all ultimately return to God.

In order to get to grips with the role of Christ in situations of human polarization, we offer a short Bible reflection for individuals or groups as a way to resource an understanding of Christ's witness amidst polarization. Read carefully the story of Jesus and the Samaritan women in John 4:4–26. This text is important because the Samaritan woman's encounter with Jesus touches upon a multitude of ways in which polarity expresses itself. How do you think polarization manifests itself in the text and context of John 4?

In Jesus' time, there was a tremendous rift between the Jews and the Samaritans. The Samaritans were the inhabitants of the northern kingdom of Israel who were left behind during the Babylonian exile when the ruling elite had been taken away to Babylon by King Nebuchadnezzar. This was done as a means of maintaining control over the conquered territory. As a matter of survival, the remnant left behind incorporated some elements of their conquerors into their own culture. They were still Jews, but they made some accommodations and "dabbled" in the idol worship of Baal. It was for the infidelity of this "dabbling" during the time of the exile that the Jews looked down on and despised the Samaritans.

In this text, we can see polarization operate at a number of levels. There is a cultural polarity between the Samaritans and the Jews. There is gender polarity between a female interacting with a male "outsider" in this context. There is a liturgical/ecclesiastical polarity expressed in the differences over where the proper center of worship should be (Mount Gezarim or Jerusalem). There is polarity in the Samaritan's implied status as an outcast within her own community.[18]

It is not very likely in any village of this time and region that a woman would have been married five times. This aspect of the narrative is possibly a parable of sorts. There are many speculations as to what the "five" represent. St. Augustine thought that perhaps the five husbands represented the five human senses that cannot help us understand God without the aid of the Holy Spirit. Others have thought that it represents the five ethnic groups that comprised the Samaritan people, or five different religions that were fused into the Samaritan beliefs. Another interpretation is that the woman is currently living with a sixth man who is not even her husband, and this is a symptom of her isolation and loneliness. Jesus, who is often referred to by the metaphor of "bridegroom," becomes the seventh. In biblical symbolism, the number seven denotes perfection. In other words, the woman's fallen denigrated state is lifted up and restored in Jesus Christ.

The fact that the woman is out at midday by herself and not with other women is indicative of her status as an outcast within the local Samaritan community. This woman is, in the eyes of an observant Jew, defiled in a number of respects: fallen woman, Samaritan, spurned by her own community. By being in contact with her, Jesus chooses to defile himself and in doing so sanctifies and cleanses her and by extension all Samaritans. It is not insignificant that this event occurs at Jacob's well which is in a manner of speaking "common ground" for both Jews and Samaritans.

In conclusion, reflect further on this text by way of the following reflection questions. If you are in a group setting, this should take about thirty minutes. If the group is quite large, please reflect on the questions in small groups of three to five people. Begin by rereading the text aloud and inviting each other to answer the questions. If you have divided into groups of three to five, reconvene at the end allowing groups to share their reflections on the questions in the larger group.

---

18. The following section is based on the work of Mary Birmingham. See Mary Birmingham, *Word & Workshop: Work for Year A* (Mahwah, NJ: Paulist Press, 1999).

1. What do you think Jesus means when he says, "But the hour is coming, and is now here, when the true worshipers will worship the Father in spirit and truth, for the Father seeks such as these to worship him?"
2. Earlier in this chapter, we referred to the idols of Baal that managed to edge their way into the Samaritan culture. What false idols are there in your own context, individually and collectively, that draw us away from God and act as barriers to the peace of God entering our world? Why do you think God allows us to put up these barriers in the first place?
3. The peace of God is manifest in how the Samaritan woman reacts to this encounter with Jesus. She simply cannot contain the Good News. She has to go out into her own community, from which she is estranged, and tell everyone of what she has experienced. In light of this text and the other issues raised in this chapter, what ways might we witness similar movement of the Holy Spirit impacting our lives, communities, and the wider world? Where else might we see God at work in this way?
4. In current situations of polarity in our culture, do we have a "Jacob's Well" or common ground for meeting and conversation? To what extent can the Church create such space?
5. What other stories, from scripture, does this encounter in John 4 bring to mind as you watch Jesus relate to those whom his society considered "outsiders?"
6. What experiences have you had or witnessed in regard to the "outsider?" Who are the "Samaritan women" in your context and what ministry priorities might your community identify?

Conclusion

Polarization as conflict is complex. We have considered it from distinct perspectives. Polarization has been considered from a historical perspective (our focus has been the United States of America and the Virginia Seminary's place in a racially polarized nation), a biblical perspective (we have reflected on polarization in reference to the stories of Cain and Abel, Jacob's sons, and the Samaritan woman), a psychological perspective (we have illustrated how polarization can be understood through family-systems analysis), and a theological perspective (central to God's witness amidst polarization is the person and work of Christ). Of course, these perspectives are not as distinct as might be first assumed. We have seen how historical, biblical, emotional, and theological issues intersect and relate in a context of polarization. As you think about the complexities of polarization in your own context, and the call and message of the gospel, take a moment to meditate on these verses from Philippians. As you read and meditate, ask the Spirit to guide you in your witness to God's peace in God's world:

> Do not worry about anything, but in everything by prayer and supplication with thanksgiving let your requests be made known to God. And the peace of God, which surpasses all understanding, will guard your hearts and your minds in Christ Jesus.
>
> (Phil. 4:6–7)

Inter-contextual Peacebuilding

Robert S. Heaney and John Y. H. Yieh

Each chapter, especially in the third section of this study, is characterized by contextual concerns, readings, and priorities. Individual scholars and practitioners—along with teams of leaders from the Middle East, East Africa, West Africa, and North America—address the specificity of conflict and peacebuilding in their settings. By way of conclusion, we make the move from contextual readings to an inter-contextual reading. That is to say, in a comparative reading of all the preceding chapters we ask—to what extent are there major themes and common practices at work across the contexts that define a particular approach to peacebuilding? The object of analysis in *Building Dialogue* has been beyond the text in the social phenomena of conflict and resolution. A narrative-based approach has, however, created a set of texts shaped by and responsive to such social phenomena. In a final move, an inter-contextual reading now asks of the text *as a whole* the three research questions asked of *each* participant to the project—what is conflict? What is the Christian vision for peacebuilding? What practices or priorities should the Church pursue in its witness to peace amidst conflict?

Understanding Conflict

In this collection, a three-dimensional approach to conflict is at work in intertextual, historical, and existential analyses. This analysis results in a complex appreciation of the nature of conflict in relation to symbols, chaos, war, loss, gender, inter-contextuality, and spirituality.

Analyzing Conflict

First, the authors in this collection analyze conflict *via* practices of *intertextuality*. This is seen clearly in the early chapters as the witness to peace is considered in the biblical text. Chilongani and Yieh, though each focus on one of the two testaments, both read understandings and visions of peace across a number of texts and contexts (see also chapters 5, 9, 11, and 12). The intertextuality of this analysis is seen in historical, linguistic, and social-rhetorical analysis. Alongside Hebrew and Greek, an appeal is made to technical intertextual analysis in Syriac and Aramaic (chapter 2). A focus on the power of text and the analysis of text is not limited to the study of the Bible. Chapters 6 and 9 bring to the fore the witness of Christians amidst the artistry of the Arabic language, and chapter 11 makes a special appeal to the role of Kiswahili.

An intertextual approach to conflict analysis will examine the role of texts, the reception of texts, and the complications of translation and retranslation that are posed for understanding identities, intentions, and communication. Beyond scripture and scriptural commentary, this study takes account of the nature and impact of distinct types of texts including legal texts (see chapters 7, 9, and 11), declarations of war (chapter 10), judicial decisions (chapters 7 and 11), and governmental edicts (chapter 11). Intertextuality is reading scripture and extra-scriptural texts alongside, in response to, or in conversation with scriptural interpretations, extra-scriptural contexts, non-biblical languages, and modern contexts (see chapters 3, 4, 5, and 7). Such intertextual analysis is further deepened when it is recognized that in *Building Dialogue* a majority of authors do not count English as their heart language.

Second, in understanding conflict, *historical* analysis becomes important. In this approach to analysis, the focus is on past actions and actors that continue to fuel conflict or frame conflict. Conflict is a recurring theme in history. Historical conflict remains present in the way it forms communities, geographies, and people (see chapters 4, 5, 6, 7, 9, 10, 11, and 12). Such historical analysis also reminds the Church that in any context of conflict it begins in weakness (see chapter 4).

Heaney points to historical success and failure in the mission of the Church as it has found itself in conflict and as it created the conditions for conflict (chapter 4). Qubti looks to historical actions that created conflict and continues to map the conflict (chapter 7). In doing so, she defines conflict in geographical terms. Past political actions and current political polices, quite literally, map the region for conflict. In chapter 10, Ankrah, Browne, Burrowes, Duncan Cassell, Fredericks Cooper, Gaye, and Williams begin with a historical reading of their conflict. They point to histories of ethnicity, colonialism, negotiation, and violence as definitive of their conflict. The land disputes in view in chapter 11 center on the exercise of political power. A historical analysis, however, ensures that the issue of land disputes is not simply reduced to the use or misuse of political power. A historical view brings into play the importance of national identity (relocating the capital to the central location of Dodoma), ethnic identity, and local customs as they contribute to and exacerbate conflict. Similar historical dynamics are at work in chapter 12 and the consideration of polarization in the United States of America. Historically, racism constructed identities and policies of exclusion, inclusion, and segregation on the basis of such constructions. Such a historical reading brings to the fore the deep work yet to be done in local communities and in the nation.

Third, important in each chapter, but especially in section C, is an analysis of conflict through an *existential* lens. Here is a focus that gives primacy to the present impact of conflict over textual or historical readings. In a number of chapters, the psychological, familial, and embodied nature of community and conflict is taken into account. Dagher (chapter 6), in part, depicts the conflict in his context in relation to a range of feelings including fear, hatred, and grief. Qubti (chapter 7) evokes feelings of dispossession, marginalization, isolation, guilt, hate, and frustration as inherent to an understanding of conflict.

In chapter 9, Far, Khadir, Lukens, Naoum, and Rahmoun speak of young people "losing their sense of Palestinian identity" amidst the conflict. Palestinians often feel they are not in control. They are afraid. They are in desperation. There is confusion, loss, and frustration that is only exacerbated by the actions of government. Chapter 10 identifies emotional categories at work in the conflict and aftermath of conflict in Liberia. Indeed, Ankrah, Browne, Burrowes, Cassell, Fredericks Cooper, Gaye, and Williams speak of violence as a deep wound in the soul of Liberia. The pain from that wound is still felt today. Ongoing trauma continues to impact the lives of young people not least as they turn to drugs and enter into abusive relationships. Feelings of sorrow, toil, pain, defilement, abandonment, revenge, and hopelessness abound. In chapter 11, Kabia, Magayo, Mdabuko, Mwihambi, Ndahani, and Yohana include in their understanding of conflict a loss of joy or serenity. In land disputes, feelings of injustice, entitlement, selfishness, and ethnic superiority are at play existentially in this conflict. It is, however, only in chapter 12 that a specific psychological theory is identified as important to conflict analysis.

Cole, Cotting, Crippen, Davis, McCormick, Musser, and Wensing appeal to the analytic potency of family-systems theory. Relational patterns are at work in situations of conflict not the least of which are unsatisfied longings and sadness. Misunderstandings, fears, unrecognized longings, and unexpressed affection help analyze the complexities of conflict and, particularly in the United States of America, the complexities of polarization.

The Nature of Conflict

Given the intertextual, historical, and existential analyses at work in *Building Dialogue*, is there a particular understanding of conflict that emerges in this study? In this section, we will suggest that conflict is characterized in relation to symbols, chaos, war, loss, gender, inter-contextuality, and spirituality.

First, conflict is *symbolic*. It should be understood that conflict as symbolic is not somehow distinct from "real" conflict or "actual" conflict. On the contrary, liturgical theology deepens an understanding of the reality of this aspect of conflict (see chapters 3 and 5). In a Tanzanian context, Christian liturgical signs are joined with non-Christian ritual (chapter 11). Symbols, at least in Anglican liturgical thought, may be more than symbolic. They can be effectual signs. They can, in a manner of speaking, act (see chapter 5). Therefore, as liturgical theology appeals to the more-than-symbolic symbols of reconciliation (found, for example, in eucharistic liturgy) so, then, symbols in conflict will be understood in distinct ways from the perspective of a theological peacebuilder. In conflict, symbols are mobilized not only as a means to marshal solidarity. They are mobilized because of their very nature as more-than-symbols. The symbols are not bare signs. Flags, passports, identity laws, and identity cards are *in themselves* sites of conflict (see chapters 7 and 9). Likewise, constructed symbols of race categorizations became not only contested as unfaithful signs but also become the locus of conflict itself (chapters 4 and 12).

Second, it is particularly in chapter 1 that conflict as *chaos* is centered. Chilongani argues that this primordial concept of conflict in the Hebrew Bible stands over against the concept of peace (*šālôm*). Chaos is manifest in a number of conditions in the biblical text including societal breakdown, exile and slavery, the failure of diplomacy, and the onslaught of war. A dominant form of chaos in the Hebrew Bible is war. War is an enemy of *šālôm*. This immediately raises hermeneutical questions on how to read the divine's involvement in war. By implication, such hermeneutical concern posits questions for any textual and theological justification for war. Chilongani concedes that certain acts of Yahweh are depicted as a battle. However, they belong to a distinct category that is distinct from war as chaos. God acts to deliver and God does not use conventional weapons of war. As the biblical text develops, however, God's action in battle is decentered in favor of human action. Whatever the hermeneutical questions and resolutions that are open to exegetes, the idea of war or conflict as chaos remains. This is seen in a number of chapters in *Building Dialogue*. For example, Yieh (chapter 2) explicitly references chaos as a feature of internal conflict in the Church of Corinth. Snyder (chapter 5) references conflict as chaos in the context of armed warfare. Chapter 10 does not directly employ the term "chaos." However, in depicting the two civil wars that Liberia experienced, Ankrah, Browne, Burrowes, Cassell, Fredericks Cooper, Gaye, and Williams speak of it as bringing destruction at all levels of society. While the biblical concept of chaos might apply to forms of conflict beyond the text, Chilongani is clear on one aspect of its ongoing relevance. The idea of war as chaos may be ancient, but it seems ever more apt as humanity increases its proficiency in war and the weapons of war.

Third, conflict is *war*. A number of authors defining peace or reconciliation emphasize that both terms mean more than the absence of war. Conflict is, however, often experienced as some type of war. This is seen across a number of chapters in *Building Dialogue*. As we have seen, Chilongani defines chaos in relation to war (chapter 1). Heaney cites the possibility of renewed Christian witness in the aftermath of World War II (chapter 4). Snyder references conflict as war in South Sudan (chapter 5). Dagher depicts his context as caught up in permanent war. Qubti references the Israeli war of independence, or the *Nakba*, as the defining moment for Palestinian people forced into a diaspora and fragmentation (see chapters 7 and 9). In defining trauma, Cotting cites war as a major contributing factor (chapter 8). In chapter 12, unresolved issues in society are particularly associated with the American Civil War. It is, however, the chapter on Liberia where conflict as war is dominant (chapter 10).

Ankrah, Browne, Burrowes, Cassell, Fredericks Cooper, Gaye, and Williams determine the meaning of conflict in the midst of Civil Wars. In the Liberian context, war has meant insurrection, coups d'état, factional violence, ethnic violence, religious violence, sexual violence, extrajudicial killings, and the destruction or desecration of religious spaces. Statistics cannot capture the nature of conflict as war, but they point to the great cost to human life. In Liberia, 150,000–300,000 people were killed. War left 1.2 million people displaced. While the war as armed conflict has passed, the impact on society continues. It continues to have psychological, spiritual, societal and health impacts.

Fourth, conflict is *loss*. In chapter 3, Browne points to peacebuilding as a redeeming of time lost (Eph. 5:16; Col. 4:5). Conflict is not only a laying waste to creation and creatures, but it is also wasted time. It is a loss of *šālôm* (chapter 1) which, according to Christian theology, is restored in the mission of Christ (chapter 2). Conflict as loss is at work in the Heaney chapter where racist and ethnic conflicts, sometimes in the context of violent colonial incursions, forestalled fuller expressions of the Christian Gospel in indigenous or contextual terms (chapter 4). Snyder's three R's of reconciliation (re-membering, re-humanizing, and re-imagination) point to conflict as loss (chapter 5). Conflict is dis-membering (a loss of wholeness), de-humanizing (a loss of humanity), and a loss of vision (a failure to imagine possibilities beyond conflict). Conflict as loss of imagination is evidenced in telling our stories in service of self-interest. It is a refusal to be creative. It is the refusal to tell our story in the presence and light of other stories founded upon the unseen, but God-given, reality that *all* are children of God (chapter 5).

In a number of chapters, conflict as loss means dispossession. This is seen plainly in the land disputes in Dodoma city (chapter 11). It is also at play in chapters that are set in, or refer to, historic or contemporary colonialism (chapters 4, 6, 7, and 9). Qubti reminds readers that one hundred years ago, 10 percent of the population of Palestine was Christian. Today Palestinian Christians make up 2 percent of the population of Israel and 3 percent of the population of Palestine. Conflict as loss is a reality each day for Palestinians.

Fifth, conflict is *gendered*. This insight is at work in chapters 10 and 11, but it is particularly pronounced in chapter 7. For Kabia, Magayo, Mdabuko, Mwihambi, Ndahani, and Yohana, conflict as land disputes has a clear gendered dimension (chapter 11). Despite the law of the land, that gives daughters the right to inherit, traditional codes remain that make it difficult for women, in practice, to inherit land. Leaders in Liberia's Women in Peacebuilding Network (WIPNET) had a particular concern for the havoc visited upon families because of war (chapter 10). For Qubti, women are present in every aspect of life and are impacted by conflict in distinct ways as women. As spouses, parents, daughters, sisters, committed church members, carers, educators, theologians, charity workers, and peacebuilders in the field, they experience firsthand the violence of the conflict. The conflict is deepened for women as they experience political and social marginalization not only in the broader context of competing nationalities but also within their very own community. Indeed, even in inclusive processes of peacebuilding, women can experience marginalization as such processes are dominated by men and the perspectives of men. In short, the gendered nature of conflict deepens the suffering and, if not taken account of, weakens any peace process.

Sixth, conflict is *intercultural.* A number of authors in *Building Dialogue* emphasize, or at least identify, the intercultural nature of much conflict. Even in the midst of local conflict, the causes or impact belong to broader relationships and networks beyond the initial site of conflict. Amidst civil conflict in Liberia agents from outside Liberia were involved in the conflict (soldiers from Guinea were involved in responding to social disorder). Cultural distinctiveness and ethnic particularities further exacerbated the conflict.

Heaney takes intercultural conflict, or contestation, to be central to the modern emergence of Anglicanism (chapter 4). The encounter, across cultures, between white missionaries and African converts and missionaries got to the very heart of what Anglicanism would be or could be. The transplantation of an English tradition would come up against the missionary zeal for translating the gospel into diverse and distinct cultures far removed from England. Dagher recognizes the cultural diversities at work in his context of conflict among ethnicities and religious identities including Jews, Samaritans, Druze, Christians, Muslims, and Bahá'í (chapter 6). From the same context, Far, Khadir, Lukens, Naoum, and Rahmoun note that interculturality is not only at work socially but can be at work, in complex ways, at an individual level. Palestinian identity is a combination of ethnic, religious, denominational, and national histories and commitments. Chapter 9 explicates an interculturality that not only complicates conflict but can also be seen by those with power to be a threat. The 2017 Identity Law works against the fact of cultural diversity apparently based on a view that such diversity is a threat and, thus, a locus for conflict. In chapter 12, Cole, Cotting, Crippen, Davis, McCormick,

Musser, and Wensing depict the United States of America as becoming less intercultural. The way to a deeper interculturality for communities and the Church remains a largely unresolved issue in the wake of the Civil War, the era of Jim Crow, and recent public demonstrations of white supremacy.

Seventh, conflict is *spiritual*. Across a range of chapters, authors explicitly cite the spiritual dimensions of conflict and peacebuilding. Ankrah, Browne, Burrowes, Cassell, Fredericks Cooper, Gaye, and Williams cite Romans 8:6 as a reminder that conflict, in the Christian imagination, is rooted in the heart. Chilongani emphasizes the holism associated with *šālôm*. It does not simply address an "inner" need but the wholeness of life. It is God's gift to a people tempted to reject or resist God's sovereignty and trust in their own power. While there was peace, and the offer of divine peace, there was also resistance and rejection of peace (*ayin šālôm*). Eventually, rebellion against God led to exile from the land (chapter 1). Cole, Cotting, Crippen, Davis, McCormick, Musser, and Wensing echo the complex relationship between humanity and the land in the story of Cain and Abel. They see in Cain's vocation a harkening back to the "first violation and alienation from God and the land." It is in the context of this Genesis 4 story that sin first appears in the biblical text. Here, the identification of the spiritual dimension of conflict names not only enmity with God and between brothers but also humanity's alienation from the earth itself.

That humanity might be at enmity with God is also a predicate of depictions of peace in chapters 2 and 5. Yieh points to the central message of the gospel in the New Testament (chapter 2). Peace between humanity and God is wrought by Christ. Relationship with God is restored through Christ and faith in Christ. Snyder is plainspoken on humanity's need for reconciliation (*katallage*). It is needed because of a broken relationship between humanity and God. Kabia, Magayo, Mdabuko, Mwihambi, Ndahani, and Yohana, reading the New Testament text, define God's reconciliation as necessary because of hostility between God and humanity and between Jews and Gentiles. In this context, there is a belief that the ancestors have agency. Thus, the blessing for reconciliation may be conferred by the ancestors. Equally, if reconciliation fails or is facile, the ancestors have the power to visit consequences on the perpetrators (chapter 11). Snyder also speaks of a brokenness and enmity not only between people but also within the human spirit itself. She reminds us that, often, the hardest person ("enemy") to love is one's self. Jesus' command to love God, neighbor, *and* self recognizes the complexity of conflict. Here are deep spiritual realities that need ongoing spiritual work.

Browne, Heaney, and Snyder point to a corporate and even liturgical spirituality that calls the Church to wholeness even in the act of unveiling the Church's brokenness. The liturgy of the Eucharist is ever calling the Church away from brokenness and conflict to peacebuilding worship and communion. For Browne, the high point of the eucharistic liturgy is the fellowship that ensues as a result of the sacrament. Here is a moment where conflict and barriers are recognized and a spiritual vision of openness, redemption, and oneness before God is revealed (chapter 3). Heaney recognizes that the Church finds itself in conflict. A spirituality of peace faces the historical and grounded reality of conflict, and the impact of conflict, in the context of discerning both judgment and grace. That conflict is spiritual is a call for the Church to more deeply experience contrition, penance, and absolution (chapter 4). Snyder recognizes that the movement for reconciliation is a key feature in a sacramental worldview. Citing Katongole, she sets before us a sacramental vision of reconciliation that unveils a holy church made up of forgiven sinners (chapter 5).

Understanding Peace

Using intertextual, historical, and existential analyses to compare and synthesize the statements, arguments, and assumptions of the twelve chapters in this volume, we can find numerous insights and remarkable experiences to reflect on and sketch out an intercontextual vision of peace. The Christian vision of peace is theological and it is practical. Together, as theological and practical, seven elements of a Christian understanding of peace emerge: definition, source, reason, scope, process, ministry, and challenges.

Theological Peace

First, definition. Peace is polyvalent and multifaceted, as expressed in Christian scripture, theology, liturgy, and practice. Peace is *shalom* in Hebrew scripture referring to the opposite state of chaos, danger, hatred, and violence. Chilongani (chapter 1) recounts the biblical narrative to show God chooses Abraham's offspring as God's people, saves them from slavery in Egypt, makes covenant with them on Mount Sinai, gives them the law to live by, leads them to the promised land, and disciplines them in exile and return. Throughout their history, the people of Israel suffer personal temptations, social enmities, tribal conflicts, and international wars. Amidst all kinds of suffering, however, God offers them God's peace in various forms of blessings. Peace is safety, prosperity, comfort, and joy.

Peace is *eirēnē* in the New Testament referring to inner tranquility in the soul, cordial relationship with others, just order in society, and genuine concord among nations. Yieh (chapter 2) explains how Jesus serves as the unique mediator between God and humanity. Offering himself as an atoning sacrifice on the cross, Jesus redeems believers and makes them children of God, enabling them to receive God's peace. Yieh also argues that God's peace is now labeled as Jesus' peace and is something the world cannot give. It is a potent peace from the Son of God who has conquered the "ruler of the world" and even death itself by his resurrection from the grave. Having experienced Jesus' peace that sustains his faith and ministry amidst violence, persecutions, and imprisonments, the Apostle Paul can remain calm in the face of death. Aptly, Paul describes Jesus' peace as a peace that "surpasses human understanding" (Phil. 4:7). In his theological reflection on peacemaking, Browne (chapter 3) underscores Eucharist as a central liturgy in Anglicanism both symbolic and effectual. The Eucharist is a commemoration and participation in the peace of God in Jesus Christ and a sharing of communion with fellow believers in the Holy Spirit. In a broken world, where humans are alienated from God and one another, the Eucharist calls and forms a church for mission-as-peacemaking.

Beyond its fundamental definitions in scripture and theology, peace is further understood in a dynamic sense as reconciliation—the action and result of fixing a ruptured relationship—between warring sides. Peace as reconciliation recognizes the problems of conflict, rivalry, and violence and seeks to resolve, defuse, and deter those problems. Heaney's critical account of Anglican missions in Africa (chapter 4) shows how the Church of England went wrong in its debate about the gospel and African culture and how in the light of postcolonial theology by African theologians, the Anglican Communion needs to find theological reconciliation. For Dagher (chapter 6), interfaith reconciliation is the goal of his community-based ministry. Focusing on science, arts, and music education programs for local children, he aims at bridging the gap between Jewish, Druze, Christian, and Muslim groups. Qubti's autobiographical narrative (chapter 7) shows how reconciling social identities is a key theme in her life journey that begins with the innocence of youth in a conservative church, continues in the struggle with complicated identities in a society in conflict, and finally comes to more mature and nuanced expression in her vocation as a voice of conscience for oppressed and marginalized women. Here, peace is advocacy for racial, political, religious, and gender justice through telling the stories of those who would be made voiceless.

Second, source. Peace is originated from and conferred by the triune God. The vision of peace in the Hebrew scripture is focused on the God of mercy who blesses people with God's peace abundantly. The generous giving of God's peace is based on a covenant relationship that the almighty God has made with the people of Israel chosen to be the light to all nations (chapter 1). The vision of peace in the New Testament highlights Jesus' peace as the amazing grace from God. Peace is reconciliation between God and humanity. The New Testament centers this peace on Christ's self-offering on the cross that makes reconciliation available, by faith, to all. This peace, wrought by Christ, is the very essence of the gospel. Coming from the Father and the Son, the Holy Spirit makes the peace of Jesus available to comfort, teach, and defend Jesus' followers so that they can conquer the evil of the world (see chapters 2 and 4).

Peace is endowed by God, effected by Christ, and empowered by the Holy Spirit. Christians have confidence, then, that by God's grace peace is attainable and reachable (2 Cor. 5:17–19). We hope and work hard for peace because God wills peace. For all the authors in this volume, the fundamental reason why the Church should pursue peace is that peace is God's gift to all people, regardless of their racial-ethnic, cultural, social, economic, religious, or gender differences. As evident in the scripture, God's peace and Jesus' peace are free gifts to the world, so God's children who have received the blessings of peace freely from God are expected to share the gospel of peace freely to others. It is a gospel mandate. God's children should imitate their heavenly Father, loving peace and making peace, as Jesus declares, "Blessed are the peacemakers, for they will be called children of God" (Matt. 5:9). For the Church, making peace is not an option but a divine command.

Theological Practice

Third, reason. Peace as self-preservation and mutual security cannot be ignored in any theological account. Dagher (chapter 6) organizes many interfaith services and education programs for children in the area west of Nazareth. He wants to increase better understanding and mutual trust in his racially and religiously mixed community so that the cycle of violence might be broken. The main reason why Qubti (chapter 7) advocates for women's rights to serve and lead in the struggle for political freedom and social equality in the Holy Land is to promote justice for all. Peace is a human right given by God that no one should take away.

Fourth, scope. The scope of peace is wide and concerns God, the world, and all realms of life. This is most evident in the four team chapters from the Middle East, East Africa, West Africa, and the United States of America. While tackling the conflicts in their contexts, the four teams explain what peace means for them. The Palestinian chapter (chapter 9) sets out a vision for peace that means coexistence. Their desire is for coexistence with neighbors of different religions in the Holy Land where everyone has identity, dignity, equality, human rights, and mutual respect. They seek an end to oppression, hatred, and fear. The Liberian chapter (chapter 10) searches for lasting peace. This means cessation of war, reconstruction of society, and new opportunities for the lost generation. They seek an end to conflict, destruction, and despair. The Tanzania chapter (chapter 11) wants a fair peace. This means legal ownership of land, fair division of inheritance between sons and daughters, and no fraudulence or coercion in government and business. Peace means no more corruption, exploitation, or greed. The U.S. chapter (chapter 12) pursues a just peace. This means a deeper understanding of history, repentance of racial discrimination, and reparation for the descendants of enslaved persons. There can be no more discrimination, amnesia, or indifference. In these four team chapters, peace becomes an umbrella concept for the common good. Rivals are reconciled, relationships are restored, the downtrodden are lifted up, and the oppressed are liberated.

Five, process. Snyder (chapter 5) proposes a practical process to help peacemakers achieve reconciliation. This process has three steps: re-membering, re-humanizing, and re-imagining. The way we make sense of our past is to pick and choose some milestones in our lives to construct a meaningful narrative about what happened. To begin the process of reconciliation, we need to remember our past honestly and listen to the stories of the other fairly to come closer to the truth of what happened. In conflicts, we often dehumanize, deface, or demonize our offenders. We allow a metaphorical wall to block our vision. We no longer see the good in others and forget that God loves them equally. Re-humanizing offenders makes it easier to accept and love them. Re-imagining is the third step, by which we recognize the shared elements between all our stories. In doing so, we will then be able to see the possibility of a reconciled future (see chapter 6).

Six, ministry. A theological approach to peace resources ministry. Many ministries of peacemaking have been proposed and tried. In the next section, we will identify principles for practice but before doing so it is important to draw attention to local ministries of peace at work in the contexts and chapters of this volume. Five ministries are noteworthy (Bible study, liturgy, social service, children's ministry, and advocacy).

Central to the approach of *Building Dialogue* has been Bible study. Foundational to understanding peace, analyzing conflict, and designing processes of dialogue has been scripture. Besides the comprehensive studies of peace in the Hebrew scripture (chapter 1) and the New Testament (chapter 2), the teams have used "scriptural reasoning" to guide and support their peacemaking efforts (see chapter 8). The Palestinian chapter (chapter 9) uses the story of Ruth and Naomi (Ruth 1–4) to find hope for coexistence and the story of Jesus calming the storm (Mark 4) to find inner peace amidst their suffering. The U.S. chapter (chapter 12) cites the story of Cain and Abel (Gen. 4) and the story of Joseph (Gen. 37–50) to reflect on the alienation and aggression between siblings that is mirrored in the racial tension and political polarization in American history.

Liturgy is particularly important as formation in Anglican thought. In this volume, the Eucharist has been interpreted as a liturgy of reconciliation that celebrates the peace between humanity and God and commissions the baptized to become peacemakers among warring parties in the world (chapters 3 and 5). In the light of African theologians' postcolonial critique on the historical debates concerning missionary bishops in Africa in the nineteenth century, Anglicans have taken part in liturgies of reconciliation. Indeed, Archbishop of Canterbury Justin Welby offered a sincere confession, a public apology, and an official restoration of Bishop Crowther's reputation at a service of "thanksgiving and repentance" (2014). Here might be a glimpse of how the Church can practice reconciliation with humility by admitting its mistakes, repenting of its sin, and repairing its broken connection with one another in the Anglican Communion (chapter 4).

Social services can speak louder than words. Often, the best way to show goodwill and reach the hearts of rivals, opponents, or enemies is to serve their needs through helping hands. Supporting war victims, feeding the poor, and educating the young are important works of charity in themselves, but they are also instrumental in building trust for lasting peace among people in the aftermath of conflict, wars, and social unrest (chapter 10). Every town or village has specific issues of concern and shared desires for the well-being of its members and families. Community organizing through active participation and generous partnership in public affairs help create an interpersonal bond and a sense of belonging in the neighborhood. Becoming a loyal and contributing member of the community makes it much easier to bring diverse groups of people together and overcome any suspicion, misunderstanding, or hatred (chapter 6).

Building peace is not only a repair job to fix past conflicts, but it is also preparation work to build a future peace. Children are open to new experiences. They have the potential and opportunity to turn the dark history of conflict to the bright future of peace for their own good. Children's ministry and youth ministry are in view at several junctures in *Building Dialogue*. Art classes, music camps, and sports, among different religious and social groups, are beneficial to their education and socialization. They become friends by learning and playing together. Their friendship may also affect their parents and their network of relationships (see chapters 6 and 10).

Advocacy is often needed for the sake of justice. In conflict and violence, those who are bullied and hurt often lose not only their identity, property, and freedom but also their voice, dignity, and opportunity. When no one even knows how the victims are suffering, how can they possibly receive necessary comfort or support to fight for their survival and resolve conflict? To pierce through the wall of domination and ignorance, the task of advocacy for the oppressed through church networks, NGOs, and digital media become useful and even indispensable (see chapters 7, 10, and 11).

Seven, challenges. Theological practice is founded on the work of God and not human naivety. As Browne (chapter 3) reminds us, peacemaking will always be partial and incomplete because of human finitude, inexactitude, and fallibility. It is eschatological. Even with the best intention and the smartest strategies, therefore, one should be cognizant of the challenges that may thwart the process of peacemaking. The defiance against peace will understandably be strong for those who have the upper hand in conflicts, and numerous roadblocks in the way to justice may indeed appear insurmountable. Those roadblocks include the long memory of violence and hatred (historical), fear of revenge or reverse aggression (psychological), corruption of power and exploitation for profit (political), racial-ethnic discrimination, economic disparity, gender inequity (social), self-centered, self-serving, and self-aggrandizing tendencies (spiritual). To overcome such challenges in human nature and social structure, Snyder (chapter 5) offers thoughtful observation and wise advice on how peacemakers may cultivate proper virtues and suitable habits, such as hospitality, empathy, and vulnerability, to become trustful, empathetic, and skillful reconcilers. Cotting's essay (chapter 8) on how to organize small group discussion in the Church to inform and inspire Christians to engage conflicts and build peace also provides good pedagogy and a practical model.

All the projects, practices, and processes presented in this volume are peaceful, proactive, and positive. They can be adopted, adapted, and adjusted for use in different contexts and diverse conditions. There is no guarantee that they will be as productive or successful in every context, but they are useful case studies showing important principles and rules of engagement for all peacemakers to take under advisement. We do not have to invent new wheels or repeat the same mistakes.

Witnessing to Peace Amidst Conflict

Given the means of analysis and the emergence of a theology of peace, what is it, in fact, that participants to this study actually *practice* by way of peacebuilding or reconciliation? Both as a summative move and a means to illustrate possible ongoing priorities for peacebuilding, we have identified three types of practice for peace in *Building Dialogue*.

First, practice *assembly*. The commitment to assemble or gather together across difference, and in the midst of conflict, is well attested to in *Building Dialogue*. The call to assembly is understood in distinct ways and includes distinct constituencies. We might think of the types of assembly in terms of concentric circles. Those closest to the center of the conflict are those directly involved in the conflict as protagonist and/or victim. Further from the center are those who assemble across difference for mutual learning. Lastly, are those who belong to one community in the conflict but who assemble together for the purpose of formation toward peacebuilding.

In Liberia, the Interfaith Mediation Committee (becoming in 1995, the Inter-Religious Council of Liberia) assembled parties to the conflict and engaged them in peace talks. The Inter-Religious Council organized dialogue promoting understanding and tolerance, advocating for human rights, promoting methods and means for conflict resolution, and serving as mediators amidst conflict. In the same context, the WIPNET acted as intermediaries amidst violence. Dagher points to the work of *Parents Circle* in the Holy Land which brings together parents who have been bereaved because of the conflict. Each of these initiatives involved creating organizations that could hold space or open space for those from different sides of the conflict. Thus, the ecumenical work of the Liberian Council of Churches joined with the National Muslim Council of Liberia to form the Interfaith Mediation Committee.

Depending on the stage or ferocity of the conflict, further out concentric circles may be easier to assemble than those directly involved in the conflict. For example, distinct forms of assembly that provide distinct forms of peacebuilding ministry are associated with processes of education and healing. In Liberia, Christian schools are open to all. This has resulted in one Christian school, in Monrovia, having 40 percent of its student body made up of Muslims. Likewise, Far, Khadir, Lukens, Naoum, and Rahmoun point to the witness of Anglican hospitals and schools as well as institutions that serve the elderly. Not one of these institutions requires a religious test. They are open to all.

A less diverse assembly further removed from the center of the conflict might be conceived. This assembly may yet represent distinct traditions though these traditions would operate within a broader constituency and align with one party to the conflict. In the Tanzanian context, this might mean the joining together of Christian and traditional African groups or approaches to peacebuilding. Traditional forms of assembly might be drawn upon as well as traditional rituals (see also chapter 10). Thus, the role of elders and rituals of reconciliation might provide a framework for assembly that is ordered toward peace. In this assembly, fines and rituals are associated with apportioning blame and offering reconciliation. Animals are often offered as a ritual sign of peacemaking followed by ritual eating together.

A further circle removed from the center is an ecumenical assembly (see chapter 8). The Christian Council of Tanzania provides ecumenical seminar training on dialogue, and tolerance across traditional and religious divides. This is particularly needed in a context with ethnic and religious diversity and increasing tension between Christians and Muslims. In the U.S. context, polarization is particularly marked by race and racism. The authors of chapter 12 are members of an Episcopalian seminary but also represent different denominations. The group was also racially diverse. Their work is a microcosm of the need for ongoing work, in assembly, between Christians whose analysis of polarization differ. Ongoing work is needed in terms of readings of history, hermeneutical priorities in reading the biblical text, and outward facing practice and witness.

Second, hear *testimony* and give testimony. A rich vein of practice at work across the diverse settings in *Building Dialogue* is a commitment to testimony. A variety of means are pursued as is a variety of postures toward public access or dissemination. The gospel is peace. Peace with God is restored through the cross of Christ. Christ's cry from the cross (*Tetélestai*) is an affirmation that the work of reconciliation he was sent to accomplish is now completed. Because of the cross, peace is restored (chapter 2). Therefore, for Kabia, Magayo, Mdabuko, Mwihambi, Ndahani, and Yohana, testimony for peace cannot be less than evangelism. For Jesus Christ is our peace (Eph. 2:14). It is Christ that is "a deep cure for the evils of racism, tribalism, and a divided humanity" (chapter 11). The Church is called to testify to this healing.

For Browne, God is not the God of Christian peace. God is God of all peace. Those, therefore, who embrace peace are a people renewed (chapter 3). Dagher attests to the positive impact of interreligious gatherings in his context that might be understood as events or processes of mutual testimony. Likewise in Liberia, testimony to deeper community has been served by the testimony of celebrating each other's tradition. For example, the testimony of Christians participating in the breaking of the fast with Muslims at the end of Ramadan was testimony that spoke powerfully in the midst of conflict.

The arts can reach across all kinds of division. Dagher illustrates this in reference to artistic work in his context. Especially through the testimony of music, religious groups, otherwise in conflict, come together. At the Cultural Center in Shefa-'Amr, diverse traditions are celebrated demonstrating distinct identities and distinct identities in relation to one another (chapter 9; see also chapter 11). God is the one who gifts humanity with a spirit of creativity. Thus, the testimony to diversity, for Far, Khadir, Lukens, Naoum, and Rahmoun, is a gift and a way of countering ignorance and prejudice (chapter 9). Such testimony, it might be added, complicates narratives of conflict when communities are tempted to understand conflict in binary terms (conflict as "us" versus "them").

Qubti writes about the *Women Behind the Wall* podcast that now has an international reach. It bears testimony to how conflict impacts the lives of women. For her, such testimony humanizes or "gives names and voices" to the women who live amidst conflict every day. In local and international peacebuilding, the experience and voice of women are largely ignored. The podcast centers the voices of marginalized women in a context where their voices are suppressed. It is the secular press that is particularly interested in this testimony. In part, then, the testimony is not only about uplifting the voices of women in the conflict. It is also a testimony that unveils the apparent disinterest Christian organizations, dominated by men, have for the cry of their sisters in the conflict. For Qubti, the success of the podcast has amounted to a methodological shift. Bringing the storytelling of women to the fore is now her priority as she increasingly moves away from peacebuilding centered on assembly and formal dialogue.

Third, prepare to *intervene*. Encounter across difference in the midst of conflict and testimony to one another amidst conflict may result in actions of intervention. In *Building Dialogue*, we have examples of religious actors precisely doing this. Such intervention may take place at individual or local level or it may take place at more public and national levels.

The psychological reading of conflict in chapter 12 facilitates a reflective and individual intervention by spiritual leaders. Practically, this is a process that calls people to *recognize* the conflict and the depth of connections between those who are party to the conflict. Those in conflict are issued an invitation to make visible the common bonds in meeting together and hearing each other's testimonies. Individuals as members of a community in conflict are called to *reflect* on how often they see issues solely from one point of view. All are summoned to practice deeper practices of confession and *repentance* (see also chapter 4).

Echoing Snyder's exhortation for reconcilers to re-member, re-humanize, and re-imagine (chapter 5), members of the cathedral congregation in Monrovia intervened. Here spiritual and local intervention meant members of the congregation welcoming so-called *Zogos* to worship. This intervention eventually resulted in the congregation supporting young people financially through drug rehabilitation (chapter 10). Local intervention was also at work in Dodoma (chapter 11). Here, among other interventions, the Church had to intervene to establish and defend its land rights. Ongoing interventions, given both good and bad outcomes surrounding land claims, are now shaped according to three principles. First, land occupancy is the right of all citizens. Second, citizens must know the law, government must be transparent in the application of the law, and traditionalists must be aware that the law forbids discriminatory practice. Third, the Church must continue to advocate for the weak against the strong and teach the God-given dignity and equality of all people.

In the gaze of the public eye, the WIPNET gathered together each day to pray for the nation. They made themselves visible in the public square donning a common dress and prostrating themselves on the ground. They went on strike forgoing cooking, washing, and sex as a protest against the conflict. Their public intervention ensured a narrative of new possibilities was brought to the national consciousness. Women were largely absent in negotiations. WIPNET's intervention changed that. Christian and Muslim women's needs were often overlooked in peace talks. WIPNET's intervention changed that. To ensure reconciliation and a lasting peace, women needed to be involved. WIPNET's intervention and ongoing commitment meant that training for women and the voice of women would be an integral part of negotiation and resolution in Liberia.[1]

---

1. See Leymah Gbowee and Carol Lynn Mithers, *Mighty Be Our Powers: How Sisterhood, Prayer, and Sex Changed a Nation at War: A Memoir* (New York: Beast Books, 2011).

The Virginia Theological Seminary intervened in the ongoing struggle against racism in the United States of America and in the telling of its own story. In 2019, the seminary established a $1.7 million reparations program. This is an ongoing project. It began when a more complicated history of the seminary was acknowledged. Money was set aside as a reparations fund. A dedicated team continue to research the scale of slavery at the seminary and trace descendants of these enslaved persons. Descendants are now receiving reparations payments and further funds have been set aside to create programs of justice and inclusion as well as to center the work and voices of Black clergy within the Episcopal Church. No amount of money can compensate for slavery. This reparative intervention supports, in practice, the repentance that the institution has made and the necessity of witness in a penitential voice (see chapter 4).

Conclusion

In contexts marred by conflict, we always begin in weakness. Yet, as Christians, we believe our weakness is met by the transforming grace of God. We have known both weakness and grace in the journey that has culminated in this publication. The book you hold in your hands is the product of dialogue. It is theological vision and theological practice for peacebuilding.

The dialogue was designed by facilitators based in institutions in East Africa, the Middle East, North America, and West Africa. As with any design, it had strengths and frailties. Opportunities were taken and opportunities were lost. Yet, by the grace of God theologians and theologian-practitioners told their stories, read scripture, and prayed together. Indeed, a clear intercontextual approach to peacebuilding has emerged. In summary, an intercontextual approach to peacebuilding defines conflict as symbolic, chaos, war, and loss. Such conflict is often marked by gendered dynamics, related to intercultural tensions, and rooted in spiritual dysfunction. Peace is theological and it is theological practice. Peace is the work of God attested to in scripture. It is centered on the person and work of Jesus Christ. As theological practice, it resources preservation and coexistence grounded on realistic processes of reconciliation and local acts of ministry. At least three principles emerge from a Christian intercontextual analysis of conflict and peace—assemble, testify, and intervene.

The rest, now, remains to you reader. Ask the Spirit of God how stories of old and testimonies from today can complicate, problematize, and enrich understandings of conflict in your context. Invite your community, or build community, to listen and discern the will of God in scripture. Then, gather around the table of the Lord. For there you will find, in broken bread and overflowing cup, inbreaking grace for a fractured world:

> The end of things is near; therefore be serious and discipline yourselves for the sake of your prayers. Above all, maintain constant love for one another, for love covers a multitude of sins. Be hospitable to one another without complaining. Like good stewards of the manifold grace of God, serve one another with whatever gift each of you has received. Whoever speaks must do so as one speaking the very words of God; whoever serves must do so with the strength that God supplies, so that God may be glorified in all things through Jesus Christ. To him belong the glory and the power forever and ever. Amen.
>
> (1 Pet. 4:7–11)

Bibliography

Abbink, Jan and Mirjam de Bruijn. *Land, Law and Politics in Africa: Mediating Conflict and Reshaping the State*. Leiden: Brill, 2011.

Ateek, Naim Stifan. *A Palestinian Theology of Liberation: The Bible, Justice, and the Palestine Israel Conflict*. Maryknoll: Orbis Press, 2017.

Baldwin, James. *The Fire Next Time*. 1963; Reprint, New York: Vintage International, 1993.

Barker, Paul A. "Rest, Peace." In *Dictionary of the Old Testament Pentateuch*, edited by T. D. Alexander and D. W. Baker, 687–691. Downers Grove: IVP, 2003.

Barth, Karl. *Church Dogmatics*, vol. 3: *The Doctrine of Creation*. Edited by Geoffrey W. Bromiley and Thomas F. Torrance and translated by J. W. Edwards, O. Bussey, and Harold Knight. Edinburgh: T&T Clark, 1958.

Bauckham, Richard. *Gospel of Glory: Major Themes in Johannine Theology*. Grand Rapids: Baker, 2015.

Bekoe, Dorina and Christina Parajon, "Women's Role in Liberia's Reconstruction." *United States Institute of* Peace, May 1, 2007, www.usip.org/publications/2007/05/womens-role-liberias-reconstruction. Accessed January 8, 2022.

Bergen, Jeremy M. *Ecclesial Repentance: The Churches Confront Their Sinful Pasts*. London: T&T Clark, 2011.

Bergen, Jeremy M. "Whether, and How, a Church Ought to Repent for a Historical Wrong." *Theology Today* 73, no. 2 (2016): 129–148.

Berlin, Ira. "Making Slavery, Making Race." In *Many Thousands Gone: The First Two Centuries of Slavery in North America*, 1–14. Cambridge: Belknap Press, 1998.

Bevans, Stephen B. "God Inside Out: Toward a Missionary Theology of the Holy Spirit." *International Bulletin of Missionary Research* 22, no. 3 (1998): 102–105.

Bevans, Stephen B. *Models of Contextual Theology*, revised ed. Maryknoll: Orbis Books, 2004.

Birch, Bruce C. "Old Testament Foundations for Peacemaking in the Nuclear Era." *The Christian Century* 102, no. 38 (December, 2004): 1115–1119.

Birmingham, Mary. *Word & Workshop: Work for Year A: For Ministry in Initiation, Preaching, Religious Education and Formation*. Mahwah, NJ: Paulist Press, 1999.

Bishop, Bill. *The Big Sort: Why the Clustering of Like-Minded America Is Tearing Us Apart*. Boston: Mariner Books, 2009.

Bjerk, Paul. *Building a Peaceful Nation: Julius Nyerere and the Establishment of Sovereignty in Tanzania, 1960–1964*. Rochester: University of Rochester Press, 2015.

Brown, Francis. *The Brown-Driver-Briggs Hebrew and English Lexicon*. With the cooperation of Samuel R. Driver and Charles A. Briggs. Oxford: Clarendon Press, 1952.

Bruner, Jerome. *Acts of Meaning*. Cambridge: Harvard University Press, 1990.

Bruner, Jerome. "The Narrative Construction of Reality." *Critical Inquiry* 18, no. 1 (1991): 1–21.

Buber, Martin. *I and Thou*, trans. Walter Kaufmann. New York: Touchstone, 1970.

Burridge, Richard. *Imitating Jesus: An Inclusive Approach to New Testament Ethics*. Grand Rapids: Eerdmans, 2007.

Byron, John. "Cain's Rejected Offering: Interpretive Approaches to a Theological Problem." *Journal for the Study of the Pseudepigrapha* 18, no. 1 (2008): 3–22.

Carter, J. Kameron. *Race: A Theological Account*. Oxford: Oxford University Press, 2008.

Chacar, Hanriette. "This Palestinian Life: Uncovering the Stories of Women behind the Wall." *972 Magazine*, August 30, 2018. 972mag.com/this-palestinian-life-uncovering-what-life-is-like-for-women-behind-the-wall/137531/.

Chacour, Elias and David Hazard, *Blood Brothers: The Dramatic Story of a Palestinian Christian Working for Peace in Israel*. Grand Rapids: Baker Books, 2013.

Childs, Brevard. *Biblical Theology in Crisis*. Philadelphia: Westminster Press, 1970.

Colenso, John W. *Village Sermons*. Cambridge: Macmillan and Co., 1853.

Colenso, John W. *St. Paul's Epistle to the Romans: Newly Translated, and Explained from a Missionary Point of View*. Cambridge: Macmillan and Co., 1861.

Constantineanu, Corneliu. *The Social Significance of Reconciliation in Paul's Theology: Narrative Readings in Romans*. London: T&T Clark, 2010.

Cook, Stephen L. *Reading Deuteronomy: A Literary and Theological Commentary*. Macon, GA: Smyth & Helwys Publishing, 2015.

Crossan, John Dominic. *Jesus: A Revolutionary Biography*. San Francisco: HarperOne, 2009.

Dancer, Helen. "An Equal Right to Inherit? Women's Land Rights, Customary Law and Constitutional Reform in Tanzania." *Social & Legal Studies* 26, no. 3 (2017): 291–310.

Dansu, Kwaku. "Mending Broken Relations after Civil War: The 'Palava Hut' and the Prospects for Lasting Peace in Liberia." *Kofi Annan International Peacekeeping Training Center*. Policy Brief 2 (May 2016): 1–6. https://media.

africaportal.org/documents/KAIPTC-Policy-Brief---The-Palava-Hut-in-Liberia.pdf. Accessed February 22, 2022.

De Fina, Anna and Alexandra Georgakopoulou. *Analyzing Narratives: Discourse and Sociolinguistic Perspectives*. Cambridge: Cambridge University Press, 2012.

De Fina, Anna and Alexandra Georgakopoulou eds. *The Handbook of Narrative Analysis*. Chichester: Wiley-Blackwell, 2015.

Diéz-Macho, Alejandro ed. *The Neophyti Targum of the Pentateuch*. Madrid-Barcelona: Consejo Superior de Investigaciones Científicas, 1968–1978.

Dillistone, Frederick W. *The Power of Symbols*. London: SCM, 1986.

Dunn, James. *Romans 1–8*. Vol. 38a of *Word Biblical Commentary*. Grand Rapids: Zondervan, 1988.

Durham, John I. "םוֹלָשׁ and the Presence of God." *Proclamation and Presence: Old Testament Essays in Honour of Gwynne Henton*, edited by John I. Durham and Joshua R. Porter, 272–293. London: SCM, 1970.

Echols, Charles L. *Tell Me O Muse: The Story of Deborah (Judges 5) in the Light of Heroic Poetry*. New York: Continuum Press, 2008.

Etherington, Norman. Introduction in *Missions and Empire*, edited by Norman Etherington, 1–18. Oxford: Oxford University Press, 2005.

Ezigbo, Victor I. *The Art of Contextual Theology: Doing Theology in the Era of World Christianity*. Eugene: Cascade, 2021.

Fitzmyer, Joseph. *Romans*. New York: Doubleday, 1993.

Franklin, John Hope and Evelyn Brooks Higginbotham. *From Slavery to Freedom: A History of African Americans*, 9th ed. New York: McGraw-Hill, 2021.

Gerlemann, Gillis. "םלש šlm to have enough." In *Theological Lexicon of the Old Testament*, vol. 3: םיִפָּרְת-הלצ, edited by Ernst Jenni and Claus Westermann, 1337–1348. Peabody, MA: Hendrickson, 1997.

Good, Edwin M. "Peace in the OT." In *Interpreter's Dictionary of the Bible*, vol. 3, *K-Q*, edited by Keith Crim, 704–706. New York: Abingdon Press, 1962.

Goodwin, William Archer Rutherford. *History of the Theological Seminary in Virginia and Its Historical Background*, vol. 2. New York: Edwin S. Gorham, 1923–1924.

Gray, George Buchanan. *Critical and Exegetical Commentary on Numbers.* Edinburgh: T&T Clark, 1903.

Guy, Jeff. *The Heretic: A Study of the Life of John Willian Colenso, 1814–1883.* Pietermaritzburg: Natal University Press, 1984.

Hall, Stuart. *Doctrine and Practice in the Early Church*. London: SPCK, 1994.

Hansen, Bruce. *All of You Are One: The Social Vision of Galatians 3.28; 1 Corinthians 12.13 and Colossians 3.11*. London: T&T Clark, 2010.

Hauerwas, Stanley. *The Peaceable Kingdom*. Notre Dame: The University of Notre Dame Press, 1983.

Heaney, Robert S. *From Historical to Critical Post-Colonial Theology: The Contribution of John S. Mbiti and Jesse N.K. Mugambi*. Eugene: Pickwick, 2015.

Heaney, Robert S. *Post-Colonial Theology: Finding God and Each Other Amidst the Hate*. Eugene: Cascade, 2019.

Hendel, Ronald. "Genesis." in *The HarperCollins Study Bible*, revised and updated, edited by Harold W. Attridge et al., 3–82. San Francisco: HarperSanFrancisco, 2006.

Henry, Patrick. "The Art of Christian Apology: Comparing the French Catholic Church's Apology to the Jews and the Vatican's 'We Remember.'" *Shofar: An International Journal of Jewish Studies* 26, no. 3 (2008): 87–104.

Herbert, Thompson. "A Black Bishop's Journey: To Reconcile. To Heal. To Liberate. To Serve." Address given at Virginia Theological Seminary, Alexandria, VA, February 24, 2005.

Horace, Zoe. "Inter Religious Council Refutes Being Opposition." *Liberia Public Radio*, April 25, 2019. https://liberiapublicradio.com/2019/04/25/inter-religious-council-refutes-being-opposition/.

Hurtado, Larry *Lord Jesus Christ: Devotion to Jesus in Earliest Christianity*. Grand Rapids: Eerdmans, 2005.

Isaac, Munther. *The Other Side of the Wall: A Palestinian Christian Narrative of Lament and Hope*. Downers Grove: IVP, 2020.

Jastrow, Marcus. *Dictionary of the Targumim, Talmud Babli, Yerushalmi and Midrashic Literature*. New York: Judaica Press, 1985.

Johnson, Charles and Patricia Smith. *Africans in America: America's Journey through Slavery*. New York: Harcourt Brace, 1998.

Junior, Nyasha. "The Mark of Cain and White Violence." *Journal of Biblical Literature* 139, no. 4 (2020): 661–673.

Käsemann, Ernst. *Commentary on Romans*. Grand Rapids: Eerdmans, 1980.

Kassis, Rifat Odeh. "Thoughts on Normalisation in the Israel-Palestine Conflict." No2BrandIsrael.org, June 3, 2015. www.no2brandisrael.org/thoughts-onnormalisation-in-the-israel-palestine-conflict/.

Katongole, Emmanuel. *A Future for Africa: Critical Essays in Christian Social Imagination*. Scranton, PA: University of Scranton Press, 2005.

Katongole, Emmanuel and Chris Rice. *Reconciling All Things: A Christian Vision for Justice, Peace and Healing*. Downers Grove: IVP, 2009.

Kieh, George and Eric Paterson. *Liberia: Religious Leaders, Peacemaking, and the First Liberian War*. Washington, DC: Berkley Center for Religion, Peace and World Affairs, 2013.

Kieh Jr., George Klay. "The Roots of the Second Liberian Civil War." *International Journal on World Peace* 26, no. 1 (2009): 7–30.

Kieh Jr., George Klay. "Religious Leaders, Peacemaking and the First Liberian Civil War." *Journal of Religion, Conflict and Peace* 5, no. 2 (2012): 1–18.

Kimambo, Isaria N., Gregory H. Maddox, and Salvatory S. Nyanto. *A New History of Tanzania*. Dar es Salaam: Mkuki na Nyota, 2017.

Kittel, George, and Gerhard Friedrich eds. *The Theological Dictionary of the New Testament*, 10 vols. Translated by Geoffrey Bromiley. Grand Rapids: Eerdmans, 1964–1976.

Ladd, George Eldon. *A Theology of the New Testament*, rev. ed. Grand Rapids: Wm. B. Eerdmans, 1993.

Lamsa, George M., trans. *Holy Bible from the Ancient Eastern Text*. San Francisco: HarperOne, 2014.

Lederach, John Paul. *The Moral Imagination: The Art and Soul of Building Peace*. Oxford: Oxford University Press, 2005.

Lewis, Clive S. *Mere Christianity*, rev. ed. New York: HarperCollins, 1996.

Lind, Millard C. *Yahweh Is a Warrior: The Theology of Warfare in Ancient Israel*. Pennsylvania: Herald Press, 1980.

Longman, Tremper III and Daniel G. Reid. "When God Declares War: The Violence of God Can Only Be Understood in the Shadow of the Cross." *Christianity Today* 40, no. 12 (October 28, 1996): 14–21.

Martin, Ralph P. "New Testament Theology: A Proposal. The Theme of Reconciliation." *Expository Times* 91 (1980): 364–368.

Martin, Ralph P. *Reconciliation: A Study of Paul's Theology*, rev. ed. Grand Rapids: Zondervan, 1989.

Mauser, Ulrich. *The Gospel of Peace: A Scriptural Message for Today's World*. Louisville: John Knox Press, 1992.

Mbiti, John S. *African Religions and Philosophy*, 2nd ed. Oxford: Heinemann, 1989.

Mbiti, John S. "Confessing Christ in a Multifaith Context with Two Examples from Africa." *Metanoia* 4, nos. 3–4 (1994): 138–145.

Mertus, Julie and Jeffrey W. Helsing. *Human Rights and Conflict: Exploring the Links Between Rights, Law and Peacebuilding*. Washington, DC: United States Institute of Peace, 2006.

Mitchell, Margaret. *Paul and the Rhetoric of Reconciliation: An Exegetical Investigation of the Language and Composition of 1 Corinthians*. Tübingen: Mohr, 1991.

Moltmann, Jürgen. "God in the World—the World in God: Perichoresis in Trinity and Eschatology." In *The Gospel of John and Christian Theology*, edited by Richard Bauckham and Carl Mosser, 369–381. Grand Rapids: Eerdmans, 2008.

Moore, Sando. "Liberia: CWA Alumni Announces Diversity Symposium." *The Daily Observer*, February 5, 2022. www.liberianobserver.com/node/1727.

Mugambi, Jesse N. K. *The Biblical Basis of Evangelization: Theological Reflections Based on an African Experience*. Nairobi: Oxford University Press, 1989.

Mugambi. Jesse N. K. "A Fresh Look at Evangelism in Africa." *International Review of Mission* 87 (1998): 342–360.

Mugambi, Jesse N. K. *Christian Theology and Social Reconstruction*. Nairobi: Acton, 2003.

Musk, Bill. *Kissing Cousins? Christians and Muslims Face to Face*. Oxford: Monarch Books, 2005.

Mustafá, Kabahā. *The Palestinian People: Seeking Sovereignty and State*. Boulder: Lynne Rienner, 2013.

Nord, Roger, Yuri Sobolev, David Dunn, Alejandro Hajdenberg, Niko Hobdari, Samar Maziad, and Stéphane Roudet. *Tanzania: The Story of an African Transition*. Washington, DC: International Monetary Fund, 2009.

Norfleet, Agnes W. "Genesis 45:1–15." In *The Renovaré Spiritual Formation Bible*, edited by Richard J. Foster et al., 79. San Francisco: HarperSanFrancisco, 2005.

Nugent, Paul. *Africa Since Independence: A Comparative Study*. London: Palgrave Macmillan, 2004.

O'Connor, Daniel. *Three Centuries of Mission: The United Society for the Propagation of the Gospel 1701–2000*. London: Continuum, 2000.

Peiefer, Claude J. "Peace According to St. Paul." *The Bible Today* 21, no. 3 (May, 1983): 170–175.

Pius XII. *Mystici Corporis Christi*. 1943. www.vatican.va/content/pius-xii/en/encyclicals/documents/hf_p-xii_enc_29061943_mystici-corporis-christi.html. Accessed April 22, 2022.

Polkinghorne, David. *Narrative Knowing and the Human Sciences*. Albany: SUNY Press, 1988.

Qubti, Shadia. "Amira's Story: Challenging Western Christian Justification of the Occupation." June 3, 2018, in *Women Behind the Wall*. Podcast, Episode 3, www.womenbehindthewall.com/blog/2018/6/3episode-3-amiras-story-challenging western-christian-justification-of-the-occupation.

Qubti, Shadia. "Eilda's Story: Holistic Healing for a Community in Ongoing Trauma." June, 10, 2019, in *Women Behind the Wall*. Podcast, Episode 4. www.womenbehindthewall.com/blog/2018/6/3/episode-4-eildas-story-holistic-healing-for-a-community-in-ongoing-trauma.

Regnault, Lucien. "Moses the Black, Saint," *Claremont Coptic Encyclopedia* (1991). http://search.ebscohost.com.libproxy.udayton.edu/login.aspx?direct=true&db=edsoai&AN=edsoai.ocn759741319&site=eds-live. Accessed January 2, 2021.

Riessman, Catherine Kohler. *Narrative Analysis*. Newbury Park: Sage, 1993.

Sachs, William L. and Robert S. Heaney. *The Promise of Anglicanism*. London: SCM, 2019.

Sacks, Jonathan. *The Chief Rabbi's Haggadah: Hebrew and English Text with New Essays and Commentary*. New York: HarperCollins, 2007.

Schreiter, Robert J. *The Ministry of Reconciliation: Spirituality & Strategies*. Maryknoll, NY: Orbis Books, 1998.

Segundo, Juan Luis. *Faith and Ideologies*, vol. 1. New York: Orbis Books, 1982.

Sirleaf, Ellen Johnson. "Annual Message to the Second Session of the 53rd National Legislature of the Republic of Liberia, Theme: A Time for Transformation." Lecture at Capitol Hill, Monrovia, Liberia, January 28, 2013. www.emansion.gov.lr/doc/2013o128_President_2013_Annual_Message_FINAL.df. Accessed August 31, 2019.

Smedley, Audrey, "Origin of The Idea of Race." *Anthropology Newsletter*, November, 1997. Found on "Race—The Power of an Illusion." PBS.org. www.pbs.org/race/000_About/002_04-background-02-09.htm. Accessed February 23, 2022.

Smith, Payne ed. *A Compendious Syriac Dictionary Founded upon the Thesaurus Syriacus of R. Payne Smith*. Oxford: Clarendon, 1985.

Sokoloff, Michael. *A Dictionary of Jewish Palestinian Aramaic of the Byzantine Period*. Rmat Gan, Israel: Bar Ilan University, 1990.

Spangler, David. *Parent as Mystic, Mystic as Parent*. New York: Riverhead Trade, 2000.

Spencer, Herbert. *The Principles of Sociology*, vol. 1. New York: D. Appleton and Company, 1895.

Stephenson, Alan M. G. *Anglicanism and the Lambeth Conferences*. London: SPCK, 1978.

Strayer, Robert W. *The Making of Missionary Communities in East Africa: Anglicans and Africans in Colonial Kenya, 1875–1935*. London: Heinemann, 1978.

Strong, Rowan. *Anglicanism and the British Empire*. Oxford: Oxford University Press, 2007.

Tutu, Desmond. *No Future Without Forgiveness*. New York: Doubleday, 1999.

Tutu, Desmond. *God Has A Dream: A Vision of Hope for Our Time*. New York: Image-Doubleday, 2004.

Tutu, Desmond and Mpho Tutu. *The Book of Forgiving: The Fourfold Path for Healing Ourselves and Our World*. New York: HarperOne, 2014.

Vanier, Jean. *Befriending the Stranger*. Grand Rapids: William B. Eerdmans, 2005.

Vatican II. *Lumen Gentium*. 1964. www.vatican.va/archive/hist_councils/ii_vatican_council/documents/vat-ii_const_19641121_lumen-gentium_en.html. Accessed April 22, 2022.

Vidler, Alexander Roper. *Essays in Liberality*. London: SCM Press, 1957.

Volf, Miroslav. *Exclusion and Embrace: A Theological Exploration of Identity, Otherness, and Reconciliation*. Nashville: Abingdon Press, 1996.

Warren, Max A. C. *Caesar The Beloved Enemy: Three Studies in the Relation of Church and State*. London: SCM Press, 1955.

Weiner, Tim. "At 14, a Liberian War Veteran Dreams of Finding a Way Home." *New York Times*, August 25, 2013. www.nytimes.com/2003/08/25/world/at-14-a-liberian-war-veteran-dreams-of-finding-a-way-home.html.

Weiser, Artur. *The Psalms: A Commentary*. Philadelphia, PA: The Westminster Press, 1962.

Westermann, Claus. "Peace (Shalom) in the Old Testament." In *The Meaning of Peace: Biblical Studies*, edited by Perry B. Yoder and Willard M. Swartley and translated by Walter Sawatsky, 16–48. Louisville: John Knox, 1992.

Wiseman, D. J. "'Is It Peace': Covenant and Diplomacy." *Vetus Testamentum* 32, no. 3 (July 1982): 311–326.

Wright, Will. "Seminary Built on Slavery and Jim Crow Labor Has Begun Paying Reparations." *The New York Times*, May 31, 2021. www.nytimes.com/2021/05/31/us/reparations-virginia-theological-seminary.html. Accessed January 10, 2022.

Yong, Amos. *Mission After Pentecost: The Witness of the Spirit from Genesis to Revelation*. Grand Rapids: Baker Academic, 2019.

Index

CPSIA information can be obtained
at www.ICGtesting.com
Printed in the USA
JSHW061425160922
30598JS00004B/4

9 781640 655881